Jungian Arts-Based R
"The Nuclear Enchai
New Mexico"

MW01283689

Jungian Arts-Based Research and "The Nuclear Enchantment of New Mexico" provides clear, accessible and in-depth guidance both for arts-based researchers using Jung's ideas and for Jungian scholars undertaking arts-based research. The book provides a central extended example which applies the techniques described to the full text of Joel Weishaus' prose poem *The Nuclear Enchantment of New Mexico*, published here for the first time.

Designed as a "how-to" book, *Jungian Arts-Based Research and "The Nuclear Enchantment of New Mexico"* explores how Jung contributes to the new arts-based paradigm in psychic functions such as intuition, by providing an epistemology of symbols that includes the unconscious, and research strategies such as active imagination. Rowland examines Jung's *The Red Book* as an early example of Jungian arts-based research and demonstrates how this practice challenges the convention of the detached researcher by providing holistic knowing. Arts-based researchers will find here a psychic dimension that also manifests in transdisciplinarity, while those familiar with Jung's work will find in arts-based research ways to foster diversity for a decolonized academy.

This unique project will be essential reading for Jungian and post-Jungian academics and scholars, arts-based researchers of all backgrounds and readers interested in transdisciplinarity.

Susan Rowland, PhD, is the author of several books on Jung, literature, gender and creativity, including *Jung as a Writer, The Ecocritical Psyche, Remembering Dionysus* and *Jungian Literary Criticism*.

Joel Weishaus is a poet and digital literary artist. He has published seven books, and his current digital and archived digitized work can be accessed at weishaus.unm.edu.

"Arts-based research claims to be transdisciplinary but lacks the methodological foundations. In this context, *Jungian Arts-Based Research and "The Nuclear Enchantment of New Mexico"* is a nice surprise. The practical and useful Chapter 6, The Nuclear Enchantment of New Mexico, blends science, religion, myth, history, poetry and anthropology. This book brings together Jung and arts-based research in the social sciences, showing them both to anticipate and require the methodology of transdisciplinarity."
– Basarab Nicolescu, author of From Modernity to Cosmodernity

"Rowland has done it again! Having brilliantly re-visioned Jung's writing through the lenses of feminism, eco-psychology and literary theory, she now directs her scholarly gaze to arts-based research. The results are illuminating. It reveals Jungian psychology as a mode of poetic enquiry into being human. In so doing, Rowland offers arts-based researchers a fresh psychological perspective within which to frame their practice. This is an indispensable book for everyone engaged in understanding the human condition."
– Dr Luke Hockley, UKCP, ADIP, FRSA; Professor of Media Analysis,
University of Bedfordshire, UK

Jungian Arts-Based Research and "The Nuclear Enchantment of New Mexico"

Susan Rowland and Joel Weishaus

 Routledge
Taylor & Francis Group

LONDON AND NEW YORK

First published 2021
by Routledge
2 Park Square, Milton Park, Abingdon, Oxon OX14 4RN

and by Routledge
52 Vanderbilt Avenue, New York, NY 10017

Routledge is an imprint of the Taylor & Francis Group, an informa business

British Library Cataloguing-in-Publication Data
A catalogue record for this book is available from the British
Library

Library of Congress Cataloging-in-Publication Data
Names: Rowland, Susan, 1962- author. | Weishaus, Joel, 1939-
author.
Title: Jungian arts-based research and 'The nuclear enchantment
of New Mexico' / Susan Rowland and Joel Weishaus.
Other titles: Nuclear enchantment of New Mexico.
Description: Abingdon, Oxon ; New York, NY : Routledge,
2020. | Includes bibliographical references and index.
Identifiers: LCCN 2020010548 (print) | LCCN 2020010549
(ebook) | ISBN 9781138310780 (hardback) | ISBN
9781138310797 (paperback) | ISBN 9780429459238 (ebook)
Subjects: LCSH: Psychoanalysis and literature. | Jungian
psychology. | Literature–Psychology. | Arts–Psychological
aspects. | Arts–Research.
Classification: LCC PN98.P75 R6937 2020 (print) | LCC PN98.
P75 (ebook) | DDC 150.19/54–dc23
LC record available at https://lccn.loc.gov/2020010548
LC ebook record available at https://lccn.loc.gov/2020010549

ISBN: 978-1-138-31078-0 (hbk)
ISBN: 978-1-138-31079-7 (pbk)
ISBN: 978-0-429-45923-8 (ebk)

Typeset in Times New Roman
by Swales & Willis, Exeter, Devon, UK

Dedicated to Jerome and Susan Bernstein "in reciprocity"

Contents

Acknowledgments

We would like to thank friends, colleagues, students and artists at Pacifica Graduate Institute who have encouraged us on the road to this book. Particular mention goes to Mary Wood, Keiron and Kathryn Le Grice, Joe Cambray and Linda Carter. We especially thank students on the MA Humanities and the Creative Life, and the Doctoral Program in Jungian and Archetypal Psychology for their enthusiasm for ideas and practices of the creative psyche. Lori Pye of Viridis Graduate Institute and Jacqui Feather have also given wonderful support.

Moreover we would like to thank kind friends in England, such as Wendy Pank, Christine Saunders, Claire Dyson, Leslie Gardner, Evan Davis and Guillaume Batz for their generosity. This book is dedicated to Jerome and Susan Bernstein for their wonderful work in New Mexico and kindness to the two of us.

Finally, we are very grateful for our editors at Routledge, Susannah Frearson and Heather Evans, for fostering new research and ideas. All of you and many more are also part of this book.

Chapter 1

Jung and arts-based research
Introduction

Overview and aims

This book proposes that the psychology of C. G. Jung and the scholarly practice of arts-based research have the potential to develop each other. In particular, I suggest that Jung and arts-based research already share ideas and strategies about knowing and being that can be furthered by forging a relationship between them. Consequently, the aim of this book is to enrich both Jungian studies and arts-based research, whether they be treated as separate domains or, more excitingly, become a dual enterprise. That is, Jungian studies expands by seeing how the creativity innate to Jung emerges into knowing through arts-based research. Conversely, arts-based research is deepened by the Jungian practice of psyche. What arises is a Jungian arts-based research, as we show by two major examples in later chapters.

Ultimately such a re-orienting of a field within psychology, such as Jung's, and the multidisciplinary endeavor of arts-based research can point to a transdisciplinary transformation of learning. Such a future would have important implications for the academy, for societies and cultures, and religions, as described by transdisciplinary theorist, Basarab Nicolescu (2014). Transdisciplinarity is a new framework for knowledge and so too is arts-based research. Key examples in both paradigms are offered in this book by Joel Weishaus' *The Nuclear Enchantment of New Mexico*,[1] (2019) and Jung's *Liber Novus* or *The Red Book* (2009).

Therefore, this book is for audiences in which disciplines are related without having to be enacted in a hierarchy, a feature of both transdisciplinarity and arts-based research. For example, this book is for those engaged in arts-based research who seek psychological dynamism within creativity. They will find it in Jungian psychology, which is based on the notion of an innately creative psyche oriented towards meaning-making. Such practitioners may come to this book seeking Jung or merely aiming to deepen and extend their practice. As the first four chapters will demonstrate, Jung provides arts-based research with theories and practices that go far beyond psychotherapy to broader concerns of image-making, historical meaning, philosophy and spiritual practice. These concerns augment existing arts-based strategies.

This book is also for Jungians who want to understand or embark upon arts-based research, not least because arguably C. G. Jung pioneered creative practice as a way of knowing in *The Red Book* (2009), which will be examined in Chapter 4. Those not directly engaged in art-making should also find this book insightful in showing that Jungian studies is already at home in this mode of academic inquiry. Arts-based research enhances what Jungian studies can be, and where it can find new domains of applicability. In short, Jung and arts-based research (often ABR for brevity) can extend the kinds of knowing and being possible in making new knowledge. Ultimately, I suggest that Jungian ABR amounts to a paradigm that brings together transdisciplinary and arts-based research more directly. For this reason, Jung and arts-based research paradigms are the subject of Chapter 2.

By expanding the definition of Jungian studies and ABR, this book also interrogates the notion of art itself. Like Jungian archetypes (see below), art in some form exists wherever humans live together while also developing specialized functions that may differ across societies. For this reason, this is not a book of art history. Yet it must be acknowledged that existing arts-based research arises from the late-twentieth-century Western depiction of art as largely separated from other meaning-making activities, such as religion and scholarly inquiry in disciplines. Art in Western modernity has been severed from many of the therapeutic, sacred and social roles of its distant past. Some of these are found today only in indigenous societies. Indeed, Western art suffers today from conventional assumptions that art is decoration, a financial investment or entertainment.

Arts-based research explicitly rejects the marginalization of art. It contests the exclusion of art from important questions of knowledge, reality and being. In fact, one crucial link between Jung and arts-based research is that both regard imagination as primal, and therefore creativity as of fundamental importance in who we are and what we can know. Creativity is how humans become both functioning adults and extraordinary beings. Engaging in creative activity is transformative and necessary in ways that deny reducing art to individual idiosyncrasy. Put another way, by cutting off art practice from major social endeavors, including education, Western society has amputated the social psyche in ways only just being recognized by the mainstream, but which are to the fore in Jung and arts-based research.

Jung shows the psyche to be spontaneous, responsive, autonomous and improvisatory. Such psychic creativity includes what we are aware of in ourselves, the conscious mind, and importantly, what we are unaware of except in dreams and other indirect manifestations, the unconscious. Specific to this psychology is the necessity of forging an ongoing relationship between conscious and unconscious. Due to the spontaneity of the psyche, making such a relationship is an innately creative and lifelong process.

"Arts-based" signifies all possible arts, including but not limited to creative writing, poetry, music, film-making, sculpture, embroidery, gardening, ceramics, and so on. On the other hand, arts-based research is not making art after doing the research; rather, doing art is an essential and revelatory part of the research inquiry. Art-making becomes knowledge-making.

For example, Jung engaged in a process he called "active imagination" to generate the images that were aesthetically crafted into *The Red Book* (Jung 1963/1983: 213). Both the active work with images and the "crafting" are arts-based research strategies. Joel Weishaus decided to research the nuclear legacy of New Mexico by evoking psychic images. These are worked into written fragments gradually patterned into forty prose-poems. As well as each page of poetry, he turned to scholarly articles in various disciplines to form a "paratext." These scholarly notes are not context to the poetry. Rather they compose a parallel framework that weaves the poetic inquiry into the styles and tones of multidisciplinary responses to nuclear weapons technology.

Both examples of Jungian arts-based research will be explored in later chapters. For now, it is time to start mapping the terrain of Jung and ABR as a prelude to bringing them together. Those familiar with Jung might skip this next section, while readers steeped in arts-based research may not require its introduction in this first chapter.

Getting started with Jung (for arts-based research)

Intuition, imaging, incompleteness

Three characteristics of Jungian psychology drive its potential union with arts-based research. They are intuition, imaging or imagination, and incompleteness. Regarded by Jung as one of four basic psychic functions, intuition has become central to the making of art since the era of Romanticism. An era of revolution in politics, science and art, Romanticism rejected the previous privileging of tradition or rule-following in favor of making something entirely new or rule-seeking. Post-Romantic art breaks rules and searches for new form. Intuition has become the creative ally of the practicing artist.

To Jung, intuition is housed in an active unconscious. It mediates perceptions via the unknown psyche in a way he described as instinctive (Jung 1971/1987: 124). Intuition is irrational and yet may engender conventional knowledge by being harmonized with rational categories. In fact, Jung cited philosophers Spinoza and Henri Bergson as presenting "*scientia intuitiva*" as a supreme kind of knowledge (ibid.). Significantly, although intuition may appear via emotion or feeling, or found in intellectual pursuits, it neither relies upon nor originates in these faculties. Intuition is the lively, embryonic meaning-desiring quality of the unconscious. It is the engine of the unconscious as a source of creativity.

Imaging and imagining require careful unpacking; for image in Jungian psychology is not the sense impression it is often taken to be in the usual use of the term. Jung was quite explicit:

> When I speak of "image," ... I do not mean the psychic reflection of some external object, but ... a figure of fancy or *fantasy-image* ... it then has a greater *psychological* value, representing an inner reality which often far outweighs the importance of external reality.
>
> (Jung 1971/1987: 113, italics in original)

An image to Jung is a manifestation emerging from the deep psyche. It is an expression of inner being, a truth of the inner world. It may eventually take material form, such as being uttered, painted, sculpted or narrated. Consequently, genuine psychic images find a home in all art practices that incorporate the unknown psyche in its processes. Imaging is therefore highly intuitive. In fact, images give form to intuition, and in doing so connect the unconscious to the conscious mind. Here it is worth recalling from above that intuition can be stimulated by external conditions, including reacting to circumstances or intellectual endeavors.

Therefore, images are the result of intuition getting involved in meaning-making. Activities conventionally found in academic research, such as reading intellectually demanding books or setting up experiments, often provoke intuition from the unconscious. In turn, intuition provides images that feed the other functions of the psyche (see below) in making knowledge. For arts-based research, the central role of intuition is focused through images that can then be materialized in the work. Hence, imaging is imagination given a new meaning-making purpose. Whereas imagination has long been regarded as a source process for art, Jung's conception of the image as fundamentally psychic and rooted in the unknown supplies a rationale for creativity as psychically generative. Imagination is the choreography of psychic images.

Incompleteness is an overlooked and undervalued aspect of Jungian ideas. Yet it provides an essential drive for Jung to be important for arts-based research. For Jung took *seriously* the unconscious as the unknown and fundamentally unknowable. So significant is the mystery in the heart of being that it must be factored into the human capacity to know the world and ourselves.

> Nobody drew the conclusion that if the subject of knowledge, the psyche, were in fact a veiled form of existence not immediately accessible to consciousness, then all our knowledge must be incomplete, and moreover to a degree that we cannot determine.
>
> (Jung 1947, CW8: para. 358)

Humans are creatures with aspects beyond rational control, such as in dreaming, where images arise that are neither summoned nor consciously "made." It follows that the human project of knowledge must forever be unfinished. Put another way, knowledge is radically incomplete if we demand it to be always ordered, coherent and comprehensible. For example, the conventional scientific assumption is that everything can be discovered by experiments where the researcher is kept out of the frame so only the conscious, rational mind participates. Such an assumption about knowledge leaves out what is irrational, ecstatic or mysterious in human experience.

The role of such incompleteness for arts-based research and its framework or paradigm will be explored in Chapters 2 and 3. However, it is worth noting that incompleteness is the starting place for all research projects. For now, it is important to consider what radical unknowing does to Jung's own project of knowledge, his psychology.

In the essay, "On the Nature of the Psyche," Jung comes to the conclusion that his psychology is not a series of proven propositions founding secure concepts (Jung 1947). Indeed, his psychology amounts to a "model" designed merely to offer an effective way of working with the psyche (ibid.: para. 381). It doesn't reveal ultimate truths, but is rather a pragmatic practice. Jungian psychology offers a perspective that is effective, while not claiming to be conclusively authoritative.

Later in the essay he calls his work "a net of reflections" that has collected material from disciplines beyond psychology, such as philosophy, religious studies and the social sciences (ibid.: 421). This notion of a net of language from different knowledges cast over a protean and mysterious psyche is the seed for an arts-based research with a transdisciplinary future, as I shall show. For now, it is time to look at Jung's potential for socially engaged research, followed by the other three psychic functions, and core concepts such as archetypes, individuation and the teleological psyche.

Jungian psychology and the social sphere

Three further characteristics of Jung's work orient the psyche to social being and knowing. These are the critical attitude within the psychology, the concern for personhood and the tendency to de-center cultural assumptions. To begin, Jung is a *critical* thinker in three ways. Firstly, he is critically important as a pioneer of working with the unconscious, a factor crucial in the intellectual history of the twentieth century. In fact, the unconscious is arguably even more significant in the twenty-first century, in which a loosening of boundaries promotes new kinds of research, including arts-based. This chapter has already noted how fundamental to post-Romantic notions of art is the engagement with the unknown. Jung's insistence on the importance of intuition and incompleteness is a framework that makes the unconscious a critically necessary part of both knowledge acquisition and art practices.

Secondly, Jung is critical to research, including arts-based research, because his body of texts impacts on knowledge far beyond his home discipline of psychology, as he himself noted. Jung is important because his work influences literary writers, visual artists and philosophers. Among notable figures where influence is acknowledged or documented are D. H. Lawrence, James Joyce, Walter Benjamin, Giles Deleuze, Herman Hesse, Thomas Mann, John Fowles, Ted Hughes, Doris Lessing, Jackson Pollock, Anselm Kiefer and filmmakers such as George Lucas, John Boorman and Derek Jarman.

Finally, Jung is critical in the sense of offering a meaningful criticism because his work provides a framework for analyzing and evaluating. Jungian psychology is an interpretative enterprise that can be used to make art and to evaluate it. By putting creativity at the heart of what it means to be human, Jung expands the perspective of art-making to disciplines such as literary studies, philosophy, history, cultural studies, politics and religion.

Even more fundamental, Jung's work is a mode of social criticism because the focus on intuition, imaging and incompleteness interrogates what it means to be a person and a member of society. A critical approach to personhood occurs because the unconscious is an actively destabilizing factor. Personhood is constantly remade. Moreover, Jung's unconscious is guided by creativity that cannot be determined by any external factor.

So, while personhood is styled by family and society, it is not inherently limited to the conventions of any one era. Jung himself was a conservative citizen in a conservative early-twentieth-century nation of Switzerland. However, he produced a revolutionary psyche that could not be fixed in any one social norm. His unconscious has priority because it always exceeds conscious knowing. Further chapters in this book will explore the implications of this model of personhood for research through creativity.

The Jungian psyche is protean to a degree that no rational structure can fully contain; therefore, the Jungian view of society is fundamentally critical because the imagination can always generate something new. Jungian personhood is built upon an unstable, generative and unpredictable unconscious. It follows that a society made up of these persons is also subject to powerful, often incomprehensible and even overwhelming irrational forces. At this point, Jung the healer and Jung the conservative express a desire for balance.

Achieving successful personhood, which he called a process of individuation (see below) depended upon a balance or relatively stable alignment between conscious knowing and unconscious being. So too should societies balance destabilizing unconscious forces with healthy ways of engaging with the irrational side of human nature. Unfortunately, according to Jung, the Western world since the Enlightenment has radically underestimated the extent, irreducibility and generative necessity of the irrational. Where once religion contained and tamed the desire for more than reason supplied, modernity has simply repressed it. The result is a fragile consciousness in modern people that requires psychotherapy, and a perilous fragility in political and social groups.

While Jung's specific historical criticisms may not be so relevant, what is of lasting value is his location of the psyche as beyond the biological person. Jungian psychology de-centers cultural norms because the intrinsically creative unconscious is always at work and cannot be absorbed wholly into any one philosophy, creed or practice. Jungian ideas are critical for all kinds of research because no set of assumptions can limit the possibilities of this creative psyche. It is time to focus more closely on how he saw the psyche operating.

Four psychic functions

Jung liked patterns of four. He defends his four psychic functions as activities that cannot be reduced to each other and occur in everyone in his long clinical experience (Jung 1971/1987: 108). He calls two functions rational, thinking and feeling, and two irrational, sensation and intuition, by which he means not fully accessible to consciousness. Each function turns out to be a little more than the common use the word indicates, and together they offer, I suggest, fertile ground for arts-based research.

Thinking as a function is not musing or idly dwelling upon an idea. It is very much directed to knowing, and includes judgment (ibid.). Indeed, this thinking means conceptual thought in which ideas are linked together by means of a concept, a basic ingredient in many research processes. Given that concepts are meant to be generally applicable, the function of thinking delivers ideas into the world of communication, and hence judgment plays a role in the process.

Feeling, too, is not as simple as it might appear to be. For Jung, feeling is an independent psychic activity where the center of consciousness, called the ego, becomes linked to something in a way that includes a sense of value. Feeling includes valuation, and hence also implies a kind of judgment, yet not the intellectual kind he ascribed to thinking (ibid.: 105). Feeling is also not synonymous with emotion. Whereas emotion implies being *moved* by some external impulse, feeling is rooted within the psyche in its relation to validation. If feeling becomes augmented enough to impact physical being, it becomes an "affect" (ibid.). Feeling is therefore necessary for ethical kinds of understanding. Together, thinking and feeling are functions of judgment that make up intellectual rigor and the capacity to value, both distinctive qualities for arts-based research, as we will see.

While the function of intuition has been explored above, that of sensation forms the partly unconscious connection to the physical body. Sensation mediates the physical senses and is therefore a way of describing perception (ibid.: 132–4). Jung calls it an irrational function because being depends upon the body. Sensation is not something added to the person, but rather what generates the person. He argues that sensation should be distinguished from feeling, even though a "feeling-tone" may accompany sensation. Feeling is internal to the psyche, whereas sensation may come from external stimuli or the internal organic processes of the body.

The distinction between sensation and feeling will become important when we examine Jung on art itself later in this book. For Jung regarded art as appealing to the function of sensation because of the physical appreciation of beauty. Here, separating feeling and sensation isolates art, at least the physically sensory aspects of art, from functions of evaluation and judgment. This will later prove important to Jung's distrust of art, although it need not impede arts-based research from developing from contact with Jungian ideas, as I shall show.

Distinguishing these four psychic functions enabled Jung to suggest that they are not equally dispersed in every person. While everyone has all four functions, some of the variety of human personalities can be classified through realizing that functions can be over- or underdeveloped. In addition, Jung coined the terms "introversion" and "extraversion" to signify inner and outer orientation respectively. The functions can also be introverted and extraverted. Here are the building blocks of what Jung called his "typology," a way of classifying personalities. For example, a largely introverted person may have most of her or his functions strongly introverted and only weakly extraverted. Many people will have a mixture of extraverted and introverted functions.

Jungian typology has received a lot of attention from scholars such as John Beebe, who developed it into a subtle, much-admired system of working with people (Beebe 2016). For these reasons, this book will not pursue typology in the weaving together of Jung and arts-based research. For, as excellent typology resources are readily available, this book will point to what is less recognized about Jung, e.g. his contrary resistance to rational organizing principles in the mysteries of the psyche. While typology may well be useful to the arts-based researcher, I suggest what is most valuable and least appreciated is Jung's adherence to the psyche as a limitless and generative source of knowledge that is as yet inconceivable. It is therefore now necessary to consider Jung's own conceptual schema as a threshold into the unknown.

Jung: the basic concepts (most significant in bold)

The psyche does not exist in fenced-off areas, and its concepts are to be regarded as helpful pragmatic tools, rather than denoting rigid structures. In fact, it is worth starting with the key notion of **individuation** because it shows that the Jungian psyche is in a state of perpetual making and unmaking. Individuation is the process of becoming a distinctive person by creatively integrating more and more unruly energies that appear from the unknown psyche.

However, individuation is not about becoming an individual in the sense of being separated from other people, or from one's physical or social surroundings. It is just the opposite! Individuation incorporates what appears separated from consciousness being as the physical body, other people, nature and society. The unconscious greets consciousness in the guise of anything *other*. Strong, irrational emotions provoked by parents, or a sunset, or an experience of divinity or a nightmare – all are channels for unconscious energies. Individuation is a never-to-be-completed process of being as constantly in touch with what is strange, new, provocative and potentially overwhelming.

Individuation defies and re-makes the psyche that Jung conceptually divided into the **ego**, as known center of consciousness, and the **unconscious** or unknowable. Propelled by the active unconscious, individuation is not only unstoppable, its regular functioning is necessary to psychic health. Blocked individuation is the main cause of psychic illness, to Jung. Moreover, individuation is collective as well as personal. In this sense, epochs need to individuate too. Blocked cultural individuation can lead to violence on a terrifying scale in an explosive eruption of the **shadow**.

The shadow is one of several important archetypal modes of largely unconscious energy. **Archetypes** are the embedded, possibly inborn, potentials for certain kinds of patterns and meanings. Jung posited that humans have evolved psychic contents as well as physical developmental characteristics. These contents are not inherited images, nor are they inherited ideas. They are the merest potential for images and ideas and what emerges will always be shaped by the surrounding history and culture. In this way, the psychic image is an archetypal image partly derived from the antecedent archetype and partly influenced by the person's conscious involvement in their world. Art as materialization of psychic, archetypal images is a physical weaving of a common archetypal inheritance that Jung called the **collective unconscious**, filtered through art/cultural traditions and the individual artist's conscious strategies.

Archetypes are inherently active. They test to manifest contrarily to conscious attitudes in order to promote individuation. If consciousness is weak or complacent or determined to repress all that is other, then a particularly overwhelming other may arise that Jung called the shadow. For the shadow is opposite to the ego in the sense that it is what the ego represses, despises, ignores or disavows in its effort to remain unsullied. For the excessively rational person, the shadow is uncontrollable desire. For the bigoted person, the shadow may be love for the other, the stranger. For the virtuous person, the shadow may be irresistible seduction into crime. Whatever the ego is not, the shadow is. The more it is repressed within the psyche, the stronger and more irrefutable it becomes.

The healthy psyche is one aware of its shadow, which immediately makes it less powerful and more capable of fertilizing rather than crushing the ego. Psychic breakdown occurs when the unconscious other is so vigorously stamped upon that it manifests as a shadow that floods or splinters the ego. Psychotherapy is then required to forge a new pattern of being that will partially contain shadow energies.

Once shadow energies are brought into relationship with the ego, Jung felt, heterosexist that he was, that the unconscious would typically offer a contrasexual gender archetypal form for potential union. He called the feminine gender archetype activated in a man the **anima**, and a woman has a corresponding masculine **animus**. Here Jungian psychology needs to move on from Jung's understanding of gender, based as it was on an essentialist and binary notion of men and women. In Jung's world, men are innately masculine and women biologically and stereotypically feminine. Gender is not separate from bodily sex and any treatment of sexuality is confined to outmoded, purely heterosexual assumptions.

Outmoded and not fit for a twenty-first-century understanding of gender as fluid, historically shaped and constructed in multiple bodily and psychic inter-actions, on the other hand, Jung, a conservative with revolutionary ideas, could be said to have a more flexible structuring of psyche and gender than he admits. For individuation, that necessary psychic deconstruction, *requires* that gender be unfixed and generated from unconscious exchanges between body and culture. Individuation means that males have to learn to integrate their feminine animas, and not just project them upon women. Similarly, women must assume and absorb their masculine energies.

Gender cannot be fixed or essentialist for Jungian psychology, even though Jung took this position as a starting point. Given psychic images enacting gender in dreams and fantasies, and so forth, will be influenced by conscious bodily existence, those archetypal images called animus and anima by Jung are actually mutable and partly culture-specific. Another fundamental point about archetypes applies here as well. Archetypes are androgynous and limitless in their potential image formations. A so-called Mother archetype could manifest as a bear, a spider, a mountain, a woman of another land, or even as a man doing nurturing work. While C. G. Jung might prefer that gender be essential-ist and welded to bodily sex, his psychology denies it.

Jung placed great emphasis on another category of archetypal images, those of the **self**. Not in any way synonymous with the conscious ego, the self is both an organizing principle of the psyche and a way of imagining a totality of being that encompasses psyche and body and reaches out into the world, and even the cosmos. The self is the sun in the solar system of being, and the goal of individuation is to securely orbit it. To monotheistic religions, the self is God, or an image of God. Its power is such that it makes the psyche teleo-logical or goal-oriented. Therefore, to Jung, the aim of individuation is union with the self.

Later Jungians, such as James Hillman, resist the gravitational pull of the self as a tendency to oneness, Christian theology, balance and coherence (Hill-man 1975). Hillman pioneered archetypal psychology, which discards the self in favor of a more polytheistic notion of multiple archetypal gods and god-desses of the psyche. Such an importation of pluralism opens up Jungian stud-ies to multicultural, multi-sexual and polyamorous configurations of desire and being. It also brings in the importance of **myth** as non-essentialist stories of being and knowing.

In his use of myth Jung anticipates archetypal psychology by regarding it as stories that are creative of being without fixing it. Myths are living stories, the stories we knowingly and unknowingly live by and make meaning from.

Myths make us who we are. Unhappy or mentally ill people may be stuck in the wrong myth; they are being blocked by the narrative they unconsciously live out. Hence, Jung coined the term "personal myth" to denote the story we discover and make in the individuation process – the myth that is our fate.

Dreams often provide clues to the current unconscious myth or story. To Jung, a significant dream is not a code for a deeper truth; it is rather a direct representation of the unconscious in its own language of images. While some dreams are just reflections of everyday concerns, powerful dreams direct us to mysteries, the unknown, and come from the collective unconscious. Combining these two types of dreams, those continuing conscious preoccupations and those that are alien and new, could become a basis for arts-based research.

One aspect of what Jung called big dreams is their capacity to exhibit what Jung named **synchronicity**. By this Jung referred to what are otherwise thought of as coincidences, specifically when something in the psyche bonds with a physical event in a relationship that cannot be causally explained. A dream that proves to foretell some unanticipated event, or a happening that is not known to the dreamer but proves later to have occurred at exactly that moment in time while separated in space – these are what Jung called synchronous. Such instances outside mainstream scientific theories on causality lead Jung to theorize that archetypes are more prevalent in the fabric of the cosmos than just the human psyche. He began to move from a notion that the psyche is unconsciously *projected* on to exterior reality to a vision of it as unconsciously interconnected.

While later chapters will dig deeper into the Jungian preoccupation with creativity and meaning, this introduction would not be complete without mentioning how the psychic image manifests in art; also his understanding of alchemy, which Jung regarded as a precursor to his psychotherapy.

In an essay on poetry (Jung 1922, CW15), a distinction was made between words as either signs or symbols. This suggestion has far-reaching consequences for arts-based research. With his liking for binary structures, Jung called signs those words with a knowable, consciously contained meaning; in complete contrast, the symbol is ineffable: it links the reading psyche to the mysteries of the collective, archetypal unconscious. Jungian ideas of both image and symbol are foundational to the potential for arts-based research and will be explored in later chapters.

In particular, Jung is definite that the psychic image can find a home in words, if words can summon irrational as well as rational connotations. Of course, Jung's distinction between sign and symbol can be applied to other modes of art. Psychic symbols can appear in paintings, films, music, and so on. In fact, the prevalence of signs and symbols in art causes him later, in an essay on literature, to expand the ideas as two artistic categories for the psychologist. He called art **psychological** if the work revealed its underpinning in the psyche overtly and explicitly. Psychological art is where the psychology has been worked out consciously by the artist. It is likely to contain more signs than symbols because the language of the medium has been subjected to careful analysis. More of the conscious thinking and feeling functions will be apparent.

By complete contrast, **visionary** art erupts from the collective unconscious with very little conscious intervention. Composed largely of symbols, visionary art is saturated by unprocessed material from the unknown psyche. It is a work of intuition and sensation with the conscious functions only weakly displayed. Importantly, Jung said that visionary art was to the culture that produced it what a significant dream is to the individual: a revelation of what is ignored, repressed or required to compensate for some imbalance in the collective consciousness (Jung 1930, CW15: para 152). Hence visionary art is a revelation amounting to an intervention for society, far more than it pertains to the individual who suffered it into being. For "[a]n epoch is like an individual; it has its own limitation of conscious outlook, and therefore requires a compensatory adjustment" (ibid.: para. 153).

Clearly both the categories of psychological and visionary art speak to the aims and practices of arts-based research. Later chapters will show that these categories can be used as interpretative and generative in the making of new knowledge. In addition, the connection with cultural currents and biases is suggestive for a Jungian arts-based contribution to social studies disciplines. Finally, the link to history hints at Jung's other exploration of imaginative practice; one now marginalized almost out of existence, that of alchemy.

Popular in the Renaissance as attempts to convert material lead into valuable gold, alchemy has a long multicultural heritage, possibly back to ancient Egypt, China and early Islam (Linden 2003: 5–10). It existed at a sharp angle to the dualism in Western modernity that eventually forced the divorce of matter and spirit. To alchemy, matter is imbued with spirit. For example, lead was a form of leaden spirit. Thus, it should be possible to distill the spirit from leaden matter and allow it to achieve its perfected golden form. In alchemical texts, Jung discovered images in woodcuts and in words that he recognized as symbols. He concluded that alchemists were in a state of unwitting projection of their psyches on to matter. The enterprise of alchemy was so intensely real for them because they were actually imaging, or imagining, their own individuation process in their chemical experiments.

From the perspective of today, alchemy is art and science as one unified enterprise, as alchemy is the ancestor of modern chemistry, which began when researchers stopped looking for the immaterial spirit. It was also art because the ingredients of symbols, philosophy and religious practices were individually combined into meaning-making ... Arguably, alchemy was arts-based *research* because of its constant speculative and investigatory quality. Later chapters will return to Jung's prescient employment of alchemy in modern psychotherapy.

In another evocative quaternary, Jung depicted psychotherapy as confession, followed by explanation, education and transformation (Jung 1933/2001: 35). Here analytic practice is more than helping with mental distress. It is rather re-making the person through an essentially pedagogic process. Confession of problems, linked by Jung to Catholic confession of more ecclesiastic times, is followed by a reassuring explanation of the various creaturely aspects of the psyche. There follows a process of education by doing, by exploring the living qualities of the psyche through its imagery. The result is transformation and a re-orienting to the world. Such a result is exactly the goal of much contemporary arts-based research. It is time to introduce this rich, diverse and challenging field of knowledge-making.

Introducing arts-based research

Research is a term with many connotations. Within its construction is the notion of re-search, or examining *again*. Hence research is to look again at what we think we know, and to critically examine it with a view to extending, revising or making it more useful. Research is purposeful. It is required to connect meaningfully to a bigger picture of the established knowing and being of a world or social group. In this way, research differs from art in Western traditions, which have diverged more and more from specific imperatives. When Oscar Wilde has a character proclaim: "the good ended happily, the bad unluckily," he was explicitly rejecting the moral teaching value of literature, which was one of its lingering social justifications (1895/1990: 22).

While artists of all kinds continue to urge the necessity of art for healthy communities, the project to restore the ancient notion of art as research, as a means to new knowledge, is a direct challenge to post-Romantic art's desire to be a thing-in-itself, art as its own justification for being. Yet arts-based research was not entirely invented by modern pioneers such as Elliot Eisner, who set up a series of institutes at Stanford University from 1993 to 2005, leading ultimately to publications with Tom Barone such as *Arts Based Research* (2012). After all, the role of imagination was treated as a proper knowledge-making tool until the rise of a "scientific method" that insisted on the researchers' detachment (Nicolescu 2014: 5). James Rolling Jnr.'s invaluable *Arts-Based Research Primer* (2013) considers the progressive marginalization of the imagination from making valued knowledge.

This split between the arts, humanities and sciences will be explored in Chapters 2 and 3. For now, Rolling Jnr. helpfully divides ABR into four categories: analytic research, or thinking in materials; synthetic, meaning re-examining communities of discourse; critical-activist; and improvisatory (ibid.: 51–8). More details will be given on these categories below, but what all four types of ABR share is their starting base, or what is presumed before the research can begin. For what makes ABR distinctive, and, in the view of many, a different research paradigm, is its lack of commitment to any specific worldview.

An arts-based research ontology accepts universal laws as they may emerge, yet does not *presume* them and does not promote the validity of outcomes on their ability to be replicated without significant variance in other contexts. Rather an arts-based ontology accepts a universe of variances and supports knowledge as a local interpretation of reality, valid within its own context, yet fully subject to reinterpretation or translation into other contexts.

(ibid.: 5, italics in original)

Ontology is the study of being. It is therefore the explicit or implicit starting place for any act of research. Looking again, or re-searching, entails encountering the academic disciplines that themselves possess one or more ontologies. Jungian ontology could be said to be the reality of the known *and* unknown psyche. Apart from the multifarious psyche, Jung does not suggest that other aspect of being be taken for granted, as we have seen. The existence of the unconscious means that all other knowledge is incomplete. Even Jungian principles can only be taken as a pragmatic working model. Rolling Jnr.'s initial sentence above could be accurately rewritten with Jung instead of ABR: a *Jungian* research ontology accepts universal laws as they may emerge, yet does not presume them.

Therefore, ABR ontology is an ungrounded theory; it insists upon nothing except the validity and being of art itself. Since art depends upon the existence of a maker, the human psyche, while not specifying anything about that psyche except the capacity to create, already Jung and ABR are united in a common ontological enterprise. Jung presumes a creative and partly unconscious psyche; ABR presumes the meaningful existences of the product of that psyche. By being what they are, they make conceptual space for each other.

A term often linked to arts-based research is heuristic, which refers to problem solving by practice rather than theorizing in advance. Heuristic research will be driven by the intuitive function in Jungian terms. Although it is true that art-making can be heuristic and almost always intuitive, it would be wrong to define ABR as inherently heuristic. For much art is guided not by the artist alone as a single being presuming nothing with regard to a problem. Rather, the artist is never just a single perspective; it is the artist-and-the-medium as a given.

A writer is always conscious of other writing, and a painter works, perhaps alone, yet aware of the ghostly presence of painting as a medium that is centuries old and cross-cultural. If heuristics implies meaning-making from the single, intuitive and improvising researcher, it does not account fully for ABR. While these qualities are very much part of art practice, they are not its sole tools, as we will see. Rather, artists work with the existing world of art and its concrete materials, even when trying to transform or revolutionize them. Arts-based research may participate in heuristics, but is not restricted to it.

Similarly, ABR is neither quantitative research nor qualitative exclusively. It rather absorbs ideas and practices from both major research types. Quantitative research derives its validity from using large amounts of data or big populations, whereas qualitative research emphasizes the researcher's perspective and immersion in the work as an organic part of the study. Although ABR might appear on the surface as securely qualitative, it lacks the research's specific and ontological location in the researcher.

Qualitative research locates meaning-making in the researcher's interaction with her subjects. ABR, on the other hand, must factor in the art as an independently meaningful entity. The art must ultimately stand alone, not dependent on the artist for its meaning. Also, while ABR is rarely interested in making large quantities of art, or in putting on a show with thousands of actors, its creativity and what counts as *art* are not excluded from quantitative rules and premises. Jung himself was keen to show that many psychic images, as evidenced in cross-cultural art, are plentiful and recurring. To him, their quantity was germane to knowledge.

Rolling Jnr. cites Harold Pearse (1983) on art-making forming systems of production, communication or critical reflection (2013: 9). Again, these characteristics make ABR stand out from traditional quantitative or qualitative practices. Art *produces* and so indicates knowledge-making that may or may not be based on knowledge discovering. Art communicates by its very nature in multiple, complex and not fully conscious ways. Traditional research is usually communicated after it is completed, and rarely seeks modes of appealing to diverse audiences or to the unknown psyche.

Finally, art is a critical reflection in its essence because it enters the world of pre-existing artistic practice, even if only to flout it. Whereas artists may deliberately use art as a medium for cultural criticism or not, they are, by the very nature of art, producing a creative, idiosyncratic response to the culture. Such individuality and idiosyncrasy can be read as critical.

Many of these dimensions of art are already present in Jungian psychology. The Jungian psyche is always producing images, some of which are symbols connecting the known to the unknown. Such images of varying psychic intensity and in any media, from the aural, visual, verbal etc., become the raw material of art. Images thus materialized in art communicate on multiple levels within the person and throughout society. Jungian individuation means that critical reflection is built into images-making-art. What is made in dialogue with the unknown psyche will intrinsically vary and challenge stereotypical assumptions. It does so to provoke more interactions with the unknown psyche, and hence more individuation.

All the above factors in arts-based research make a distinct paradigm, or knowledge-making worldview, according to Rolling Jnr. ABR is a reflexive practice with formational and informational and transformational properties (Rolling Jnr. 2013: 13). While research paradigms will be considered more fully in the next chapter, these notions do bear uncanny resemblance to Jung's

four stages of psychotherapy: confession; explanation; education; transformation (see above). For example, any process of reflection in research means
identifying problems or gaps, a kind of confession of what is wrong or absent.

Of course in psychotherapy a new patient will be pre-occupied with themselves, and a researcher is looking at problems in a more collective sense, but
the notion of beginning with a wound or absence is suggestive. Rolling Jnr.'s
informational aspect of ABR is close to Jung's stages of explanation and education, while formational and transformational moments recall Jung's psychic
transformation through enlivened and less painful individuation. For just as
much modern art seeks form, even when abstracting it, rather than presuppos-
ing it, so too does the Jungian psyche search for its own myth, its unique
story's arc of being. Similarly, just as one genre of art takes form in relation to
other art genres, so too does the personal myth spark meaning from other, culturally available myths.

Ultimately, ABR is transformational, of the artist researcher and, as we will
see, aims to be so for the culture. While conservative-minded Jung concentrated on individual transformation in psychotherapy, he was also a cultural
critic who saw that Western society was sick because it had repressed too
much that was "other" to its rational, patriarchal and colonial structures. He
knew that individual psychic health could not be separated from cultural
health. He suggested that art was one potent means for the collective unconscious to rebalance the world (Jung 1930: para. 161). It is time to look a little
closer at Rolling Jnr.'s types of arts-based research.

Types of arts-based research

Analytic arts-based research, or thinking in materials, is arguably empirical or
experiential. It means that the artist researcher is immersed in the medium *and
that very immersion* is the guiding direction towards meaning. Rolling Jnr.
quotes Barone and Eisner on the way that the term "empirical" has become
diverted from its roots.

> [W]e find it ironic that what is regarded as empirical focuses upon studies
> in which numbers are used to convey meaning … Indeed, it is interesting
> to note that the word *empirical* is rooted in the Greek word *empirikos*,
> which means experience. What is hard to experience is a set of numbers.
> What is comparatively easy to experience is a set of qualities.
>
> (Barone and Eisner 2012: xi, italics in original, quoted in
> Rolling Jnr. 2013: 21)

C. G. Jung also regarded creativity as empirical, in that his work with psychic
images was immediate contact with the material, the image as a thing itself
(1963/1983: 205, 336). To him, his psychology was scientific because it
encountered images from the deep psyche, empirically, without pre-judging

them. Here we remember Jung's assertion that his principles and concepts were a model, or a net thrown over psychic experience. The experience of images is, in his mind, an empirical act of knowing to be offered in the hypothetical frame of the psychology as a set of ideas. In a sense, the concepts are meaning-making forms by which to encounter the raw empirical matter of psychic images. Moreover, it is worth emphasizing how close Jung and ABR are in how their empiricism runs counter to what is meant by empirical research in modern times.

So-called mainstream empirical research is supposed to be repeatable, or replicated by another researcher. Neither the psyche nor the production of art works that way. Psychic images may share generic archetypal themes, yet they are unique as expressions of a particular moment. The empiricism of the psyche and of art combines what is transcendent or general (archetype, art in genres) with what is immanent, unique and particular (for the artist and the audience).

So analytic arts-based research is led by empirical practice in the medium, whether that medium be paint, music, film or writing or some other. Rolling Jnr. quotes from his analytic ABR paper, "Messing with Identity Constructs: Pursuing a Poststructuralist and Poetic Aesthetics" (Rolling Jnr. 2004). He demonstrates through poetic writing that his art is not an example, or a vehicle for ideas for pre-existing ideas. It is rather an *exploration through making* of the relationship of words, memory and being (ibid.: 79).

> In this writing I present myself as a child again, reconstituting blue worlds, regaining alternative homes, extra-normal realities, positioned outside of adult constraints and considerations. Outside the home of my father. Outside of schooling. Outside of my anxious body.
>
> (ibid.)

For analytic ABR, the art medium is a dynamic, creative, molten entity and a full partner with the researcher-artist. The artist does not shape the medium to a predetermined subject or outcome. Rather, the act of immersion, thinking in the materials (where words are materials too) becomes a mode of being and knowing. Similarly to Rolling Jnr.'s example, *The Nuclear Enchantment of New Mexico* in this volume is not prose-poems *about* nuclear New Mexico. It is a thinking/being in poetry to explore and investigate how the land, people and their psyches have been scorched by nuclear technologies. It is analytic ABR that, like many other such projects, has aspects of Rolling Jnr.'s other types as well.

Synthetic arts-based research practice reinterprets existing published research and dominant assumptions through the making of art. Rolling Jnr.'s analytic ABR above was also synthetic in undermining and repositioning categories and genres of traditional research writing (ibid.: 98). Research generally is characterized by forming and re-forming communities around ideas and practices in disciplines and fields. Synthetic research directly addresses these knowledge-making activities or discourses. In the making of art, synthetic ABR will enter a dialogue with multiple perspectives.

Its aim is not to force the research conversation into one dominant view because art is conceived as inherently fluid and open to many and various interpretations. Rather, synthetic ABR enters discourse as a space of mutability and transformation to adopt and switch between voices. It may offer new yet temporary theoretical notions; it always continues the productive dance of generating new positions (ibid.: 87–90). Such research could take explicitly theatrical or performative form, while it is also conducted through private acts of writing, painting, sculpting and so forth. The synthetic aspect of *The Nuclear Enchantment of New Mexico* is both within the poetry and in its dialogue with what Weishaus calls "paratexts," which bring scholarship from multiple disciplines into a unique and generative relationship with the poetry (see Chapter 5).

Given that synthetic ABR re-orients the existing research field, it is not difficult to see that it may overlap with critical-activist arts-based research. Here research is ex-centric. The art resists and disrupts the centralizing tendency of powerful ideas or powerful groups. The theorist most influential to exploration of power as a centralizing force on language and society is M. M. Bakhtin. In *The Dialogical Imagination* (1981), Bakhtin has a metaphysical notion of primal centripetal forces of power in language that are countered by the way actual practice dilutes the discourse of power in what he calls heteroglossia. Every act of speech and writing is in one sense individual, and yet also framed and constrained by only partly conscious structures of permission and prohibition.

Power focuses language and aspires to an impossible purity. Such perfection of pure power in utterance is impossible because it only gets enacted by individuals affected by multiple divergent energies that shape psychic embodiment every day. Hence, critical-activist arts-based research exploits the eccentric, destabilizing potential of the artistic imagination. By engaging with powerful ideas and groups through making art, there is emphasis on its heteroglossic capacity to disrupt.

Critical-activist ABR detonates conventional narratives such as the work of the street artist known as Banksy, who turns graffiti into an investigation of how public spaces are made to reinforce dominant social groups, while in *The Nuclear Enchantment of New Mexico*, poetry disrupts the typical scientific and military terminology around nuclear weapons. The work reveals how the positioning of certain types of language has enabled weapons of mass destruction to be hidden from full consciousness.

Resemblance between the work of Bakhtin and Jung was first considered by Raya A. Jones (2003) and explored in my *Jung as a Writer* (2005). If language does work in the centrifugal (heteroglossia) and centripetal way proposed by Bakhtin, then it presupposes a corresponding psychic patterning rather like Jung's archetypes. A sense of Bakhtin for the critical-activist ABR artist will be energized by a psyche that destabilizes fixed meanings. The Jungian psyche de-centers meaning and makes it fluid because that is how individuation works. Therefore, the critical-activist artist would be enthused by understanding the Jungian psyche as *inherently* challenging of the existing forms and language of power.

To C. G. Jung art is innately critical-activist, not because he wanted any kind of actual revolution, but because he saw that repression of all that is "other" in psychic terms is enacted in repression of all that is other to hegemonic powers in social and ecological terms. Art imbued with psychic images as symbols of the unconscious destabilizes power as a necessary attempt to heal modernity's sick psyche. Whether its aim is reforming or revolutionizing society, critical-activist ABR gains by the opportunity of a Jungian underpinning.

All art is dialogical in Bakhtin's sense, because it is always in a tension between the idea of perfect form incarnated in medium or genre, and its enactment, which inevitably brings in individual heteroglossic immanence. Arguably, genre in art is itself a centripetal idea pushing towards conformity, tradition and the way art has previously reinforced the powerful. Take the genre of portrait painting, for example, where the tradition points to the artefact as a display of worldly dominion. In this context, the ABR painter might disrupt the heritage of portraits as a celebration of an individual's social position. A portrait can aim to enact immortality (as an icon of the state), or suggest his or her mortality.

Here I have stressed that critical-activist research need not be an overt act of protest to qualify. This is not to undervalue ABR that is demonstrably subversive in its material processes, such as turning a nuclear weapons base into a theater or guerrilla gardening, making artful gardens in neglected or contested public spaces. Above all, critical-activist ABR is sited on the Jungian archetypal psyche as endless encounters with the other, whether it is aware of it or not.

The fourth type of improvisatory research practice is a modality more familiar to the artistic community. It corrals intuition in the full Jungian sense of being guided instinctively by the energies of the unknown psyche. Here the self as in the whole being of the researcher becomes the instrument of the process. What most distinguishes this type of ABR is the commitment to an unknown destination before the artist begins.

Crucially, the researcher is not always the subject or goal of research, as improvisatory ABR can be directed to interior or exterior material. Indeed, improvisatory research can range from the purely instinctual to the fully cognitive (Rolling Jnr. 2013: 133). In between these polarities is the realm of intuition, which Rolling Jnr., quoting Wilson (1998), expands in a dynamic and comprehensive way. Intuition enables creative play that is not restricted by the rigid demands of instinct, nor the rational demands of logic.

> Between these two distinct modalities of knowing [instinct and cognition] lies the intuitive, defined as that "which allows us to escape the inflexible world of instinct by mixing unlike entities," relying neither upon inexplicable precognitive impulses or careful logic but on that which is wholly and simultaneously "inventive and unreasonable" (Wilson 1998: 31). This range of instinctual, intuitive, and fully cognitive modalities are all at play in the creation of new knowledge through improvisatory arts-based research.
>
> (Rolling Jnr. 2013: 133)

While this is an exciting arena for the researcher, neither Rolling Jnr. nor Wilson includes Jung's development of intuition as embracing both body and non-material psyche. However, the point about mixing unlike entities is important. For Jung, archetypes, as embodied energies, link the deepest precognitive instinctual base, where body and psyche are indistinguishable, to the parts of the psyche where cognition is possible. His understanding of intuition and sensation is how the body becomes psyche through images that can be as diverse as obscure bodily symptoms, or as impactful as the astonishing effect of a powerful painting. Intuition is the autonomous mobilization of images in which the unknown psyche is most alive. In this way, it mixes unlike entities, as it demands that such images be treated as meaningful and *their* energy, their independent being, be trusted.

Moreover, Jung integrates intuition as one of the four key psychic functions that can be distinguished from each other, as we have seen above. Intuition is important because the unknown psyche is actively trying to individuate the person by means of its autonomous creative energy. The unconscious will, of its own accord, try to supply the ego with what it lacks, or has repressed. Here lies the great connection between art-making and individuation, a connection, not an identity. While the archetypal unconscious will generate images to compensate or remedy a fragile ego, art psychotherapy has risen to operate in the Jungian psyche's teleological drive to wholeness.

A work of art may be the outcome of art therapy, yet art is not the goal of art therapy, which is always the therapy and not the art. Artists in any media are linked by seeing art as possessing a life and integrity *independent of themselves*, to the extent that art has to be prioritized over self-healing considerations. In fact, Jung came closest to understanding art in this way by acknowledging that visionary art may be demanded by wounds, or gaps, in the culture, not the person. Jung's ambivalence about art will be returned to. For now, it is important to stress that improvisatory ABR, using a range of human qualities from instinct, intuition to cognition, will not be limited to therapeutic aims, whether of the maker or of society.

Jung's framework of four key functions of thinking, feeling, sensation and intuition is a tool for working with the experience, process and results of improvisation that could – perhaps should – include exploration in each psychic property. Arguably, Jung's model of the psyche can in this way expand

ABR significantly at the level of process. Sensation, which Jung saw in the participation of the physical senses in art, can be a springboard for intuition that can be further developed by thinking, valuing and feeling. We begin to see that Jungian psychology is a map for building a more integrated model of artistic process. That such an account of psychic creativity can help ABR address modernity's way of knowing and being will be the subject of the next two chapters.

To conclude this introductory chapter, I offer Rolling Jnr.'s succinct summary of the way ABR challenges previous structures of research, more on Jung's ambivalence over art, and a research context that ABR itself is slowly approaching, that of transdisciplinarity (Nicolescu 2014).

Arts-based research as challenging knowledge conventions

Rolling Jnr. argues that ABR is by nature radical and challenging because it questions not only how we make knowledge but also what we call knowing (4–18). It does so in three ways, all of which undermine any claim of knowledge to be transcendent or beyond dispute, universally applicable and accepted. Transcendent knowledge would exist in a realm above any considerations of history and cultural partiality. It would be abstract and not subject to revision. On the other hand, ABR brings ideological, rhetorical and socially constructed considerations to bear on existing disciplines and paradigms.

First of all, he stresses that art-making is a *process* directed to an audience that is not limited to a specific group at any one moment. It is therefore ideological in the sense of engaging with current political and social norms and yet also must reach beyond them. In doing so, rather like the critical role of Jungian psychology in revealing what is not yet known, ABR refuses to simply replicate ideological conventions. ABR will of its nature subvert and reveal what is ideological about existing knowledge.

Moreover, ABR engages rhetorically with traditional research genres and forms. Rhetoric is the art of persuasion, and is therefore a vital under-recognized component of all research. For example, columns of numbers are presented for rhetorical value as well as content value if they are enacting a research paradigm that is generally accepted (see Chapter 2). Rolling Jnr. gives an example of his own ABR of creative writing, pointing out that "[m]y approach was literally to undermine traditional research writing practice" (Rolling Jnr. 2013: 98). His work interrupts the rhetorical strategies of typical social science writing about identity in order to examine, critique and offer alternative models of knowing. In this sense all ABR is rhetorically innovative and critical as it brings not only the newness (to modernity) of making knowledge through art, but also the newness of rhetorical form enacted by every individual piece.

Finally, ABR reveals the socially constructed nature of knowing by fore-grounding the *making* of knowledge, even if it is also discovering knowledge. Knowing is socially constructed if we accept that it arises out of embedded social conditions and agreements about what is real and what is not. Since art is never stripped of a cultural context that is prepared to engage with the arte-fact, even if to recoil in horror, then it foregrounds the fragile social contract over what is art and what is not art. In this setting, ABR makes visible the socially encoded strategies that go into knowledge producing and disseminating.

Indeed, ABR often provides far more diverse audiences for academic know-ing. Typically in academic research access is limited by its rhetorical conven-tions that only the initiated can penetrate. In this way, traditional forms of research encode privilege by only being accessible to the highly, if narrowly, educated. ABR questions such privileging by using the broader communicative strategies of art to make and disseminate knowing. Such an overturning of how research is received reveals how far the academy and its research is repli-cating rather than critiquing social exclusion. In doing so ABR again uncovers social construction in knowledge production.

Above, I have suggested that ABR and Jung offer similar positions to know-ledge-making, in aiming to bring the new or previously unknown into con-sciousness (ABR through embedding in communicable art). Given such cordiality, what about Jung's own ambivalence about art as key to psyche?

Not art but nature?

In his autobiography, *Memories, Dreams, Reflections*, Jung records a famous exchange with a figure in his psyche.

> I once asked myself, "What am I really doing?" … Whereupon a voice within me said, "It is art." … This time I … said, "No, it is not art! On the contrary, it is nature," and prepared myself for an argument.
>
> (Jung 1963/1983: 210–11)

> If I had taken these fantasies of the unconscious as art … The anima might then have easily seduced me into believing that I was a misunderstood artist, and that my so-called artistic nature gave me the right to reject reality.
>
> (ibid.: 211–12)

Jung is in the midst of a psychological crisis in two senses. His break with Freud is partially due to his inability to accept Freud's dictum that all psychic energy is fundamentally sexual. To Jung, psychic energy was not fundamen-tally any one thing; it was mutable and extended into mysterious realms that could equally manifest in a religious or spiritual manner. The quarrel with Freud over ideas in psychology precipitated Jung's own mental breakdown, with visions, and voices, such as the anima above. These images from Jung's unconscious eventually find form in his unfinished, and unpublished by him, *Liber Novus* or *Red Book*, which will be the subject of Chapter 4. Meanwhile, what of his visceral rejection of the role of the artist?

Tjeu van den Berk's excellent book, *Jung on Art* (2012) unpicks the psychologist's suspicion of aesthetics, a term often folded into ideas about art, and refers to the study of what makes beauty (Berk 2012: 57–60). As one immersed in German Romanticism, Jung took aesthetics from Alexander Baumgarten, who in 1735 argued that aesthetics was the "science of the quality of sensory sensation," and so an instinctual and bodily matter only. From this perspective, Jung saw the aesthetic, or beautiful, sensory qualities as confined to sensation and intuition, the more unconscious of his four functions. Art may employ aesthetics, but is not identical with it. He realized that an artwork can also demand ethical qualities of thinking and feeling as well.

> Jung believed that when a person adopts an aesthetic viewpoint, that is to value something as beautiful or not, it is mainly intuition and sensation that are activated in him. Not thinking and feeling. An aesthetic viewpoint is not at all the same as an ethical viewpoint. Jung … fundamentally disagreed with the opinion that art is the same as aesthetics.
>
> (Berk 2012: 57)

Today, aesthetics is considered as the dimension of art that was engaged with beauty in any sense, including its rejection and destruction. As we will see in later chapters, art-based research vigorously disputes Jung's Romantic heritage, because it sees the aesthetic as a summoning of what Jung might describe as all four functions. The aesthetic is a way of engaging with art that in ABR extends to ethical considerations that are integral to all research. However, Jung does discover ethics in his later encounters with art, as we will see. His famous concern that identifying as an artist would be a rejection of reality, and hence his patients, is only the beginning of the story of Jung as unwitting contributor to arts-based research.

A transdisciplinary future

In the *Handbook of Arts-Based Research*, its editor and contributor, Patricia Leavy, uses the term "transdisciplinary" to invoke the way ABR has greater communicative and hence social potential than traditional forms of research (Leavy 2018: 24). Nowhere in the *Handbook* is the term "transdisciplinary" defined as anything other than a way of blending hitherto separate and sometimes hostile disciplines. By contrast, Basarab Nicolescu has produced a vision of a transdisciplinary future that would not only welcome ABR but also would provide a new relationship between knowledge, power, culture, religion and the individual.

Originally a quantum physicist, Nicolescu describes transdisciplinarity as a rejection of any hierarchy of access to the truth among academic disciplines. No branch of science, no one psychology, philosophy, art or humanities subject can claim to be more "true" than any other. While different disciplines construct and/or explore different realities, none of these is more fundamental to who we are and how we know. Rather, the cosmos is made up of different kinds of reality, and so are human beings. Above all, the presumed superiority of the subject/object split in knowing is explicitly denied by transdisciplinarity. The importance of this move will be considered in the following chapter.

Nicolescu's book, *From Modernity to Cosmodernity*, shows an ancient division in Western culture between two forms of knowing. Reductive classical science relies upon the subject/object split and repeatable experiments, while what Nicolescu calls "Tradition" is knowledge fostered by religions, spirituality, bodily practices and the occult. Such knowing is tended by revelation, vision, feeling and intuition (Nicolescu 2014: 19–24). Despite the presence of the sacred in Tradition, it is, like the classical science that denies it, affected by history and culture.

What Nicolescu does not say is that the arts are a key means by which Tradition is renewed and perpetuated. The arts preserve and disseminate spirituality and revelation through their media. For art has forms with ancient origins that enact historically inflected ways of knowing and being. As we will see, ABR has a lot to say about splits in a culture's attitudes to knowledge. Jung and ABR together offer unique opportunities to re-weave the torn fabric of our research.

Future chapters will consider Jungian ABR as providing a psychology that extends to a philosophical approach that is innately holistic and embodied. Moreover, Jungian ABR can serve to address such twenty-first-century anxieties as technological alienation: it will propose a new human subject not limited to the human. Jungian ABR is also historically embedded in the multicultural practice of alchemy; it can be ecological, and of necessity is transdisciplinary. Jung can help make arts-based research into a paradigm for change that this era urgently requires.

Note

1 Joel Weishaus' "The Nuclear Enchantment of New Mexico" was originally a joint exhibition with photographer Patrick Nagatani that premiered at the Albuquerque Museum May 19–August 11, 1991, and went on to the Stanford University Museum of Art, October 19–December 12, 1993. Afterwards, under the title, "The Deeds and Sufferings of Light", Weishaus exhibited and further developed the texts on the Internet. In 2018–19 they were further revised with regard to recent research on nuclear weapons. Here they've been returned to their original title, for their first publication in book format.

References

Bakhtin, M. M. (1981) *The Dialogic Imagination: Four Essays*. ed. M. Holquist, trans. C. Emerson and M. Holquist. Austin, TX: University of Texas Press.

Barone, T. and E. W. Eisner. (2012) *Arts Based Research*. Los Angeles, CA and London: Sage Publications.

Beebe, J. (2016) *Energies and Patterns in Psychological Type: The Reservoir of Consciousness*. Hove and New York: Routledge.

Berk, T. V. D. (2012) *Jung on Art: the Autonomy of the Creative Drive*. New York and Hove: Routledge.

Hillman, J. (1975) *Re-Visioning Psychology*. New York: Harper & Row.

Jones, R. A. (2003) 'Mixed Metaphors and Narrative Shifts: Archetypes', *Theory & Psychology*, *13* (5), 651–672.

Jung, C. G. (1922) 'On the Relation of Analytical Psychology to Poetry', *Collected Works, Volume 15: The Spirit in Man, Art and Literature*, 65–83.

Jung, C. G. (1930) 'Psychology and Literature', in *Collected Works, Volume 15: The Spirit in Man, Art and Literature*, pp. 109–134.

Jung, C. G. (1933/2001) *Modern Man in Search of a Soul*. London and New York: Routledge.

Jung, C. G. (1947) 'On the Nature of the Psyche', in *Collected Works, Volume 8: The Structure and Dynamics of the Psyche*, pp. 159–234.

Jung, C. G. (1963/1983) *Memories, Dreams, Reflections*. Recorded and Edited by Aniela Jaffe. London: Fontana.

Jung, C. G. (1971/1987) *Dictionary of Analytical Psychology*. Ark Paperbacks. London and New York: Routledge & Kegan Paul.

Jung, C. G. (2009) *The Red Book: Liber Novus*. ed. S. Shamdasani, trans. M. Kyburz, J. Peck and S. Shamdasani. New York: W.W. Norton & Co.

Leavy, P. ed. (2018) *Handbook of Arts-Based Research*. New York and London: The Guilford Press.

Linden, S. J. (2003) *The Alchemy Reader: From Hermes Trismegistus to Isaac Newton*. Cambridge: Cambridge University Press.

Nicolescu, B. (2014) *From Modernity to Cosmodernity: Science, Culture and Spirituality*. New York: SUNY.

Pearse, H. (1983) 'Brother, Can You Spare a Paradigm? The Theory beneath the Practice', *Studies in Art Education*, *24* (3), 158–163.

Rolling Jnr., J. H. (2004) 'Messing around with Identity Contructs: Pursuing a Poststructural and Poetic Aesthetic', *Qualitative Inquiry*, *10* (4), 548–557.

Rolling Jnr., J. H. (2013) *Arts-Based Research Primer*. New York: Peter Lang.

Rowland, S. (2005) *Jung as a Writer*. Hove and New York: Routledge.

Wilde, O. (1895/1990) *The Importance of Being Earnest*. New York: Dover Publications.

Wilson, J. M. (1998) 'Art-making Behavior: Why and How Arts Education is Central to Learning', *Art Education Policy Review*, *99* (6), 26–33.

Chapter 2

Paradigms for Jungian arts-based research

Introduction

Research is not an isolated, nor wholly individual, activity. It happens in connection to existing bodies of knowledge called academic disciplines, even if the connection is highly critical. Moreover, disciplines relate to something larger that frames what they posit about reality and knowing. This larger frame is a paradigm, a worldview shaping and validating what can be known in any era. In *The Structure of Scientific Revolutions* (1962/2012), Thomas Kuhn points out how disciplines such as those of science work within models that go largely unchallenged.

> Somehow, the practice of astronomy, physics, chemistry or biology fails to evoke the controversies over fundamentals that today seem endemic among, say, psychologists or sociologists. Attempting to discover the source of that difference led me to recognize the role in scientific research of what I have since called "paradigms." These I take to be universally recognized scientific achievements that for a time provide model problems and solutions for a community of practitioners.
>
> (Kuhn 1962/2012: p. xiii)

For Kuhn, a paradigm provides a framework and sustenance for a certain kind of knowing. It operates until a scientific revolution, or paradigm-breaking weight of research, forces a new worldview on the community. What elevates scientific paradigms into a worldview is the rise of science, or a particular kind of science, as exemplified by the paradigm known as the "scientific method."

In the seventeenth century, Galileo, who has been called "the father of the scientific method," proposed the existence of universal mathematical laws of nature (Nicolescu 2014: 5). He then suggested that these laws can be discovered by scientific experiments, and that these procedures must be reproducible by an independent laboratory. Such a procedure for garnering knowledge gathers within it a vision of what is fundamentally real. Once this vision and its scientific method ascend into acceptance by the educated elites, they become the standard by which all research is measured.

In short, the scientific paradigm as depicted above is hegemonic in the sense that it dominates a culture's idea *of what reality is*, and how to know it. Above all, this paradigm of knowledge is profoundly dualist, because it places the knowing subject as separate from the object to be known. After all, in order for research to be reproducible, it cannot be contaminated by the singularity and uniqueness of the researcher. The subject cannot be identified with the object, or whatever the researcher is in the midst of discovering. Knowledge becomes predicated upon the subject/object split that appears everywhere in modernity as a founding assumption about what is real. Indeed, this model of research attempts to know the world as a series of objects that can be approached, but not participated in.

Art and Jungian studies have been deeply affected by the notion of a fundamental subject/object split. Arguably, the assumption that art consists of discrete "objects" with autonomous existence in the world, entirely separate from the artist, is influenced by this idea. Jung's psychology also is shaped by such duality in dividing the psyche into oppositional pairs, such as ego versus unconscious, ego versus shadow and so on. With the "other" in each pair, the unconscious element, Jung termed it the objective psyche.

On the other hand, Jungian psychology is profoundly committed to ending psychic dualism. It is devoted to the project of individuation by which the duality of the psyche becomes multiplicity and wholeness. To counter the split in modernity of a rational consciousness, or subject, cut off from the unknown collective psyche, Jung advocates integration. Thus, archetypes provide patterning energies by which the other or object is taken into being. Individuation occurs whether the other/object is projected on to other people or the nonhuman. Jungian psychology dissolves the subject/object split, and not just inside the psyche. Rather the aim of individuation is to find oneself as indivisible from the realities of society, nature, planet and the heavens, as we shall see. The subject/object split is turned into an ensouled world.

Similarly, arts-based research challenges and re-visions the conventional subject/object split of traditional research. Chapter 1 referred to the division in research between quantitative and qualitative approaches. By engaging in large amounts of data, quantitative research embraces the ethos of the subject/object split by minimizing the entanglement of the researcher or researchers with the work. By contrast, qualitative research draws the so-called object of knowing into the subjectivity of the researcher.

Arts-based research appears to be more qualitative, by making knowing through immersion in embodied, generic and creative processes. However, as shown in Chapter 1, ABR goes beyond the qualitative. It produces tangible artworks that are heirs to traditions of knowing in art history and its material connections to society. As seen in Chapter 1, art-based research is empirical yet not reproducible: artists begin with the uniqueness of their individual psyche.

Given that both Jungian studies and ABR reject the subject/object paradigm, it is worth considering some of the problems with this ubiquitous structure of knowledge. Surely objectivity is desirable, even necessary for research?

Problems of enchantment with the subject/object split

Lee Worth Bailey, in *The Enchantments of Technology* (2005), argues that in the history of thought, some notions become more substantial than the realities they purport to describe (Bailey 2005: 41–3). Such is the subject/object split as fundamental to knowing what is authentically real. Whereas the word "object" derives from something thrown before, since the Enlightenment it possesses two meanings: that of a material thing, and as a standard for an objective truth.

His argument continues to show that the object in the subject/object split is far from objective. On the one hand, the insistence on this paradigmatic severing endows the object with obtuseness, depriving it of its own agency and autonomy. The object is conceived at best as mechanical, at worst as dead. The consequences for relations with matter and nature in this notion of knowing subject versus dumb object are everywhere around us in the present climate emergency.

Moreover, the object as obtuse is insufficient to account for its hidden effects. Rather, the split into subject/object is always psychological, Bailey insists. Hence the object is not a product of objectivity, but rather is unconsciously endowed with all kinds of irrational and largely unknown passions. For one attribute created by this overblown subject/object split is the illusion that the mind, or psyche, is locked in the human skull. As Jung also demonstrates, this is far from the case. We encounter the psyche in archetypal energies we have unconsciously bestowed upon the world. Put another way, technology, a distant cousin of art, has been falsely presented in modernity as a series of human-designed soulless objects (Bailey 2005: 41–57).

In fact, technologies are not the obtuse tools the subject/object myth imagines them to be. From cameras to flying machines to nuclear bombs, the notion of their inertness is a powerful enchantment from which they fundamentally derive, and which they, in turn, install in future generations. This is enchantment as a dangerous spell woven by the unconscious and enacted everywhere the subject/object split is taken as the ultimate paradigmatic guarantor of truth and reality.

While separating the subject from the topic to be known has made possible our modern society, Bailey suggests that the elevation of this dualism to supremacy results in a modernity perilously enchanted. Modernity is in thrall to its own technology because it is so unconscious of it. Here technology is the unconscious hidden in plain sight in apparently obtuse objects. For example, the subject/object split can be enacted in the saying that guns do not kill, only people do. In a superb analysis, Bailey unpacks the heroic, phallocentric, masculinist fantasies at work in the matter of the firearm (guns are firearms), just as the modern myth of the space cowboy requires bigger and bigger missiles (Bailey 2005: 122–54).

Bailey reminds us that if the object is far from objective, then we can see this problem also in the modern meanings of subject (Bailey 2005: 59). In one sense, the subject is the ego as centre of modern identity, the fragile shell containing "I." It is also considered as the interior mental realm as opposed to the exterior in the subject/object division. Finally, subject refers to an internal area of desires, instincts and feelings, so-called subjectivity. Again, we see a construct that is contrary to the realization that psychic reality is not a series of balloons, or "thought bubbles," inside a head. The inside/outside dichotomy is yet another version of the subject/object split. What was once a useful fiction has morphed into a dangerous enchantment.

> One of the most deeply entrenched enchantments of technological culture is this theory that the mind is contained in a subjective mental region of the brain, looking out onto a separate world of objects … It [the mind] does not know itself entirely, it is not fully "internal," nor is it "present" to itself, for unconscious passions lie below its well-lit control room and send powerful forces up to disrupt and guide it. Many of the "unexpected" outcomes of technology result from these dark, concealed forces, as we see in road rage.
>
> (Bailey 2005: 58)

Published in 2005, before the ubiquity of social media, how much more transformational are the unforeseen results of technology such as Facebook and Twitter? In the 2016 American election these inventions were far from an obtuse and neutral medium. In fact, social media proved to be an enchanting cauldron from which complex algorithms sought to manipulate populations. Social media was unleashed upon a public already enchanted by the technology of the imaginary subject/object split to believe that its seductions cannot be consequential. In fact, the hard-to-fathom impact of the Internet and its delights confirms Bailey's Jung-inspired contention that the human subject is bottomless.

> The subject seems like a tight container but when we descend into the depths of the soul and the world, we find the notion of subjectivity to be bottomless. All the passions and images that the theory of projection attempts to separate into the objective psyche flow from endless mysterious, bottomless depths of existence itself, more primordial than the subject/object divide and its mechanical models.
>
> (Bailey 2005: 82)

Bailey here disputes Jung's long reliance on projection as a way of understanding the psyche as an interior projected outside. Jung, too, reluctantly renounced this last shred of dualism when he discovered synchronicity (Jung 1952, CW8). Long fascinated by practices that challenged the assumption of the objectivity of the external object, such as spiritualism, the topic of his doctoral dissertation, Jung came to believe that the archetypal subject was indeed bottomless, because it could be affected by the external world in ways inexplicable by the scientific paradigm.

Synchronicity and the goddess for arts-based research

The subject/object split sets up a notion of causality in a universe of discrete material objects that can impact each other. No such physical cause can be found for dreams that appear to record events far away, of which the dreamer has no conscious knowledge. Moreover, some dreams seem to be prophetic, or to be linked to the "outer" world in a way that is meaningful rather than causal. Such a phenomenon Jung termed "synchronicity." With this discovery, Jung directly addresses the problem of the scientific method when the object is regarded as separate from its subject.

Of course, to Jung the subject/object split always ignores the guiding principle of his work regarding the autonomous reality of the psyche. However, with synchronicity Jungian psychology is no longer predicated upon unconscious projection, a way of simultaneously having and not having a split between a person's inner and outer world. Instead, synchronicity opens the archetypal psyche to a cosmos that also becomes psychological. In suggesting that archetypes exist in the so-called material universe, as well as imagined as within the human skull, Jungian psychology is holistic. It discerns independent pattern-making in all reality, and ultimately presents a vision of truth ripe for the quest of arts-based research.

Synchronicity proposes an underlying acausal archetypal ordering where psyche meets matter, which Jung called the psychoid. Hence, synchronicity is an on-going activity animating the universe. In particular, archetypes are not the causal origins of synchronous events; rather, they are factors structuring their meaning. So Jung calls synchronous events "*acts of creation in time*" (Jung 1952, CW8: para. 965).

The importance of the resistance to causality within synchronicity cannot be overstressed. Jung is not presenting another version of the mechanical, clockwork universe, this time with unconscious archetypes in control. Instead, synchronicity means that the cosmos itself is creative, always finding new forms for emerging fluid, never fixable, meanings. Synchronicity is the universe itself making what we might call mutable forms of art in every fabric and mode of reality. Such acts of creation in time can never be wholly accounted for by rational or cause-and-effect ways of knowing. Synchronicity is the end of the subject/object split as the dominant paradigm of research.

One often overlooked aspect of Jung's writing about synchronicity is its archetypal embodiment in a goddess.

> For [experimental science] there is created in the laboratory a situation
> which is artificially restricted ... The workings of Nature in her unre-
> stricted wholeness are completely excluded ... [W]e need a method of
> enquiry which ... leaves Nature to answer out of her fullness.
>
> (Jung 1952, CW8: para. 864)

This invocation of reality as feminine Nature is probably the closest Jung gets
to allowing the ancient pattern of a mother goddess into his thinking. The conventional trope of Mother Nature in modernity has a complex history, as
shown in *The Myth of the Goddess* by Ann Baring and Jules Cashford (1991).
"She" is today the submissive projection of the Father God of the monothe-
isms, Judaism, Christianity and Islam, who represents a gendered attitude to
the Divine and His creation. The notion of one supreme God sets up
a foundational dualism of God and not-God. This God creates everything,
including nature and human beings, as separate from Himself. The same religious pattern of God alone and not part of His creation becomes the dominant
template of modernity. From a God unconnected to the nature He made comes
the scientific subject/object split, and knowledge as reproducible because it is
wholly separate from the knower.

Mother Nature in this paradigmatic perception of reality is passive, receptive
and non-creative. *Mater* becomes matter as inert, essentially dead. Of course,
this is not the sole, archetypal understanding of nature in history, nor in other
societies. Cultures more closely embedded in the life of the planet as well as
glimpses of a pre-monotheistic past offer nature as itself divine. Nature is the
all-powerful Mother, from whom all life, being and knowing extend. The
planet is herself a goddess; her matter is sacred mater of everything. One way
that this goddess paradigm of wholeness and interconnectedness is enacted is
in animism, the understanding that everything is endowed with spirit that
humans can sometimes interact with.

Nature as Mother Goddess is therefore plurality within a wholeness, not
singleness of being and meaning, because that would be no life or spirit. She
is feminine in the sense that she is Mother, but not in the binary sense of not-
masculine, as she contains and supports all potential modes of gender and
sexuality. She is not "for" women as opposed to men. Rather, she supports creativity in all its possible iterations.

It is indicative of the potential of this alternative paradigm of the feminine
within all life and genders that it has returned to us in modernity in the form
of the theory of evolution, and also in ecology. Evolution means all life evolving from the planet's innate creativity – a secular theology. Ecology's defining
perception of interconnectedness, rather than subject/object division, represents
a paradigmatic shift only now being taken seriously in the West. (It has long
been a central tenet of East Asian metaphysics.)

Put another way, Jung's synchronicity goddess puts psychic interconnectivity
into ecological research. Synchronicity as the divine creativity of the fabric of

the universe is also woven into our being. Mother Nature perceived as synchronous is poised to become the divine partner of the arts-based researcher. She is necessary as the matrix or paradigmatic web that can begin to counter the toxic legacies of enchanted obsession with the subject/object split.

For, as suggested above, excessive dualism enchants and stagnates into a subject/object split that includes gender. The enchantments of technology have been exaggerated by, and in turn exaggerate, gender as one mode of splitting. Patriarchy fuses with scientific method. As a result, and the notion of subjectivity and objectivity as forever severed genders the dominant scientific knowing as masculine. Such a development is no longer just about extending knowledge. Rather it is enacted in power structures and colonial insurgencies.

Similarly, the Western conception of art has been shaped by the artist as essentially masculine divine creativity that produces an inert feminine object. The artist is then literalized as male seeking the feminine for inspiration for his raw material. Perhaps the synchronous goddess can unpick the patriarchal contamination of art? The aim would be to liberate as yet unimagined, holistic, plural, collective and protean ways that art can know the as yet unlived potential of being *with* the planet, rather than just on it.

In order to emphasize that Jungian arts-based research provides a paradigm that is not a total break with all academic knowing, I want to look at its precursor, the arts-based research known as alchemy[1].

Jung, alchemy and arts-based research: the historical paradigm

From the point of view of the modern scientific paradigm, alchemy was a doomed attempt to convert cheap lead into precious gold. Fortunately for alchemy, it resisted the rise of modern science with its subject/object split for as long as possible. Eventually alchemy's scientific claims were entirely rejected and its operations on minerals in test tubes were renamed chemistry. Even then, artists and poets continued to practice their alchemy by being deeply involved with matter through participatory imagination. The death of alchemy as *both* science and art was a severing that has only recently begun to be reconsidered. Once the dominance of the subject/object paradigm in knowing is challenged, alchemy can return, characterized by including the alchemist in a transforming process.

Another important paradigmatic attribute of alchemy is its long history and multiculturalism. Alchemy was an ancient practice in China, India and Africa long before it became important to medieval Islam, and from there passed into Europe (Linden 2003: 1–12). Jung was fascinated by European Renaissance alchemy books after being sent a translation from the Chinese *The Secret of the Golden Flower*, by Richard Wilhelm, in 1928 (Jung 1963/83: 230). Diverse by origin and practice, alchemy has been undervalued for its practical potential as a mode of research that engages both psyche and matter without privileging either. To the alchemist, the world is ensouled and the psyche has material dimensions.

Jung became captivated by alchemy because he saw that it was a science of symbols. In writing and in woodcuts and paintings, alchemists depicted a world ignorant of the subject/object split. Hence, it does not regard nature as existing without the creativity and imagination that are also part of human beings. Creatures today considered mythical, such as dragons, inhabit landscapes peopled with human figures with heads that are the sun and moon. A tree grows from a man's penis, or depicts stages in a great transformation. Alchemical books read like prose poetry with narratives of death and resurrection, serpents, a shapeshifter called Mercurius and intense desires to release a god trapped in matter.

The latter notion reveals the Christian influence on European alchemy as it pulls towards transcendence and a split of the divine, true reality (and the object in knowing) from the human subject. Jung, too, could not take alchemy on its own terms. For much of the alchemical studies in *The Collected Works*, Jung insisted that alchemists were mistaken psychotherapists of themselves. They projected, without conscious deliberation, their unconscious psyches on to the matter they were seeking to change. It was their own psychic individuation that lured them into the seemingly hopeless task of converting lead into gold (Jung 1937, CW12: para. 564). Jung was well aware that such a dualist paradigm was not that of the alchemists themselves. When he finds himself writing of mental or material realms, he corrects himself to say that for these figures there was no such separation (Jung 1937, CW12: para. 394, p. 266).

> [F]or that age ... there did exist an intermediate realm between mind and matter, i.e., a psychic realm of subtle bodies whose characteristic it is to manifest themselves in a mental as well as a material form.
>
> (ibid.)

The subtle body is where the psychic image or symbol becomes palpable, has material aspects and participates in the world of matter. Symbols as a way of knowing for Jungian arts-based research will be explored further in Chapter 3. Here it is worth remembering that in adopting synchronicity, Jung moved to embrace the paradigm of alchemy, and not the other way around. And in exploring Renaissance alchemy, Jung comes to portray these figures as fully immersed in what today would be called arts-based research, for they are working in a world of imagination, forming images that are part of the same order of doing and being as matter. This alchemical category of matter includes language, paint, clay, wood, music ... any material that can be animated into images.

The alchemist made images in psyche and matter without regarding psyche as separate from matter. She was doing so in order to provoke a great transformation, which alchemists believed was a hastening of natural processes. They thought that metals ripened in the earth, eventually to produce gold (Eliade 1956: 42). This was to be an investigation of nature, which did not regard Her as a machine to be disassembled, but rather as a living interconnected organism to be aided to pro-duce or release a divine spirit.

Gold was not inert metal, but a life-giving substance with multiple forms such as the ultimate medicine, a panacea, or giver of immortality, a god. Today alchemy is often cited as the ancestor of modern chemistry, with the idea of abstract research into chemicals. However, just as chemistry can be applied to finding new compounds for industry and pharmaceuticals, so alchemists were often also pharmacists. Many practiced as physicians, such as John Winthrop Jnr. (1606–76), alchemist and governor of the English colony of Connecticut (Woodward 2010).

Alchemists did creative research. The common ultimate goal was transform-ation, not easy riches. So too does arts-based research aim for transformation: there is a transformation into art that becomes a knowing *and transforming process* of the research topic (see Chapter 1). In fact, the common ground between Jung's research into alchemy and ABR is evident both from what he quotes of alchemists as well as what he writes. For Jung, alchemy and ABR meet in what alchemists called the true imagination, or *imaginatio.* Here Jung quotes from the *Rosarium Philosophorum* (1550).

> Nature carries out her operations gradually … let thy imagination be guided wholly by nature. And observe according to nature, through whom the substances regenerate themselves in the bowels of the earth. And imagine this with true and not with fantastic imagination.
> (Anonymous 1550, quoted by Jung 1936, CW12: para. 218)

Jung's commentary on this passage makes clear that he is witnessing a participatory, creative imagination that is embodied, seeking for the truth of the material and spiritual cosmos.

> *Imaginatio* is the active evocation of (inner) images *secundum naturam*, an authentic feat of thought or ideation, which does not spin aimless and groundless fantasies "into the blue" – does not, that is to say, just play with its objects, but tries to grasp the inner facts and portray them in images true to their nature. This activity is an *opus*, a work.
> (Jung 1936, CW12: para. 219)

Jung uses "inner" here twice, in an attempt to structure the subject/object para-digm where it does not belong. Fortunately, he presents enough of understand-ing of the alchemist's fidelity to creative nature to portray the figure as a genuine historical model for the arts-based researcher. For Jung's alchemists are working with what he termed embodied, largely unconscious intuition. They do so to facilitate images or symbols in a paradigm of incompleteness, since the divine qualities of matter escape rational capture.

Significantly, the alchemist's paradigm resembles that of transdisciplinarity, as we will see. Transdisciplinarity eschews the subject/object split in favor of multiple realities. These are considered in a dialogue with wholeness that must include the as yet unknown and what is unknowable by rational means. Alchemy in turn favors wholeness with divine unknowing in tension with a sense of multiplicity in the never predictable, creaturely, never controllable symbols. Both paradigmatic approaches to knowing infer the importance of arts-based research, and both are significantly prefigured by Jung. In consequence, it is worth looking a little further into Jung's account of alchemy.

Jung's alchemy processes and arts-based research

Jung was fascinated by the various stages of alchemy, which he argued were analogous to the individuation process by integrating aspects of the unconscious in different modes. For example, *putrefaction* or *nigredo* would be the rotting or dark encounters with the shadow; *conjunctio* or the *chymical wedding* is a profound erotic union with the unconscious other; and of course achieving the goal of a "golden" spirit corresponded to the full realization of the Self. As noted in Chapter 1, the union with anima or animus does not require the heterosexuality that Jung assumed as axiomatic.

Little noticed today is how far the stages of alchemy could be interpreted as a design for a research project. Alchemy was rejected for knowledge-making when the rise of the subject/object split made nonsense of its attempt to turn one apparently dead metal into another. Today arts-based research via Jung can restore to alchemy its place as a holistic engagement into being as knowing. The artist becomes the alchemist-partner in research. Suggestively, Jung notes that every alchemist operated differently while discerning common themes and stages in the process.

Stages to Jung manifest in colors of black, red and white, with yellowing a fourth color that fell into disuse. Colors may be animated in assuming figurative forms such as animals, or the trickster Mercurius who can appear as a black devil or a virgin white Queen ready for a *chymical* marriage. In fact, Mercurius is a personification of the infinite capacities of the collective unconscious (Jung 1963b: para. 660). The red King is a stage close to divine assumption into alchemical spiritual gold.

More pragmatic language brings alchemy closer to individuation as a research process. *Prima materia*, sometimes also called *massa confusa*, is the starting place. Here is the research task in all its initial confusion and multiple possible pathways. *Massa confusa* speaks for itself as a condition painful to endure and desperately in need of careful attention. Jung lists twelve alchemical processes in the Latin common to his sources: "*calcinatio, solutio, elementorum separatio, coniunctio, putrefactio, coagulatio, cibatio, sublimatio, fermentatio, exaltatio, augmentatio, projectio*" (Jung 1937: para. 340).

While stressing yet again that alchemists, like artists, follow no prescribed format, these terms lend themselves to research. For example: hardening into specifying a topic, dissolving of material by psychic immersing, for example by reading relevant literature. *Separatio* suggests separating out the essential parts or elements, whereas *conjunctio* must be a profound mental and physical union with those elements, including the erotic love of beauty. Death or destruction of that union occurs in *putrefactio*, as the artist-researcher takes a step back. Perhaps then there is *coagulatio*, a new solidification of material followed by *cibatio*, further feeding of the material, getting new data or art-making material, such as paint, words, etc.

By this time *sublimatio* can sublimate the bond to the work that will allow a further stage of creative fermentation. Then comes the joyful expansion into a final form of the art: *exhaltio*, followed by *augmentio*, completing the writing part of the project that cements the bond of the artwork with knowing. Lastly, *projectio* projects the knowing art into the world as something that will live and transform others. The individuated alchemist as arts-based researcher has been, of course, herself transformed.

For a streamlined version of these complexities, Jung decided that alchemists depicted three, ideally consecutive, types of transforming union. In the first place they fostered a conjoining with the unconscious. This would then be followed by a profound re-orienting of soul with body (Jung 1937: para. 664). Lastly came what was signified by a term that Jung later adopted, the *unus mundus*, where being becomes cosmos; alchemy transmutes the ensouled, bigendered being into a relationship with the stars. Earlier in his career, Jung saw alchemists trying to discover the self archetype by projecting it on to the heavens. Later, by working through his discovery of synchronicity, he renounced the necessity of projection as a dualist notion (ibid.: para. 662–4).

Unus mundus represents a mysterious and extraordinary interconnectivity where the individual is inseparable from the whole. She is joined to the universe, quantum conundrums and unknown wonders. Proposed by alchemists, the *unus mundus* became Jung's preferred term for what synchronicity revealed about the cultural partiality of the subject/object split. In addition, Jung wrote of alchemy's sense of the "tertium quid" or third thing, the way that the *unus mundus* comes between. *Unus mundus* utterly confounds subject and object in a reality that will remain sacred because never fully rationally available (ibid.). Jung says this unknowable third is what is signified by mandala paintings done by himself and his patients to express intimations of divine order emerging (see Chapter 4 on *The Red Book*). Mandalas point to this third thing as *unus mundus* and, of course, to synchronicity (ibid.).

I emphasize that Jung draws out the notion of the "third" and *unus mundus* from alchemy because these are also terms and ideas adopted by transdisciplinarity, the twenty-first-century framework of research that best fits the radical nature of Jungian arts-based research. As a final note on Jung and alchemy, Jung noted two relationships to the Christian religion in his alchemy texts. One group of adepts wanted to extend Christianity. Yet another group wanted to replace Christianity with their own mystical attitude to knowing (Jung 1937: para. 456). Both of these attitudes constitute paradigm shifts to Christianity's dominant dualism. They are also perspectives within transdisciplinarity, as we will see. First it is appropriate to consider how Jung may aid what already exists within the developing paradigm of arts-based research.

Jungian arts-based research and ungroundedness: two directions

Arts-based research is its own paradigm in being neither limited to the so-called objectivity of quantitative approaches, nor the immersion in the subject of qualitative research. ABR is empirical yet not reproducible, as noted above. It draws on centuries of art traditions and may also seek inspiration from art in other cultures. One way ABR differs from qualitative premises is by rejecting grounding in any particular theory or methodology. As Lorri Neilson (2004/18) argued, ABR departs from qualitative strictures by being "groundless theory," in refusing to assume any prior reality of mode of knowing (Neilson in Leavy 2018: 4–5).

Chapter 1 showed how Jungian psychology embraces groundless theory in its radical proposal of the inevitable incompleteness of all knowledge (Jung 1947, CW8: para. 358). Nothing can be taken for granted in research as absolute except the unknown creativity of the psyche. Yes, Jung does have a ground, but it is a dynamic ground of creative possibilities for knowing. Jungian psychology is therefore an open field ready for the artist open to plant whatever tradition, or non-tradition, she desires. We could say that grounding ABR in the Jungian psyche protects its ungroundedness by prioritizing openness to what emerges from radical incompleteness. Additionally, and in particular from synchronicity, Jung explicitly offers ABR what Bailey calls the bottomless subject, one that wants to connect to the cosmos (Bailey 2005).

The paradigm issue of fundamental principle has produced a variation in arts-based research identified in the field as two distinct forms. There is what might be called mainstream arts-based research, because it works with existing genres and forms. There is another, more experimental movement, called a/r/tography (Irwin et al. 2018, cited in Leavy 2018: 37–49). From this duality in ABR arises another possible paradigm meeting with Jung in issues of structuralism and poststructuralism, as considered below.

Holly Tsun Haggarty, in a volume of multi-authored essays on literary ABR, identifies arts-based research with structuralism as put in place by modern founders Elliot Eisner and Tom Barone.

Drawing from philosophers Kant, Dewey and Chomsky, Eisner and Barone have referred to their philosophical position as cognitive pluralism. However ... they have reworked the meaning of cognitive, moving it from positivism's abstract rationalism to embodiment in a perceptual, sensual, mindful being. Arts-based research's epistemology is strongly semiotic, and therefore structuralist, but is also informed by the ideas of constructivism, hermeneutics and, especially, by pragmatism.

(Tsun Haggarty in Sameshima et al. 2017: 73)

Epistemology in ABR and Jung is the subject of Chapter 3. For now, I want to consider the paradigmatic impact of its structuralism in relying upon relatively stable hidden structures that do not refer directly to perceived reality (Barry 2017). Indeed, Barone and Eisner begin their 2012 book, *Arts Based Research*, by contending that the inherited forms of the arts have capacity to generate knowing through symbols that do not refer directly to the world.

One might ask how a symbol system without clear connection to a codified array of referents can be useful in doing something as precise as a research study is meant to be ...? The answer to that question that we formulate is the clear specification of a referent by a symbol is not a necessary condition for meaning. In the arts, symbols adumbrate; they do not denote.

(Barone and Eisner 2012: 2)

Instead of research writing as signs that are supposed to represent a shared objective reality, art's inherited forms provide systematic and not directly representative ways of making meaning. The meaning of art becomes knowing as inherently shareable because of the way the arts have accrued semiotic resonances in their use over the centuries. Art is therefore a vehicle of knowing and being through culturally and historically mediated forms.

This semiotic notion of ABR is countered explicitly by the radical practice of a/r/tography that embraces poststructuralism. It does so by refusing to treat art as a source of a relatively stable system of signs in traditional forms. A/r/tography was pioneered by Rita Irwin as a challenge to positivism, the notion that all knowledge can be rationally proven by science or mathematically ascertained. To positivism nature is inherently knowable through rational means; it dismisses the unknowable unconscious, the sacred and the marvelous.

Using poststructuralists such as Jacques Derrida and Giles Deleuze, a/r/tography opposes Western traditions of knowing based in dualism, including, of course, the subject/object split. It seeks disorder and chaos as aspects of rupture, splitting, "fragmentation and multiplicity" (Tsun Haggarty 2017: 74). Encounters with decentered meaning and decaying traditional forms and certainties drive a/r/tography These researchers endorse Deleuze's notion of knowledge as rhizomatic; it proliferates horizontally with no centering stem (ibid.). Knowledge cannot be imaged as a tree of secure structuralist principles where stable forms produce ever more branches and twigs. Barone and Eisner's arts-based research grows from the forest of artistic forms. By deliberate contrast, a/r/tography is rhizomatic moss.

A/r/tographers may not be aware, however, that Deleuze was influenced by the work of C. G. Jung, who also used the figure of the rhizome (Jung 1963/83: 18). In addition, their dedication to overturning dualistic or binary thinking takes them into the evocative space of the "third."

> A/r/tography engages spatial metaphors to offer alternatives to binary knowledge, metaphors such as *thirdness, in-between,* and *without.* A/r/tography also resists representing thinking as structuralist and emulates a disjunctive writing style, favoring the disruptive writing techniques of postmodernism …
>
> (Tsun Haggarty 2017: 74)

Both Jung and transdisciplinarity are very interested in the "third," as we will see. For now, in characterizing the arts-based research paradigm as possessing both structuralist and poststructuralist domains, there is another correlation to Jung. For in a very real sense Jungian psychology is both structuralist and poststructuralist. Jung is a classic structuralist in his theory of archetypes as (probably) inherited potentials forming recurring types of images and meanings. He is also poststructuralist in his understanding of the unconscious as that which undermines certainty and secure knowledge.

> It is not a question of … asserting anything, but of constructing a *model* which opens up a promising and useful field of enquiry. A model does not assert that something is so, it simply illustrates a particular mode of observation.
>
> (Jung 1947, CW8: para. 381)

Jungian psychology is here a practical perspective for comprehending the psyche. One could almost call his psychology a work of art that is personal to its creator and yet partakes in traditional genres such as academic disciplinary knowing. Such a speculative comparison of Jungian psychology to an art form is helpful when approaching Jung's own categorizing of literature. In the essay "Psychology and Literature" (1930, CW15), he suggests two modes, only one of which is particularly interesting to the psychologist (Jung 1930, CW15: para. 139).

Ironically, the literature Jung calls "psychological" is not what fascinates him. Here the psychology, or finding the logos, knowing of psyche in ordered form, has been completed by the author. Often extended to all kinds of art, Jung's "psychological" art objects are transparent to rational knowing. The artist here is also a psychologist, whether deliberately or not.

What truly grips Jung is the art he calls "visionary." For this category of art, the artist is virtually helpless in the face of the overwhelming power of the unconscious. The work pours out and remains mysterious to its hapless maker.

> it is so dark and amorphous that it requires the related mythological imagery to give it form … It is nothing but a tremendous intuition striving for expression.
>
> (Jung 1930, CW15: para. 151)

In this quotation, Jung shows the partly unconscious function of intuition taking the lead in the creation of visionary art. He also chooses a suitable language in endorsing myth for such work. To Jung, myth both describes the relations between ego and unconscious and can help to shape them. Therefore, he suggests that myth can arise immanently from visionary art. It may arise entirely unknown to the artist while she is immersed in the process.

Visionary art is an eruption from the deep psyche. For this reason, it has profound implications for the society in which it first appears. Jung infers that visionary art is to the collective culture what a cryptic dream is to the individual in revealing what is unknown, ignored or repressed (ibid.: para. 161). In this way it can compensate for stale conventional biases in a society that is stuck in its conventions. Moreover, visionary art stems from an intrinsically forward-looking, or teleological, psyche, and so can indicate as yet unknown trends. It can intimate possible futures.

Jung's depiction of visionary art takes it close to the deliberately poststructuralist practice of a/r/tography. Rita Irwin calls a/r/tography a living inquiry, or living practice, because discovery and process cannot be disentangled (Irwin et al. 2018, cited in Leavy 2018: 37). Reality is not found but rather co-created through embodied, immersed creativity: "[r]ather than discovering that which already exists, a/r/tography embraces each movement, each new idea, as new reality" (Irwin 2013). Above all, flow and intuition become guiding forces that break down conventional boundaries between art, research, teaching and learning.

> It is a dynamic force that is forever becoming entangled in the materiality of all things, human and nonhuman. To do so, it embraces the practices of artists, researchers, and teachers/learners as a way to linger in this entanglement and to pursue the practice of living one's inquiry.
>
> (Irwin et al. 2018, cited in Leavy 2018: 37)

Innate to a/r/tography is the notion of breaking through conventional forms in how we process experience such as abstract, rational, creative, aesthetic, somatic types of knowing. This unbounded disruption brings a/r/tography to visionary art as open to any intuitive eruption. Neither practice is limited or measured by boundaries or conventions. Indeed, Irwin's embrace of living inquiry is cognate to Jung's insight into the living mystery of the psyche. For it, too, cannot be known by forms of knowledge that prioritize concepts and theories.

> We have to break down life and events, which are self-contained pro-cesses, into meanings, images, concepts, well knowing that in doing so we are getting further away from the living mystery ... But for the purposes of cognitive understanding we must detach ourselves from the creative process and look at it from the outside ... In this way we meet the demands of science.
>
> (Jung 1922, CW15: para. 121)

Science in the subject/object split demands separation from what is to be researched. Art-based research nurtures a connection to the living mystery in the intuitive and image-realizing practices of art. A/r/tography goes further and partakes of Jung's visionary domain where the artist-researcher-teacher need not seek anchor in rational structures of knowing, such as disciplines and genres. Although the a/r/tographer will have more self-consciousness about being in states of uncertainty and ambiguity than Jung suggests of the vision-ary artist, both quest for something distinctively new. For a/r/tography is "the feel of new forms of vitality" (Triggs et al. 2014, cited in Leavy 2018: 37). For the visionary artist, it is to similarly fathom "the deepest springs of life" (Jung 1922, CW15: para. 130).

Indeed, Jung could be initiating a/r/tography when he depicts the radical, even uncanny, aspect of visionary art.

> Sublime, pregnant with meaning, yet chilling the blood with its strange-ness, it arises from timeless depths: glamorous, daemonic, and grotesque, it bursts asunder our human standard of value and aesthetic forms ...
>
> (Jung 1930: para. 141)

This sense of creative energy in destruction could go alongside a/r/tographer Natalie Le Blanc as she articulates her similar rejection of the subject/object split.

> This materiality teaches me that the abandoned school is more than a mere object. It is a force with its own trajectories and propensities – it is a power of life.
>
> (LeBlanc in Leavy 2018: 49)

Clearly, there remain some differences in emphasis between what Jung calls visionary art and a/r/tography. Jung is keen to point out the compensatory and future-oriented possibilities of this art because he is a conservative with revolu-tionary ideas. He wants the deep, unknowable psyche to heal and restore, rather than subvert and provoke social change. Not so a/r/tography, which embraces the poststructuralist instability of knowing as also a condition of being and making. A/r/tography does so with a view to challenging the status quo.

However, Jung contributes something both distinctive and coherent to this paradigmatic spectrum of structuralism and poststructuralism in arts-based research. He offers to structuralist ABR his patterning archetypes and to post-structuralist a/r/tography the radical role of the unconscious and the example of visionary art. In addition to both types of art-making as research, his psychology provides an embodied innate creativity. Jung's psychic creativity is oriented to respond to the world, but very importantly, is not determined by external forces. The world and its systems of power and control do not control the psyche, according to Jung. To the extent that arts-based research of all kinds sticks to groundless theory or a beginning without presuppositions, it draws creative current from Jung.

This theme of the relationship between the radical potential of the ABR paradigm and existing boundaries and divisions in knowing inevitably brings in the matter of academic disciplines. Although ABR is used within existing disciplines, its radical potential requires something different. Put another way, ABR is not fully a *paradigm* (as opposed to a collection of methodologies) without transdisciplinarity, as suggested in Chapter 1. The next section of this chapter will explore in more detail how Jung fits into transdisciplinarity and aids ABR.

The problem of academic disciplines and a Jungian reaction

Academic disciplines not only divide up knowledge, they also divide up the knowing human being. Whereas the humanities, such as philosophy, history and the study of art, have long been devoted to what it means to be human and embedded in a world, the dominant scientific paradigm has cut off subjectivity from it. As noted previously, the subject/object split turns reality on to potentially knowable objects. Basarab Nicolescu argues that classical science remains in thrall to the methodology of Galileo based upon his long-lasting scientific method. This relies upon the following paradigmatic beliefs:

1) The existence of universal laws of mathematical nature.
2) The discovery of these laws through scientific experiments.
3) The reproducibility of experimental results (Nicolescu 2014: 5).

This version of science has reigned supreme for so long that it has come to dominate modern culture's perception of what is real, and even what is human. One result is that academic disciplines are imagined in a hierarchical pyramid, with this version of science at the top as the most powerful engine for making knowledge. Other disciplines and methodologies, such as those of qualitative research and now arts-based research, are presumed to offer valid knowing only insofar as they subject themselves to this paradigm. Of course, as we have seen, arts-based research is one of several challenges to this hegemony.

Here it is important to note the value of Jung's groundless theory of the psyche that supports ABR's groundless theory. Both presume no universal laws, but will accept them if they emerge. Not only does Jung declare all knowledge provisional (because of the unconscious) and that living mystery cannot be pinned into concepts, he also explicitly rejects any hierarchy of disciplines. Perhaps appropriately, in an essay on poetry he declares that studying a child's still developing psyche will not endorse any discipline as foundational; for despite the potential for science and art in infants, "all of this does nothing to prove the existence of a unifying principle which alone would justify a reduction of one to the other" (Jung 1922, CW15: para. 99).

In Jungian psychology there is no unifying principle or distinguishing paradigm that would make one form of knowledge or one discipline superior to any other. For Jung, arts-based research is poised to discover by co-participation in living mystery. There is no required attitude to what is most fundamentally real, such as the universal laws in Galileo's science above.

Such a paradigmatic embrace of openness acknowledges that subjectivity is always part of something bigger because of the unknown psyche. It denies the pre-eminence of the subject/object split and situates it as yet another culturally specific construct of modernity. By denying disciplinary hierarchies, Jung becomes transdisciplinary, as we will see below.

First of all, it is worth substantiating Jung's contribution to the ABR paradigm through his intimations that art and nature can be one. For Jung suggests that art, rooted in the collective unconscious, is an expression of our nonhuman nature. Visionary works that flow from the collective unconscious, that are minimally consciously shaped, materialize the very reverse of the subject/object split. Such art makes visible nature within and outside us a continuum.

The Jungian arts-based research paradigm includes nature

To Jung, art results from an activation of the archetypal unconscious. The intuitive and sensation aspects of the mind are stirred, and the artist is stimulated into a creative process. From this point, Jung would see alternatives in the way the artist works that result in his two categories of art. One artist will incorporate the more rational functions of thinking and feeling, a so-called psychological approach. Another artist may be so gripped by archetypal energy that contents simply pour out to become what Jung calls visionary art.

Given that archetypes provoke synchronicity, they must inhabit nature and human nature. Just as nonhuman nature speaks through synchronicities, so too nature finds material expression in art. In fact, synchronicities are potentially contributions to art. By making meaning from moments of interchange between the psyche and the world, synchronicity suggests an underlying patterning, an aesthetics in the cosmos. So, when Jung claims that "the unborn work in the psyche of the artist is a force of nature," he suggests art can be a reciprocal exchange between human and nonhuman (Jung 1922, CW15: para. 115). This possibility will be explored further with Jung's notion of symbols, in Chapter 3.

The paradigmatic implications of Jung's archetypal psychology have been extended by Robert Sandford in *Tending the Fire: Imagining the Source of Our Creativity* (2019). He pursues the mythical and alchemical aspects of Jung to investigate the tensions between psychology and creativity and their cosmological implications. Pointing out that what is annihilating to the ego is creative of being in the unconscious, Sandford suggests that the "I" of the artist is a figure for the Jungian self, that intimation of impossible-to-conceive wholeness (Sandford 2019: 46, 103).

This is an exciting departure from Jung's typical assertion that the self is an archetypal patterning that ultimately stitches being into the cosmos. For Sandford, the creativity of the artist mimics divine creativity, and participates in it through synchronous revelation. The artist co-creates with Jung's nature goddess. Moreover, we can witness Jung also realizing this symmetry between self and artist in his experimental essay on James Joyce's modernist novel, *Ulysses*, explored below (Joyce 1922/2010; Jung 1932, CW15).

Sandford is an orthodox Jungian, in seeing mythical narrative as the ultimate patterning of archetypes. He sees the creative person as Hephaistos, the club-footed immortal who is wedded to unfaithful Aphrodite, goddess of divine and aesthetic beauty. Hephaistos is the craftsman god who tends the fires of archetypal energy. Where Sandford helps Jungian arts-based research is in seeing creativity as both cosmological and sociological. He points out that all narration enacts the relationship of ego to unconscious; or, put another way, a dialogue between self and other that removes the illusion of the subject/object split.

Such a notion of creativity is a "relationship in action" (Sandford: 10). It is innately relational and co-operative, because connecting to unknowable archetypes may happen by means of other people, even though we also encounter them from an-other that has nothing to do with people. Either way, a Jungian relation to the unconscious cannot exclude any type of other, for that would be to block out the creative psyche itself. Archetypes do not arrange themselves into subject/object splits, or any other kind of absolute divisions. What Jung perceived in alchemy and embraced in synchronicity is further revealed by Sandford in that psyche and matter exist together as one cosmology, a *unus mundus*.

> The creative work imitates the cosmogony; at its center is the *axis mundi* connecting earth, heaven and underworld that births the creative space as an *imago mundi*.
>
> (Sandford 2019: 63)

Sandford portrays creativity as that which rehearses the origin of the universe. Images that are the core matter of creativity are divinely born. The "I" of the artist as self-image traces the path of a god bringing a world into being. Hence, for Sandford, "the creative drive is a homing instinct," because it brings us to our true home in an ever-creative cosmos (Sandford 2019: 62). It is time to look more closely at the cosmological paradigm for Jungian ABR by means of transdisciplinarity.

A transdisciplinary cosmological paradigm for Jungian arts-based research

Authoritative theorists such as Patricia Leavy claim ABR to be "transdisciplinary" without much exploration of the implications for disciplines and ontological assumptions (Leavy 2018: 4). However, one argument of this book is that Jung provides a bridge to the transdisciplinarity presented by Basarab Nicolescu. His transdisciplinarity is paradigmatically expansive and magnanimous enough to encompass the social, ecological, ontological and epistemological necessities of the twenty-first century. Jungian ABR therefore becomes part of an inter-weaving spectrum of knowledge-making designed to address a political and planetary crisis.

Replacing Galileo's scientific method of subject/object-based science (shown earlier in this chapter), Nicolescu offers three axioms for the paradigm of transdisciplinarity.

i) The ontological axiom: *There are, in Nature and in our knowledge of Nature, different levels of Reality and, correspondingly, different levels of perception.*

ii) The logical axiom: *The passage from one level of Reality to another is insured by the logic of the included middle.*

iii) The complexity axiom: *The Structure of the totality of levels of Reality or perception is a complex structure: every level is what it is because all levels exist at the same time.*

(Nicolescu 2014: 207)

Two of these axioms set out the fundamental reality proposed by Nicolescu's transdisciplinarity, while the other is a methodological axis. Multiple realities leading to multiple levels of perception are core concerns of both Jungian psychology and the arts. Just as the importance given to the unconscious by Jung testifies to intimations that cannot be fully explored by the rational functions of thinking and feeling (see Chapter 1), so too does art incorporate, make visible or substantial, that which is not immediate to consciousness.

Complexity here refers to developments in computing and evolutionary science that acknowledge that the complex systems such as natural environments, the human body, the psyche, massively complex computing networks all behave in ways that cannot be accounted for by linear, cause-and-effect approaches (Shulman 1997). Rather, the interaction of complex systems results in unpredictable *creativity* that emerges in a way that can't be attributed to any one aspect. Nature appears to change and transform, evolve, by interactions of these complex adaptive systems, or CAS, as they are known (Wheeler 2006: 67–8). Several Jungians have explored the way the Jungian mind–body relationship could be attributed to such autonomous complexity (Shulman 1997: 129). Where the psyche and world interact synchronically, this too is complexity at work (Cambray 2012).

Transdisciplinarity adopts complexity as the way reality and the disciplines that are working to know it co-operate. Complexity's creative interactions are how multiple realities interact, such as in Jungian individuation, and how disciplines encounter, influence and transform each other. For an academic discipline can be a complex adaptive system, just like those in nature. Disciplines don't consist of any single source; rather, they grow through the emergence of ideas as a result of countless interactions, mostly untraceable when we take into account unknown and unconscious processes in the mind of scholars.

At certain, never entirely predictable or controllable moments, disciplines will find their complex interactions transformational of their very premises: this is a paradigm shift. The move from disciplines in a hierarchy based on the subject/object split to the complexity/emergence vision of transdisciplinarity is one such example. This book argues that such a move is desirable, and can be facilitated by Jungian arts-based research.

Ultimately, a paradigm shift rests on a change of logic in the basic assumptions of both the old and the new paradigms. What was the logic of the subject/object split and its hard dualism becomes the notion of *thirdness*, as the axiom above proposes. Dualist logic says that A and B are simply separate. The logic of the third says that between A and B is a state that is both A and B. Here the third stands for the multiple realities and complexities within which A and B are contained. In this sense, the third stands for the *unus mundus* intimated by both the alchemists and Jung (see above). It is also evoked in a/r/tography as the realm of an arts-based research discovery that is also creativity.

To Nicolescu, the hidden third (hidden because not rationally available) makes the paradigm of transdisciplinarity one of simultaneous oneness and manyness (Nicolescu 2014: 127–32). That is, multiple realities and disciplines cannot be reduced to a single state or absolute, overarching, governing truth. Nor are they separate from each other in the sense of a subject/object split. Rather, this multiplicity is complex; realities and disciplines exist in relation to each other, always capable of creative interaction and transformation.

> The Hidden Third, in its relationship with the levels of Reality, is fundamental for the understanding of *unus mundus* described by cosmodernity. Reality is simultaneously a single and a multiple One.
>
> (Nicolescu 2014: 209)

All levels of Reality are interconnected through complexity. In fact, complexity is the modern form of universal interdependence. The principle of universal interdependence entails the maximum possible simplicity that the human mind can imagine, the simplicity of the interaction of all levels of reality. This simplicity cannot be captured by mathematical language, only by symbolic language.

(ibid.: 211)

One important consequence of this commitment to oneness and manyness is a relationship that removes the split between academia and other kinds of knowing. Much has been repressed by academic disciplines because of modernity's obsession with the subject/object split. It is time for science to unite with what Nicolescu names Tradition, a Tradition that includes art practice.

Jungian arts-based research as a transdisciplinary practice

Tradition to Nicolescu means the learning not organized by powerful educational establishments, but rather handed down by myth, spiritual and esoteric practices and social-moral principles. It includes all practices that stand the test of time. Crucially, Tradition is shaped by, and gives shape to, histories and cultures. It does not seek to escape specificity and embodiment in a particular time or place. Tradition is immanent and engaged with everyday life.

But Tradition also exists in space and time. Although its content is unique, its form of expression and language … are of great diversity, under the inevitable influence of history, and of the cultural environment. One of the fundamental ideas of Tradition: *unity in diversity* and of *diversity through unity*, applies to Tradition itself.

(Nicolescu 2014: 20, italics in original)

In this way, Tradition exemplifies the transdisciplinarity tenet of oneness and manyness in a perpetual dialogue. Nicolescu points out that modernity's subject/object science and Tradition exist in a contradictory spectrum. Where Tradition has knowing through revelation, contemplation and direct embodied perception, science only values the human brain for rational and so-called objective purposes (ibid.: 21).

Traditional research places great importance to the body, to sensations and feelings; scientific research excludes the researcher's own body, sensations, feelings, and faith in the field of observation … Different experimental instruments are supposed to be equipped with an intrinsic objectivity, an almost absolute independence against the will of the researcher.

(ibid.: 21)

Notably, in Nicolescu's schema qualitative research draws on Tradition. He also infers the obtuse object of modern technology explored by Bailey in the so-called objectivity of machines or research instruments (Bailey 2005). If we could discern the myth or fantasies driving these research technologies from the test tube to the particle collider, their apparent objectivity would be revealed as perilous unconscious enchantment.

Returning to Nicolescu's Tradition is an opportunity to include the arts through their legacies and heritage. Like spiritual seekers and religious novitiates, artists serve an apprenticeship, whether self-taught, in art schools or with a mentor. Such training is not only devoted to ideas carried by the arts, but also to embodied practice. Artists begin by a vital immersion in art as history, as Tradition. Moreover, art, despite contamination by the ideology of the subject/object split, is far more than the production of objects. By being *art*, it intervenes in the culture with ambitions to become part of an ongoing legacy. Artwork, by its striving toward the unknown, becomes a spiritual practice.

Nicolescu tacitly welcomes art to Tradition later, in *From Modernity to Cosmodernity*, by looking at experimental theater as transdisciplinary, cosmological research (Nicolescu 2014: 153–61). For example, the work of director Peter Brooks amounts to quantum theater in simultaneously discovering and making meaning that is non-linear and profoundly interconnected.

> A linear unfolding would signify a mechanistic determinism, whereas here the event is linked to a structure that is clearly not linear at all but rather one of interrelationships and interconnections.
>
> (ibid.: 156)

Basic to Nicolescu's transdisciplinarity is valuing the knowing of Tradition, bringing it into the paradigm from long exclusion. Jungian arts-based research imports the resources of art in Tradition, as well as the unconscious, also innate to Tradition. In effect, Jungian ABR mobilizes part of Tradition into the knowledge-making of the transdisciplinary paradigm. As Jung was never tired of saying, religions work psychologically by providing symbols that knit the personal and collective psyche into cohesion. To him, this is *unus mundus*, a condition of experiencing wholeness in manyness, the very map later spelled out by Nicolescu.

Jung saw that transdisciplinary Tradition inherits alchemical practices by supplying symbols in many modes – from the working body to the material substances to the images in pictures and words. Similarly, Nicolescu insists that transdisciplinary knowledge must be open to its own unconscious, its own failings, with an infinite capacity for revision. In other words, like Jung and arguably ABR, transdisciplinarity requires the language that Jung found in symbols. This epistemology in and of symbols will be pursued in Chapter 3.

Above all, Nicolescu's transdisciplinarity is hospitable to Jungian arts-based research because the hidden third is imaged in art that Nicolescu calls "open" and Jung calls "visionary." If the archetypal unconscious is evoked in art-making then the cosmos is invited to be co-participant in the work. A/r/tography most obviously endorses visionary and transdisciplinary principles by its attempt to be naked before the invisible pattern growing the energies of the *unus mundus*. However, I argue here that mainstream ABR need not exclude what Jung calls the collective unconscious and Nicolescu the hidden third.

Hidden within the traditions of art are its unknown practitioners. These forgotten artists live on in the evolving forms of novels, poems, paintings and sculptures and so forth. Within these practices are the myths of a collectivity haunting the consciousness of the artist-researcher in her legacy. Here Tradition invites the artist to include the as yet unknown or unknowable. Consciously invoked or not, the hidden third/archetypes are always present; their energy shapes and is nourished by the image-generating imagination.

It is time to end this chapter with a brief example of the flexible Jungian ABR paradigm emerging in Jung's own attempt at a/r/tography (although he had passed away before this practice was named).

Jung's paradigmatic arts-based research into *Ulysses* by James Joyce (1922)

Ulysses is disenchanting

Jung's essay chronicles his extraordinary journey through James Joyce's modernist novel, and is paradoxically entitled "*Ulysses*: a Monologue" (Jung 1932). Perhaps the echo of drama is a clue to its performative tone. More speculatively, perhaps Jung anticipates what will later be identified as arts-based research. After all, the Jung depicted here begins in failure. He cannot manage to read this challenging work without falling asleep (Jung 1932: para. 165). Even when this disturbing symptom drives him into considering therapy upon himself, he can find no reasonable cause, nor meaningful strategy, in Joyce's book.

When stuck, find an image for the stuckness, is Jung's key method for the recalcitrant psyche. So he conceives his image for *Ulysses*, the novel, of a worm that later becomes a tapeworm paralyzing his own body, for the "whole work has the character of a worm cut in half" (ibid.: para. 165). By using active imagination with this procreative worm, Jung finds its brainless physicality has much to infer about the novel as a metonym for the modern world. For example, he discovers what Sandford later makes explicit, that the one who creates, whom Jung calls Ulysses, is the "dark hidden father," or the archetypal self of the writer James Joyce (ibid.: para. 198).

> Ulysses is the creator-god in Joyce ... a microcosm of James Joyce, the world of the self and the self of the world in one.
>
> (Jung 1932, CW15: para. 192)

Here, of course is transdisciplinarity's hidden third, the image of the *unus mundus*. Anticipating Nicolescu, Jung, too, sees the unity in multiplicity and multiplicity in unity.

> Who, then, is Ulysses? Doubtless he is a symbol of what makes us the totality, the oneness ... Try to imagine a being who ... consists also of horses, street-processions, churches, the Liffey, several brothels and a crumpled note ...
>
> (ibid.: para 198)

In this splendidly evocative dramatic writing, Jung achieves the arts-based research paradigm as well as that of transdisciplinarity. His freefall into *Ulysses* re-composes the novel as arts-based research into the fragile consciousness of the modern European. He makes the novel into ABR and achieves it himself. In this essay, Jung writes about Ulysses by becoming Ulysses in actively imagining into the text; for he comes to see that novel as profoundly excavating Irish Catholicism. For that very archetypal depth, the novel extends to the post-medieval world everywhere (ibid.: para. 181). Jung's performative art in writing makes reading into arts-based research by transforming what is read.

In addition to discovering the hidden third, *unus mundus* and the Jungian self as the one-who-creates, "*Ulysses*: a Monologue" engages the body more explicitly than elsewhere in Jung (ibid.: para. 163). Visceral physical responses invoked in the book are taken into the act of reading and, naturally, produce the tapeworm image of the invasive somatic quality of the book. As well as bringing the body of the artist to ABR, such an analytic approach to reading propels this essay into one of Rolling Jnr.'s four categories: analytic, synthetic, critical-activist and improvisatory.

Indeed, "*Ulysses*: a Monologue" could fulfill all four categories of arts-based research. It is certainly analytic of the reading process and its potentially devastating effects upon consciousness. As synthetic, the essay brings together Jungian ideas in an unpromising context of writing in another genre (fiction), in another language and from a foreign culture. More specifically, "*Ulysses*: a Monologue" synthesizes Jungian, Joycean and their overlapping modernist approaches to propose a new understanding of the peril surrounding the modern person. For, surprisingly, Jung comes to see *Ulysses* the novel as a precise psychological and theological indictment of the subject/object split.

> O *Ulysses* you are truly a devotional book for the object-besotted, object-ridden white man!
>
> (ibid.: para. 201)

Making such a link in modern consciousness between two senses of being beset by objects, as capitalist desire and in the sense of a fundamental separation, brings the unlikely possibility of Jung as a critical-activist arts-based researcher. As a conservative thinker with revolutionary ideas, Jung's usual stance was to shore up consciousness in order to restore psychological and social balance. Left-wing radical, he was not. However, by diagnosing whiteness as a state of unhappy obsession with objects, this essay is an act of what Bailey would call disenchantment. After all, technology includes the modern printed novel, here fetishized into an object.

And yet, Jung in the fourth category of Rolling Jnr.'s ABR, improvisatory, performs a monologue in writing that exposes the false consciousness around objects and objectivity in his world. The novel connects this reader to deep roots in the Catholic culture of the suffering body (of Christ). It also embraces the historical paradigm of alchemy, when the novel is described finally as "eighteen alchemical alembics" (ibid.: para.201).

Moreover, the essay also fulfills Rolling Jnr.'s depiction of ABR as reflexive practice with formational and informational and transformational properties (Rolling Jnr. 2013: 13). Beginning with despairing reflection, the ABR of the *Ulysses* essay dives into form-making with the migrating tapeworm, only to discover the reading processes taking Jung to a better historical perspective of his age. Finally, the book is declared a transformational process by means of alchemy's distilling of a new consciousness (Jung 1932: para. 201).

"*Ulysses*: a Monologue" is an act of improvisatory creative reading showing that literary criticism is capable of transdisciplinary arts-based research. It fulfills in microcosm what Jung reveals elsewhere to be a transdisciplinary approach to his psychology. For in his book *Aion*, CW9ii, Jung describes succeeding genres of symbolism that knit together the European psyche. These include Gnosticism, astrology, Christianity, alchemy, to now, Jungian psychology (Jung 1951). The succession here is not to a perfect and complete form in his theories. Rather Jung agrees with Nicolescu in that all knowing must be open because the hidden third, or "dark hidden father," is forever mysterious to rational language. What is most necessary for a transdisciplinary paradigm is what is essential to ABR, knowing providing an epistemology of symbols, the subject of Chapter 3.

Note

1 See John Winthrop Jnr, alchemist, physician and colonial governor of Connecticut Prospero's America.

References

Bailey, L. W. (2005) *The Enchantments of Technology*. Champaign, IL: University of Illinois Press.

Baring, A. and J. Cashford. (1991) *The Myth of the Goddess: Evolution of an Image*. New York and London: Vintage.

Barone, T. and E. W. Eisner. (2012) *Arts Based Research*. Los Angeles, CA and London: Sage Publications.

Barry, P. (2017) *Beginning Theory: An Introduction to Literary and Cultural Theory*. 4th edition. Manchester: Manchester University Press.

Cambray, J. (2012) *Synchronicity: Nature and Psyche in an Interconnected Universe*. Carolyn and Ernest Fay Series in Analytical Psychology. TX: Texas A & M Press.

Eliade, M. (1956) *The Forge and the Crucible*. Evanston, IL and New York: Harper & Row.

Irwin, R. L. (2013) 'Becoming A/r/tography', *Studies in Art Education*, *54* (3), 198–215.

Irwin, R. L., N. LeBlanc, J. Y. Ryu and G. Belliveau. (2018) 'A/r/tography as Living Inquiry', in P. Leavy, ed. *Handbook of Arts-Based Research*. New York and London: The Guilford Press, pp. 37–53.

Joyce, J. (1922/2010) *Ulysses*. New York: Wordsworth Classics.

Jung, C. G. (1922) 'On the Relation of Analytical Psychology to Poetry', in *Collected Works, Volume 15: The Spirit in Man, Art and Literature*, pp. 65–83.

Jung, C. G. (1930) 'Psychology and Literature', in *Collected Works, Volume 15: The Spirit in Man, Art and Literature*, pp. 109–134.

Jung, C. G. (1932) '"Ulysses": A Monologue', in *Collected Works, Volume 15: The Spirit in Man, Art and Literature*, pp. 127–154.

Jung, C. G. (1936) 'Individual Dream Symbolism in Relation to Alchemy', in *Collected Works, Volume 12: Psychology and Alchemy*, pp. 39–213.

Jung, C. G. (1937) 'Religious Ideas in Alchemy', in *Collected Works, Volume 12: Psychology and Alchemy*, pp. 215–463.

Jung, C. G. (1947) 'On the Nature of the Psyche', in *Collected Works, Volume 8: The Structure and Dynamics of the Psyche*, pp. 159–234.

Jung, C. G. (1951) *Aion: Studies in the Phenomenology of the Self, Collected Works, Volume 9, Part 2*.

Jung, C. G. (1952) 'Synchronicity: An Acausal Connecting Principle', in *Collected Works, Volume 8: The Structure and Dynamics of the Psyche*, pp. 417–532.

Jung, C. G. (1963/83) *Memories, Dreams, Reflections*. Recorded and Edited by Aniela Jaffe. London: Fontana.

Jung, C. G. (1963b) 'The Conjunction', in *Collected Works, Volume 14, Mysterium Conjunctionis*, pp. 447–453.

Kuhn, T. (1962/2012) *The Structure of Scientific Revolutions*. Chicago, IL: University of Chicago Press.

Leavy, P. ed. (2018) *Handbook of Arts-Based Research*. New York and London: The Guilford Press.

LeBlanc, N. (2018) 'Variation III: Living Inquiry as "Becoming" in and through Practice', in Leavy (2018), pp. 46–53.

Linden, S. J. (2003) *The Alchemy Reader: From Hermes Trismegistus to Isaac Newton*. Cambridge UK: Cambridge University Press.

Neilson, L. (2004/18) 'Aesthetics and Knowing: Ephemeral Principles for a Groundless Theory', in A. L. Cole, J. G. Knowles and T. C. Luciani, eds. *Provoked by Art: Theorizing Arts-Informed Research*. Halifax, NS, Canada: Backalong Books, pp. 44–49.

Nicolescu, B. (2014) *From Modernity to Cosmodernity: Science, Culture and Spirituality*. New York: SUNY.

Rolling Jnr., J. H. (2013) *Arts-Based Research Primer*. New York: Peter Lang.

Sameshima, P., A. Fidyk, K. James and C. Leggo eds. (2017) *Poetic Inquiry: Enchantment of Place*. Wilmington, DE: Vernon Press.

Sandford, R. (2019) *Tending the Fire: Imagining the Source of Our Creativity*. Hove and New York: Routledge.

Shulman, H. (1997) *Living at the Edge of Chaos: Complex Systems in Culture and Psyche*. Zurich: Daimon Verlag.

Triggs, V., R. L. Irwin and D. Donoghue. (2014) 'Following A/r/tography in Practice: From Possibility to Potential', in K. Miglan and C. Smilan, eds. *Inquiry in Action: Paradigms, Methodologies and Perspectives in Art Education Research*. Reston, VA: National Art Education Association, pp. 253–264.

Tsun Haggarty, H. (2017) 'Fish Eyes: Investigating the Philosophy of Poetic Inquiry', in Sameshima et al. (2017), pp. 69–85.

Wheeler, W. (2006) *The Whole Creature: Complexity, Biosemiotics and the Evolution of Culture*. London: Lawrence & Wishart.

Woodward, W. W. (2010) *Prospero's America: John Winthrop, Jr., Alchemy, and the Creation of New England Culture, 1606–1676*. Chapel Hill, NC: University of North Carolina Press.

Epistemology and methodology for Jungian arts-based research

Introduction

Chapter 3 explores epistemology, those questions of how knowledge is made and justified. It will also include methodology, what it means to apply the various methods of Jungian arts-based research. Methodology can be distinguished from methods, which are specific techniques for addressing research questions and collecting data. By contrast, methodology can encompass everything in the research project from the identification of a topic or area to choosing a method coherent with a specific epistemological approach. In a sense, mainstream ABR uses art genres as methods, while ABR itself constitutes a methodology. Methodology maps why the methods are appropriate. In this sense methodology spans the implied paradigm and its ontological assumptions, including the epistemological strategies to clarify the focus of its knowledge.

The previous chapter explored paradigms as large frameworks of belief about how the universe relates to human beings, and therefore how to make knowledge. The subject/object split forms the core of the scientific experimental method derived from Galileo. It is an epistemology suited to the ontology or reality of a universe of mathematical laws discoverable through repeatable experiments. This became the ontology of the scientific paradigm. Dominant paradigms influence the individual ontologies of disciplines, such as Jung's initial contention of the primary reality of the human psyche as something separable from the world. He considered that this psyche was unconsciously projected, until his discovery of synchronicity led him to envision a more interconnected cosmos.

Such an ontology of projection sustained Jung through most of his explorations of alchemy, even though he recognized that the alchemists themselves held an alternative paradigm of correspondence and interconnectedness. Correspondence is where phenomena ostensibly on one level of reality, such as the sun, are somehow implicated in another plane of reality, such as a divine spirit and/or the metal (in this case) gold. If this reminds us of Nicolescu's transdisciplinary paradigm of inter-influencing levels of reality, he acknowledges this return of something ancient (Nicolescu 2014: 192). Above all, the transdisciplinary paradigm brings art and science together as epistemologically valuable ways of knowing (Nicolescu 2014: 181).

It is the argument of this book that Jungian psychology can enlarge and facilitate the ontologies, epistemologies and methodologies of arts-based research. To Jung, the primary reality of the psyche is human and more than human through synchronicity. His psychology supplies a methodology of knowing through images and what we might call a principle of meaning-making through symbols. Such an epistemology of symbols is rendered even more explicit by transdisciplinarity, as we will see.

The starting place of ABR is that of art as a material expression of spiritual value, meaning that it is neither determined nor limited by the codes of other social interactions. For example, the artistic value of a novel is set neither by the price of its materials nor by the labor of the writer (much to the regret of writers), nor by any financial value that might be put on a first edition, and so forth. Rather, one value of literary art, for example, is its inspirational properties for its readers, which are not limited to the first audience for whom the novel might be said to have been written. Such "spiritual" value is attributed to something mysterious in what the artist does. Art is in-spirited, taking material form in the images that make art, whether in words, paint, musical notes, and so on. Therefore, art enters Jungian psychology in locating the source of inspiration in images generated by the psyche, or through the psyche, entangled with a boundless cosmos.

Therefore, arts-based research receives from Jung endorsement of its methodology in what inspires, in-spirits; while Jungians can find in ABR art physical, often durable, manifestations of psyche in various cultures *in a way that can be formally known* within the discipline. For the diverse practices of arts-based research, including a/r/tography (see Chapter 2) and Jungian psychology converge on the epistemology of the psychic image. How such images become knowing and connect to disciplinary and art sources for making meaning will be the subject matter of this chapter.

Starting methodology and epistemology in arts-based research

Chapter 1 already noted some methodological language of art-based research in the discussion of the term heuristic. Heuristics, problem solving by practice, concentrates on the researcher as organ of knowing, and is often partnered with grounded theory as a knowledge-making structure. Sticking to a carefully chosen theory should save the research from the researcher's own fantasies. By contrast, art-based research prefers ungrounded theory, similar to Jung (see Chapter 2), and does not isolate the researcher-artist. Rather art-based research makes art as something that can function meaningfully in the world. It must *work* apart from the person of the artist. Calling pieces of art "works" indicates more than the effort that is necessary to make art. Rather, art must continue to affect its public, whatever the circumstances.

In this sense, arts-based research requires entering a living tradition and taking its social and moral premises seriously, even if only to challenge them. Art-based research is socially implicated, even if the address of the art to the world is antagonistic or nihilistic. Barone and Eisner put more positively the social aspect of the methodology of arts-based research.

> Arts-based research is an approach to research that we define as a method designed to enlarge human understanding ... the aim is to create an expressive form that will enable an individual to secure an empathetic participation in the lives of others and in the situations studied.
>
> (Barone and Eisner 2012: 8–9)

Not all arts-based research aims to increase empathy for other lives. Given James Rolling Jnr.'s four types of ABR – analytic, synthetic, critical activist and improvisatory – empathy may not be the most prominent result of some projects. However, Barone and Eisner's insistence on art as enlarging collective understanding via empathy is an important example of how ABR can use the communicative dimension of art to press for, or even enact, social change. Above all, Barone and Eisner claim that such empathy is knowing, which reminds us of their symbolic epistemology. As noted of their structuralism in Chapter 2, art, they argue, can know the world while not pretending to depict from pure, unmediated observation: "in the arts, symbols adumbrate; they do not denote" (Barone and Eisner 2012: 2).

I will develop symbols for their Jungian ABR epistemology below. First of all, it is important to emphasize that the artist as researcher is a very different being from the researcher in the world of the subject/object paradigm. Whereas classical science only invites rational consciousness into the enterprise, arts-based research celebrates all human capacities and sees the psyche as indivisible from the body. Tacit knowing, or body-based knowing that is barely conscious, was described by Michael Polyani in *The Tacit Dimension* (1967). It is celebrated for psychotherapy by Jungian teacher of ABR, Shaun McNiff (1998).

> Michael Polyani's classic study of tacit knowing (1967) describes how "explicit" knowledge in science and relatively closed methods of inquiry limit the generation of new knowledge by blocking access to what we know "tacitly." Within the arts, tacit or unspoken knowledge permeates virtually everything we do. Polyani makes it clear that the insistence on "exact" and "comprehensive" will result in the eventual "destruction of all knowledge" (Polyani 1967: 20).
>
> (McNiff 1998: 132)

Tacit knowing is where psychic images stored in the body barely intrude into consciousness. Such tacit images allow people to operate complex machinery such as cars without much knowledge of its internal mechanics. Also, tacit knowing inhabits the body of the trained artist in moving the paint brush or generating words via Jung's unconscious function of bodily sensation. To transdisciplinarity, tacit knowing is a vital epistemology of Tradition, so confirming the presence of the arts within that corpus of spiritual ontologies. Above all, tacit knowing supports the epistemology of a body-infused psyche.

Although rarely mentioning Jung, McNiff does draw on the post-Jungian archetypal psychology of James Hillman that emphasizes the image as always protean (McNiff 1998: 127). Noting archetypal psychology's precept of sticking to the image, McNiff celebrates its refusal to regard any psychic image as a fixed immutable object. The image is a living psychic being that envelops the person. The artist-researcher will be in the image, not "have" the image in the sense of being an owner or claim to be its sole origin.

By such a commitment to the human and beyond the human psyche, archetypal psychology encourages ABR away from the tendency to label images. McNiff astutely observes that "[a]rt-based research requires methods of inquiry that extend directly from the physical presence of the image as well as the person's experience of it" (ibid.: 128). He thereby sees archetypal psychology as confirming the necessity of materializing the psychic image in art, concentrating on the visual arts in his study.

McNiff also introduces research by Leonard Shlain on the crucial yet largely unacknowledged role of the psychic image in traditional science research (Shlain 1991: 42). From the role of creativity in images, one could argue that art is always involved in science because, alongside rational deductions, scientists use intuition. It is images that make intuition comprehensible as the early stages of complex ideas (McNiff 1998: 80).

Psychic images are already embedded in research processes. They are the precursors of meaning. What distinguishes Jungian and post-Jungian ABR on the image is the assertion of its importance. Regarding the psychic image as crucial to making meaning entails treating it with care lest it harden it into an object, which would freeze its animate qualities. At that point, the subject/object split is reinstated with the image left spiritually bereft.

In refusing the binary of subject/object, arts-based research is disrupting all sorts of rigidities, including another key guardian of that outworn paradigm, that of fact and fiction. To see story as a fundamental human quality suggests that all researchers are essentially storytellers, scientists included. Such an approach is fundamental to recent literature on ABR (Barone and Eisner 2012; Leavy 2018). Story is also basic to Jungian psychology. There stories come in the form of myth as narratives shaping relations between the known and unknown psyche. How Jungian myth and ABR story can support each other epistemologically and methodologically will be considered later in this chapter.

First of all, both Leavy and Barone and Eisner list advantages of ABR in ways that make epistemological claims. Crucial to Barone and Eisner is their structuralist assertion that form is expressive and inherently meaning-generating (164–72). Artistic forms and genres are the collective heritage of the human desire to make sense of the world and also be intrinsically connected to social structures. Forms generate worlds and every work of art has an implicit worldview (7–14). However, they argue that arts-based research is not a machine for generating fixed answers to social problems. It is rather a way of raising new or more empathetically informed questions. Above all, ABR can provide the kind of knowing that measurement cannot. It can provide knowing that is compassionate. Not reserved for trained artists, ABR will diversify research rather than replace existing disciplinary strategies.

Recent arts-based research will often problematize and question instead of wanting to discover a fixed and knowable reality. ABR typically rejects static and absolute modes of knowing. The images that become art in ABR are meaning-rich and yet not definitive. Similarly, Leavy's list of the advantages of ABR in the *Handbook of Arts-Based Research* presents it as a methodology to address problems by doing something different (Leavy 2018: 9–11). ABR offers insights by means of diverse ways of describing, discovering and problem solving.

Particularly Jungian, although Leavy does not say so, is noting that ABR is holistic and can make microcosmic internal connections to the social or macrocosmic dimension. The psychic image crucial to art-making can be taken into the widest possible context. It is holistic in art's capacity to integrate such various strategies as tacit knowing, trained expertise and what Jung would call the four functions of thinking, feeling, sensation and intuition.

Furthermore, Leavy joins Barone and Eisner in seeing ABR as evocative and potentially productive of empathy with social implications. Additionally, it can become a critical approach that raises new awareness and challenges stereotypes. On firm transdisciplinary ground, Leavy shows ABR to be participatory in promoting multiple meanings. Arts resist fixity and are capable of infinite reinterpretation. Finally, arts-based research takes knowledge-making into the public domain, because art by definition addresses audiences.

Again, ABR reaches towards Nicolescu when he argues that transdisciplinarity is necessarily transcultural and transreligious (Nicolescu 2014: 13–16). Multiple meanings are the sign of multiple realities that require recognition of oneness and manyness in perpetual tension. The multiple meanings of arts-based research are the substance of the diversity of Tradition (including the many traditions of art) that also embraces a holistic cosmic vision. With the transdisciplinary not fully articulated by Leavy, and Jung left mostly implicit for McNiff, it is useful to turn to Jung's explicit treatment of the arts for further epistemological and methodological potential.

Jungian epistemology for a methodology of arts-based research

Ultimately, Jungian psychology offers a number of broad epistemological strategies for arts-based research. These could be summarized as follows: Jung's proto-transdisciplinarity approaches to the personal psyche, the four functions explored in Chapter 1 as deployed in Eros and Logos (shown below), the psychic image as signs or symbols, active imagination and amplification, myth, the collective unconscious, parallels with alchemy, synchronicity and the *unus mundus*. Some of these have been introduced in earlier chapters.

However, this chapter is dedicated to Jung's strategies towards his overall epistemological principle that individuation as the growth towards wholeness is oriented to making meaning. Given that individuation requires the creative pro-active participation of the unconscious, art-making for him is also meaning-making, with an important proviso that art's images are not to be reduced to fixed meanings for making consciousness completely rational and exclusionary. For Jung too, art evokes and resonates; it does not provide simple answers. To this end, Jung the psychologist does not collapse art into psychic health, for that would frustrate his emphasis on mystery, as we will see.

Jung's proto-transdisciplinarity, the personal psyche, or why a work of art is not a disease

Jung's essays on poetry and literature are remarkable for their admission that epistemology in art cannot be the same as that of psychology. Put more simply, psychology cannot govern art. In fact, in the poetry essay he explicitly rules out a unifying principle in the infant psyche that would produce psychology as a superior mode of knowing (Jung 1922, CW15: para. 99). As noted in Chapter 2, Jung rejects disciplinary hierarchy at that very moment. By crediting the literary critic with knowledge not to be contradicted by the psychologist, Jung welcomes what would later be called transdisciplinarity. Moreover, psychology, or psyche-logos, becomes possible for an arts-based epistemology that is welcoming to any laws that might emerge, yet will not presume them. Here is ABR's groundless theory.

On the other hand, not privileging psychology over art is not the same as having no epistemological contribution to make. Jung spends much of both essays debating the role of the artist's personal psyche in the collective arena of art. While Jung leaves to specialists the matter of artistic forms and their legacy, he has a lot to say about the artistic personality and how that may or may not impact the work. Above all, he rejects causal interpretations of art: "A work of art is not a disease," meaning that it cannot be used as a diagnostic tool on the artist (Jung 1922, CW15: para. 108). Nor can the artist be used to determine the truth of the work.

This does not stop Jung. In his essay on Picasso he uses the artist's destruction of conventional form to hypothesize two groups of patients in relation to (but not identical to) such disordering visualizations. Neurotic patients, Jung decides, are searching for meaning and feeling, while the schizophrenics – producing images closest to Picasso's work – are overwhelmed and swallowed up by meaning (Jung 1932, CW15: para. 209). This liking for pairs or dualism continues in the poetry essay, again on the personal proclivities of the artist. For Jung depicts the introverted and extraverted artist as prototypes for his "psychological" and "visionary" types of art that are later defined in his essay on literature (Jung 1930, CW15).

Extraversion and introversion are Jung's terms for a duality in orientation of psychic being. The extravert is geared to participation in the world, while the introvert tends towards her inner life. Perhaps surprisingly, the introverted artist is the one so dedicated to her own consciousness that the art is largely concerned with knowable intentions (Jung 1922, CW15: para. 111). By contrast, the extraverted artist heeds the call of the "other." Such an artist will hear calls from elsewhere and give priority to what comes from the relatively unknown. Indeed, Jung is so taken with the extraverted artistic personality that he describes the inspiration as an "alien will" that is planted in the artist (ibid.: para. 113). It is the extraverted artist who listens to the Sirens of the collective unconscious.

In Jung's discourse on Picasso's shattering of conventional forms, as well as his depiction of artistic extraversion and introversion, we have epistemological strategies that could be used in arts-based research that is not necessarily dedicated to psychology. Notions of extraversion, introversion, neurosis and schizophrenia are ways of directing the making of meaning in art that does not have to be reflected back to the artist. After all, Jung distinguishes Picasso, as he later does James Joyce in his Ulysses essay, from actual patients. They are not ill, even if their art exhibits symptoms. For both artists, Jung sees a *cultural* diagnosis happening in the art.

For Jungian ABR, it is important to note that psychological arguments on the artistic personality are presented by Jung as ingredients of much larger and potentially multidisciplinary ways of making meaning in arts-based research. Personal wounds and basic orientations of the artist *matter*. They will surface in the art, yet they do not determine it. For a succinct demonstration of this principle, Jung offers a delightful meditation on Plato's famous cave myth as a creative vision.

At this moment in the poetry essay, Jung is making his famous distinction between signs and symbols as part of his quarrel with Sigmund Freud. Signs are motifs with straightforward meanings, while symbols connect to the mysteries of the unconscious. Jung accuses Freud of being reductive about art by discovering only signs. For example, Freud would take Plato's famous cave metaphor as a mere sign of infantile obsessions with the womb. What Plato does with his cave, by using it to show how people do not see reality, only flickering shadows on the wall – this would be ignored by Freud. Contra Freud, by calling Plato's cave a symbol, it could be seen to point to the complexities, creativity and metaphysics of the whole philosophy (Jung 1922, CW15: paras. 105–6).

While not exactly generous to Freud on art, Jung does credit the diagnosis he attributes to him. Plato's cave probably does indicate that a genuine level of infantile sexuality was a significant feature of the philosopher's personality (ibid.: 105). Jung's real argument is that Freudian psychology would remain stuck in looking for such signs as knowable indication of the actual person. It would miss the real achievements and meanings of the art. The approach Jung alleges as Freudian could not be useful for an ABR that wants to use art to do more than explore the psyche of the artists.

In fact, Jung provides a vivid example of how something personal to the artist, womb pre-occupation, could generate something far more universally applicable. Jung valuably emphasizes that psychology must not seal off knowing in a box of signs. Without the cave as a Jungian symbol, "we would have completely overlooked what Plato actually created out of the primitive determinants of his philosophical ideas" (ibid.: 105). Jungian epistemology in art offers meaning in a state of continuous growth; *it is never closed off or final.*

The four psychic functions and Eros/Logos

It is worth returning briefly to Jung's four psychic functions as epistemological principles and to consider them in the gender context of Eros and Logos, his dualistic structures of consciousness.

With thinking being bound up in the capacity for discrimination and judgment, feeling includes the ability to connect empathy and ethical impulses. Clearly, traditions of academic research in the subject/object paradigm have privileged Jung's thinking function and correspondingly sought to marginalize, or even eliminate, feeling. The two less conscious functions of sensation and intuition are also deeply valued by Jung as ways of knowing that seek to include the whole psyche, the unconscious included. In this sense, Jungian psychology locates knowing in all psychic dimensions and, as we will see, provides methods for arts-based research to draw on those traditionally ignored qualities of feeling, sensation and intuition.

Also worth noting here is how Jung genders thinking and feeling, in part through his binary gender archetypal patterns of anima and animus. While the Greek word Logos was considered by Heraclitus to mean universal reason, Jung takes Logos to be a masculine principle associated with spirit rather than matter, as well as thinking and discrimination (Samuels et al. 1986: 86–7). Using words such as "love, intimacy and relatedness," he proposed a corresponding feminine principle he called Eros (ibid.: 87). In his essentialist gender mode, Jung considered male consciousness to naturally be led by Logos, while women would nurture Eros.

A further dichotomy occurs in the archetypal patterns of anima and animus, which are the route by which these qualities could be accessed by the other sex. Anima makes Eros available to men, and the animus would potentially bring Logos to women through the deconstructive process of individuation. It is very unfortunate that by placing women's access to spirit and reason in the unconscious, it becomes irrational and disordered. Calling women's Logos as a "regrettable accident," Jung tellingly admits in the same paragraph that Eros and Logos are merely "conceptual aids" (Jung 1951, CW9ii: para. 29).

Therefore, I suggest following Jung's admission that the gender essentialism in these concepts is strategic rather than necessary. Jungian arts-based research could take Eros and Logos as conceptual aids to the gender politics of research modes. As described in Chapter 1, there is a buried goddess in Jung's psychology, in synchronicity, that deserves to be acknowledged, especially given the way patriarchy, the divine and rational knowing, has for centuries been gendered as male. Jung may have a problem in openly celebrating what has been denigrated as feminine knowing in Eros modes of relating and connecting, but his psychology is nevertheless a plea for wholeness and the restoration of what has been repressed.

As a conservative Swiss, Jung had a problem with women who sought their Logos. As a depth psychologist, Jung restores the feminine to research epistemology in those connected and embodied ways of knowing: sensation, intuition, feeling and Eros.

Epistemology and methodology of the psychic image as signs or symbols

Returning to the psychic image as signs and symbols is important in fully excavating the epistemology of the Jungian symbol for arts-based research. We recall that when discussing the language of poetry Jung distinguishes some words as signs with straightforward meanings, while others are symbols, images that connect to the mysteries of the unconscious.

Indicatively, a symbol is not a puzzle to be decoded. It may well yield further meanings to the enquiring or intuitive mind, but should it cease to be enigmatic or mysterious, then it becomes sign not symbol. Above all, symbols animate. Furthermore, their animation of the psyche is a facet of individuation because they promote the writer or reader's integration into the unconscious. Arguably, symbols are the language of the intuitive and/or sensation function manifesting the archetypal energy of an embodied psyche. To encounter symbols is to be opened by the psychic other to unfathomable, yet meaningful, realms beyond the conscious ego. Such a numinous meeting serves to validate life.

> A symbol really lives only when it is the best and highest expression for something divined but not yet known to the observer. It then compels his unconscious participation and has a life-giving and life-enhancing effect.
>
> (Jung 1921, CW6: 819)

Symbols materialize the arts-based researcher's sensate intuition in the process of making art. For, of course, symbols cannot be limited to words, and hence literary art. Given that symbols are types of Jungian images that are manifestations of the deep bodily psyche, then they can occur in any medium that the psyche needs to evoke beyond rational cognition. Symbols can be musical, choreographic, photographic, painterly, sculptural and so forth. They are Jung's way of accounting for the enhanced liveliness in making and viewing art.

In a previous book, *Remembering Dionysus* (2017), I suggested that symbols are part of a Dionysian narrative in individuation. Archetypal psychologist James Hillman wrote that Jung valued the Dionysian for its focus on bodily dismemberment, a particularly visceral anticipation of the deconstructive capacity of individuation (Hillman 1972). Hillman proposed that Dionysian dismemberment preceded a re-membering of consciousness that would not return to the style of the aging monotheistic God that haunts modernity. Rather, Dionysian re-membering is that of an ecstatic instinctual body that knows itself as *parts*, linked, evocative of each other, but whose wholeness is also multiplicity.

My addition to Hillman's ingenious theory is to situate the Jungian symbol as the figuration of Dionysian re-membering, and to apply it to academic disciplines via transdisciplinarity (see below). As Jung notes above, the symbol is an intuitive apprehension of a larger mystery. It propels "life-giving and life-enhancing" consciousness because it re-members the psyche–body connection in the instinctual realm where archetypes have their somatic base. Just so does Hillman suggest that Dionysian re-membering connects us to *zoe*, the divine Dionysian experience of endless, instinctual life (Hillman 1972: 29).

Of course, mere mortals cannot live in *zoe*, for our life is neither divine nor endless. Rather, the re-membering symbol gives us a taste of *zoe* as it evokes divine mysteries. Put another way, the artist using symbols is another figure in the story of Dionysus, his eventual wife, Ariadne. She is an artist with significant research concerns as she enables Theseus to navigate the labyrinth with her thread. Theseus kills the devouring Minotaur, and like many heroes who too soon celebrate slaying the monster the unconscious shelters, he undervalues the unconscious in another way: by abandoning the feminine. Ariadne is left marooned on the island of Naxos, where Dionysus later finds her.

Cast off by the masculine as conqueror, Ariadne is wooed by the masculine animated as the god of dismembering and re-membering. They marry, and Ariadne is taken into the heavens, becoming divine herself. It is worth recalling that Dionysus is also the god of theater, particularly of comedy and tragedy. Ariadne experiences both dramatic forms in her tragic abandonment and the divine comedy of her assumption into the heavens. For comedy fosters rebirth and survival, stemming from Dionysian spring fertility rites. Tragedy is dismemberment at its most abject.

I suggest that Jungian symbols enact the divine marriage of Ariadne and Dionysus. By tasting the symbol, in whatever kind of art, we participate in the

Mysteries. We intuit and embody meanings that are never reducible to rational or measurable kinds of research. For symbols are that which overcomes the subject/object split that has beset modern consciousness. By joining the ego to the wild unconscious, we are wedded to its participation in body, in nature, and in the cosmos. Truly, the symbol is a divine marriage. Given that art is often the best hope for finding symbols in an era of extreme splitting that believes reality is merely "out there" to be penetrated by experiments subjected to falsification, the Jungian symbol reveals the subject/object split to be cultural, not natural, art re-membering Dionysus.

After all, Jung makes it very clear that symbols are not something "out there," by showing that they depend upon the psychic openness of the observer.

> Whether a thing is a symbol or not depends chiefly on the attitude of the observing consciousness; for instance, on whether it regards a given fact not merely as such but also as an expression for something unknown.
>
> (Jung 1921, CW6: 818)

He is also explicit that the living mystery of the psyche is not to be found in the way traditional science butchers reality into chewable slices that can be digested by the ego (Jung 1922, CW15: para. 121). In fact, Jung points out that science already requires symbols if it is to be allowed to progress. Those scientists who truly seek in their mathematics what is not yet known are using symbols.

> Since every scientific theory contains an hypothesis … it is a symbol.
>
> (Jung 1921, CW6: para. 817)

Symbols are not limited to art; or rather, art is not prevented from being an inquiry into the nature of the universe. As with alchemy, Jung shows that art and science are not separable if we are to address all that humans are, and all the ways they interact with the cosmos. Symbols are a powerful epistemology for arts-based research. They are where known and unknown meet in the making and witnessing of art. Symbols re-member Dionysus, a god whose divine creativity rescues the human psyche once the ego abandons the pose of heroic domination of the other.

Ariadne is a prototype arts-based researcher who helped her society overcome a terrible atavistic ritual of human sacrifice. She suffered for her daring, and through that ordeal found divine inspiration. May she in-spirit us all for practices that develop symbolic consciousness, those of active imagination and amplification.

Active imagination and amplification as ABR

In a concrete way, active imagination is Jung's response to the loss of the symbolic attitude through the prevalence of the subject/object split. Cutting personhood from the other, be that other the unconscious, nature or other people, imposes a binary relationship where A, or ego, is not B, or other. The symbol is what transdisciplinarity calls the included middle, as I discuss below. It is A and B together, and by definition requires a willingness to participate in a mystery, or non-rational ways of making meaning. Active imagination was devised by Jung as a therapeutic method of creating meaning by generating symbols.

Jung presents active imagination as enabling the spontaneous growth of psychic images, and of using them as a mode of healing. When a patient is trapped in negative feelings, like Ariadne abandoned on Naxos, she is prompted to allow the sheer power trapped in the unconscious (by the subject/object split) to produce an image. Alternatively, the patient might be asked to invite an image from a dream that is already alive to them. By relaxing conscious control the overwhelming other will develop images of its own accord.

> But active imagination, as the term denotes, means that the images have a life of their own and that the symbolic events develop according to their own logic – that is, of course, if your conscious reason does not interfere.
>
> (Jung 1968: para. 397)

Either with the analyst or alone, patients establish a relationship with this active, previously alien, part of themselves. Often a dialogue develops, with the image becoming a symbol by forging a connection to the ego. For the "active" in active imagination includes ego as well as the unconscious. In this sense active imagination is a way of facilitating individuation, that healing development of an ever deeper connection between ego and unconscious archetypal energies. Put another way, by harnessing the unconscious functions of intuition and sensation in particular, active imagination is a method for making meaning through images becoming symbols. It is an epistemology of the unknown psyche and the unknown other of any kind.

Where active imagination goes deep into the psyche to heal the split from the other, Jung's amplification, it is an epistemology of the collective psyche. For amplification considers the image alongside parallel or congruent images from culture or mythology (Jung 1935, CW18: para. 173). Amplification is not personal. It is not a matter of personal association with the image. Instead, amplification involves researching the image from a source external to the psyche, as with a reference book. Such a source should contain examples from as many cultures and historical times as possible. Jung used books; today, in addition, we have powerful Internet search engines.

The artist-researcher's psyche is involved in amplification by choosing images from somewhere else to amplify, enhance or evoke more from the initial image. This starting image can be from a dream or active imagination, or from an artistic endeavor. However, *looking up* the image is another way to allow the psychic energy materialized in it to become a symbol. Finding a congruent or resonant correlate to the starting image promotes liveliness in the psychic matter. It may promote a spontaneous active imagination; it may become more active in making meaning and art.

Amplification discovers the image in its collective setting, the collective consciousness that is the emanation of the collective unconscious (see below). Like active imagination, amplification is a ritual where the ego is put aside for collective, archetypal resonance. Both are rituals for overcoming the subject/ object split, and for making symbols that join us to the universe. Such rituals generate meaning from intuitive sensation. They are therefore art-making as research.

We can also see both active imagination and amplification as Dionysian processes. For both, the ego suffers a dismembering of its illusion of control over the psyche as knowable subject split off from the world. By co-creating a symbolic connection to the other, we are re-membered in a psyche that tastes bodily rejuvenation by *zoe*.

The ego, afraid of Dionysus at first in the overwhelming images of active imagination, begins to talk to the image as *real*, other, creating of being, and thus divine. The image in active imagination takes on Dionysian divinity, not only because it is other to the ego in a destructive sense; it is also constructive because, in allowing it to *be* itself, it provides an exchange, a dialogue. The image is (Dionysian) god because it supplies energy. It re-members the divided psyche in the intimacy of exchanges *between* parts. The re-membered psyche is Ariadne as artist symbolically connected to the cosmos.

Amplification also expands meaning by substantiating the connection between ego and collective. For example, by finding that the loquacious image of an owl in active imagination resonates with a Welsh princess turned into an owl for unfaithfulness, the symbol is stronger, more dynamic, offering more narrative directions for its energy to be part of a bigger creative process. In short, in ABR active imagination and amplification are epistemologies of the image or methodologies of intuition and sensation. They bring Dionysus to ABR as an initiatory experience of *zoe*; instinctual life without limit.

The Jungian artist-researcher is a celebrant of Dionysus, not by conscious choice, rather by necessary process. Ginette Paris reminds us that Dionysus can only be encountered safely in collective rites (Paris 1998: 12). To ignore Dionysus, as Pentheus did by denying the divinity of Dionysus, is to be torn apart by his maenads. Art is either a collective ritual or a ritual offering to the collective, or it risks having no being at all. Every artist encounters Dionysus and is dismembered by his energies. It is a necessary separation of ego from other, or the realization (making real) of the subject/object split as a cultural, not inevitable, division.

The artist is re-membered making art through symbols or images that generate meaning without end. Dionysus is the god of arts-based research ontology. With his foundational stories of being, making *and* meaning, we turn to Jung and myth, or story as research epistemology.

Myth, personal myth and finding stories in ABR

To Jung, myths are stories that express and mold the psyche (Jung 1954, CW9i: para. 7). The mythology of past cultures is not an attempt at science. Rather, myths are, as they have always been, archetypal form-making entities that knit the individual to the collective psyche *on a conscious and unconscious level.* Myths are stories that function as the engine of psychic processes. They counteract stuckness.

> In the majority of my cases, the resources of consciousness have been exhausted; the ordinary expression for this situation is: "I am stuck." … the theme of many a fairy-tale and myth.
>
> (Jung 1933/2001: 70–1)

Myth begins with archetypes as potentials for form, pattern and meaning. In practice, the energies of archetypes structure the psyche in images. Such images are attracted to each other, making patterns and stories. These stories are both individual and collective, because archetypes seed archetypal images in a creative dialogue with an individual's history and culture. Archetypal images are sticky with divine or numinous energy. In turn, their stories generate meaning because they are individual, cultural and transcultural.

For example, Jung regarded the Catholic Church of medieval Europe as a satisfactory center of myth-making that sustained social dynamics. Meaning was generated to and within the psyches of the population because the symbols that the Church provided were numinous. They conjoined the individual psyche to the collective because archetypes found physical and ritual expression in Catholic symbols. Put another way, the Church was psychologically powerful because its images and rituals *were* symbols: they linked the population to a mysterious divine. By those symbols, people found a structure for their individuation.

Of course, Jung did not suggest that this particular religious gathering of mythical stories was the only one to fully express the human psyche. In *Aion* (1951), Jung proposed a succession of symbolic cultural systems that provided psychological myths for Europe. These included astrology, Gnosticism, alchemy and, more recently, his own psychology. Indeed, he made clear that as the age changed so would its myths; so that future eras could require different psychologies. Jung was not essentialist, even about his own work.

This is an important factor in the Jungian use of myth to both express and, if necessary, encourage pattern-forming in a chaotic psyche. Myths are not fixed stories, but rather the expression of recurrent human situations and the necessity of finding the right psychic container or form. Myths do not exist except as a dialogue between transcendent formless energies (archetypes) and their embodied cultural and immanent expression in archetypal images. Myths are epistemological because they generate meaning by connecting the individual to a mystery. The meanings that Jungian myths offer are contingent and universal. They suggest larger collective stories rooted in a particular time and place.

In this sense, myths are the psyche made visible. They are the partly conscious storying or historying of groups, families, tribes, nations, epochs, religions. As seen in the previous chapter, myths contribute intimately to paradigms of knowing and being. For example, *The Myth of the Goddess* by Ann Baring and Jules Cashford (1991) looks at paradigmatic creation myths as structures of consciousness that have haunted Western modernity. Their Sky Father monotheistic masculine god of fundamental dualism set up an epistemology based on separation from what is to be known. Ultimately, of course, it produced the subject/object split.

In mitigation of that drastic hegemony, myths offer an Earth Mother, a version of the planet as divine Mother to us all. Her knowing is based on the primacy of connection. Arguably, these creation stories contain narrative elements found in different mythologies all over the world. They find psychological being as Logos and Eros in Jung's gender binaries (Rowland 2017). However, they are also myths of how we make meaning. Sky Father, in his insistence on separation, will look for abstractions as ultimately meaningful in research. By contrast, Earth Mother is always involved, invaginated. For her, story-making is an ongoing creative process, just as she appears in Jung as the nature behind synchronicity, as *acts of creation in time* (Jung 1952, CW8: para. 965).

To the focus on story in arts-based research, Jung offers a psyche in which making narratives to provide meaning is indigenous and necessary. For Jung, psychic health requires on-going individuation, which means story-making as the innate creativity of archetypes encounters embodied experience. Direct that experience to research and art and Jungian myth makes meaning in the paradigm proposed by transdisciplinarity, that of oneness and multiplicity. Jungian myth invokes oneness in a sense of something with collective implications, and manyness in the sense of a uniquely embodied and temporal moment.

An example of Jungian myth in ABR has already been provided in this chapter by Dionysus. His sponsoring of dismembering in myth is epistemology, a way of making knowledge, *because* of the psyche's embodied participation in research as art-making. Whether the actual ABR project consists of making stories or not, the myth transitions personal creativity into collective wonderment and rejuvenation. Moreover, Jung provides his own example of myth as epistemology in his discussion of what has come to be known as "personal myth."

Personal myth

Jung's autobiography, *Memories, Dreams, Reflections*, records an epistemological crisis (Jung 1963/1983). His whole sense of meaning and knowing in his life breaks down. This "Confrontation with the Unconscious" occurs after the painful detonation of his professional and personal relationship with Sigmund Freud (Jung 1963/1983: 194–225). He realizes that for him, as for many of his contemporaries, the Christian myth no longer provides psychological security and a way of making sense of the world (ibid.: 195).

> But then what is your myth – the myth in which you do live?
>
> (ibid.)

Here myth is a personal quest for meaning in narrative form. So too is story for the arts-based researcher. Jung in *Memories, Dreams, Reflections* develops the notion of a personal myth begun as an individual response to a psychological crisis at the level of collective stories, his religion. By engaging with the unconscious in dreams and visions, by evolving what came to be called active imagination in word and painterly form, Jung begins *Liber Novus* or *The Red Book* (2009). His psychological principles emerge from this crisis, to become the concepts of his psychology: "[t]hrough this dream I understood that the self is the principle and archetype of orientation and meaning ... Out of it emerged a first inkling of my personal myth" (Jung 1963/1983: 224)

Jung's personal myth is closely related to his psychology from *his* psychology, his own life experiences. Given that the processes that went into *The Red Book* are poetic and artistic, Jung could be accused of pioneering arts-based research as a major, though not sole, methodology from which Jungian psychology came to be formulated. Chapter 4 will examine *Liber Novus* as arts-based research.

Jung himself did not want to be considered as an artist, but as a scientist. As noted earlier, he rejected the aesthetic as a mode of making meaning. Although he calls the time of delving into these images the "*prima materia*" or foundation for his life's work, he does not give that title to *The Red Book* itself, as we will see in the next chapter (Jung 1963/1983: 225). Rather, he asserts in *Memories, Dreams, Reflections* that reality, science and "concrete conclusions" are necessary for the psychologist and not to be found in "this aestheticizing tendency" (ibid.: 213). Jung refuses to be the pioneer of arts-based research, which regards the aesthetic as integral to science, not separate from it.

And yet, through the art practice that is given material form in *The Red Book*, Jung makes a personal myth that is a worthy counterpart to his psychological precepts. Narrative that is co-created with an intrinsically creative unconscious is a respectable epistemology for Jung. His own personal myth, reliant upon the self as archetype of wholeness and organizer of meaning, not surprisingly resembles his native Christianity. Jung spent decades examining verbal and visual images of God and the Trinity in a quest for their psychological meaning.

Of course this does not mean that he expected every personal myth to resemble Christian epistemology. Different cultures and religions would supply different styles of individuation. Personal myth shows what individuation *does* in providing a meaningful narrative by which to live. The alienated modern person will be re-integrated (by individuation) into the collective at an unconscious level that will be realized, made *real*, by simultaneously discovering and constructing a personal myth. Although Jung did not recognize his artistic journey into personal myth as the most appropriate for *his* project, Jungian arts-based research is not so limited.

Personal myth may prove to be a way of examining spontaneity in ABR and what is found to be psychically potent. It is a notion of story as a way of bonding or belonging to larger collectives. These collectives may be groups and tribes, nations or epochs, the planet and the cosmos, and so forth. For this epistemology of the previously unknown and invisible threads of belonging in arts-based research it is worth looking again at Jung's consideration of art and the collective unconscious.

The collective unconscious or art is culture and history speaking

Jung's amplification of images considered above is a way of making knowledge by including the collective unconscious. Given that dreams and the deep psyche of others are not directly accessible, the researcher looks up the image or story in an external source. In this way, the psyches of a whole community are invited into the process of meaning making. However, a work of art in any medium has already included the collective in two ways: the psyche of the artist, and that of the method or genre. Hence Jung saw that the collective unconscious as the universal psychic heritage of mankind might communicate directly through a work of art.

In his poetry essay comes the definition of the symbol and its openness to mysteries. Later on, Jung produces the notion of visionary art made of symbols that are mysterious to their creator and often to their audiences. What he also adds is that visionary art is a way of knowing the unconscious of a culture, not so much the individual. Therefore, the idea of visionary art is an epistemology of cultural and historical research.

> Therein lies the social significance of art: it is constantly at work educating the spirit of the age, conjuring up the forms in which the age is most lacking.
>
> (Jung 1930, CW15: para. 130)

Art that draws upon the collective unconscious will produce new knowing because it provides what the age lacks. Jung held that the psyche, collective or singular, would strive for balance. So visionary art will generate what is needed in the cause of general psychic stability. Visionary art has the capacity to tell us what we do not already know about our society. Jung calls visionary art of the collective unconscious "a creative act which is of importance for the whole epoch" (Jung 1930, CW15: para. 153).

Moreover, according to Jung, visionary art could even predict the future. The teleological psyche works for the collective unconscious too. Visionary art could reveal previously unknown tendencies that will become important in the future. It points to where a culture is going (ibid.: para. 154). Jung is insistent that such art arrives to restore the psychic balance, whether of the person or the age, thereby signaling both his social conservatism and his love of opposites (ibid.: para. 160). A particular emphasis in one society, or era, must to Jung call forth an opposite, to cancel out the extremes and restore harmony. But what if society is not fair, stable or harmonious to begin with?

What epistemology can find in Jung's collective unconscious and its visionary art is that the art of the sensation and intuitive functions know *more* than purely conscious reasoning can supply. The idea that art can be prophetic is not new, and does not originate with Jung. Works as various as Shakespeare writing about the *end* of European colonialism in his 1611 play, *The Tempest*, and the prophetic nature of technology imaged in Mary Shelley's 1816 novel, *Frankenstein, or the modern Prometheus*, testify to the viability of this epistemological approach.

It is worth repeating that Jung does not envisage art as a research methodology. His treatment of his own *Red Book* is a mute testimony. However, in discussing the relationship between art-making and its importance for society, he does reveal it to be a surprisingly specific and effective form of making knowledge. Art of the collective unconscious is to an era like a significant dream to an individual, he asserts (Jung 1930, CW15: para. 161). It provides mysterious truths that can continue to evolve and meet current and future needs.

Also, Jung is helpful to the cause of ABR, by insisting that the personality of the artist is not an essential epistemological focus for the art. Both his essays on imaginative writing campaign for art to be disentangled from the artist. Art should be regarded as meaningful manifestations of the collective in a particular social setting.

Of course, the drive to disentangle art from the artist's psycho-biography is somewhat disguised by the division of art into psychological (as in entirely contained by the conscious intentions of the artist) or visionary (an eruption from the collective unconscious using the artist merely as a "nutrient medium") (Jung 1922, CW15: para. 108). The two categories are extremes between an art dominated by conscious functions of thinking and feeling, and that of the unconscious, sensation and intuition. No artist, or work, is fully one or the other, as Jung tacitly implies by dividing Goethe's *Faust* between these two types (Jung 1930, CW15: para. 142).

Almost as an afterthought, in "Psychology and Literature" Jung says that the collective unconscious content of visionary art will have an individuating effect on audience as well as artist (Jung 1930, CW15: para. 161). Art of the collective unconscious is transformative of both creator and consumer. With art, knowing is connected to being as a mutually informing process. Ultimately, visionary art provides an epistemological process of social, historical and cultural concerns by and through transforming being into knowing. In so doing, it eradicates the subject/object split, for this artwork is no mere object! Jung's visionary art is made of the archetypal stuff that weaves us into the fabric of the universe.

Jung's alchemy, synchronicity symbols and transdisciplinarity for epistemology and methodology

Jung's perspective on alchemy can also be epistemological and methodological for arts-based research. In previous chapters I suggested alchemy as an important historical precedent. One factor stands out when alchemy is considered for research epistemology – its obscurity. Alchemy is not friendly to the usual aim of modern research of dissemination and reciprocal exchange. Alchemy does not want to communicate to the public. Rather, it revels in language that seals up its many possible meanings in obscurities and enigmas.

Of course, this esoteric opaqueness to rational discourse was precisely what attracted Jung to alchemy. Mysteries, impenetrable accounts and weird metaphoric language mean symbols to Jung. It was precisely the impossibility of decoding alchemical texts into a coherent practice that convinced Jung that alchemy was a projection of individuation for alchemists themselves.

To Jung, alchemy was a methodology for achieving psychic wholeness in an age not yet prepared for psychotherapy. The toxic metal mercury is also trickster Mercurius, who could poison at one moment, then transform into the Virgin Mary. There is also a king and queen who mated as sun and moon, a bath of dissolution and baptism, etc.; all these were symbols holding fast the mystery of the unconscious. As such they could participate in the radical dismembering and re-membering of the ego. They were archetypes materialized for agency.

Given that alchemy includes what we now call art, and later was redefined as a science that excludes art, alchemy is relevant to ABR in general and Jungian-informed ABR in particular. In the individuality of alchemy's reports and outcomes lies something of the specificity proper to art. Like alchemists, artists who reach into the unknown psyche find their own mysteries. Art invokes psychic images that, *as psychic*, are unique and incommunicable, except when made substantial in art. One could say that art is thereby epistemological in essence: it converts individual psychic experience into matter that generates multiple and on-going interpretations. Art is a methodology for psyche to become research.

One example of the symbol-making practices suggested by alchemy, and later developed in Jung's psychology, is synchronicity (see Chapter 2). The meaningful coincidence of psyche and material world in synchronicity is a basic epistemological move. The psyche seeks meaning in a way that the habitual assumption of the subject/object split denies. Yet the desire to find significance when a dream is proved true, for example, is an individuating eruption from that which has been denied to the ego. Such impulses to credit synchronicity propel the psyche's innate urge for meaning into an epistemological act of knowing.

That the knowing of synchronicity is ultimately mysterious is readily apparent; synchronicity could be said to create symbols. It is an artistic practice of nature itself, a nature that extends into human nature. Synchronicity is an epistemology that evokes the alchemical and transdisciplinary *unus mundus*, or interconnectedness of cosmic being and knowing. Basarab Nicolescu includes Jungian alchemy in his project by saying that transdisciplinary science must be written in symbols (Nicolescu 2014: 30–4).

Transdisciplinarity epistemology adopts symbols for writing and knowing because they are understood, as Jung proposed, to be always open to mystery. Symbolic writing here means that language is enriched, and knowing becomes permanent *because* it is open to endless revision. The literal rational language that Jung termed "signs" is liable to degrade because it cannot be open to the multiple realities of transdisciplinary epistemology.

> A symbol-theory is potentially capable of continuous improvements, of perpetual development in an attempt to find more and more of the undefined richness of the symbol. Theory based on a symbol-idea is thus an open theory. The symbol provides the *permanent* nature of such a theory. An open theory can change, over time, its shape and its mathematical formalism, but its *direction* remains always the same.
>
> (Nicolescu 2014: 34)

Nicolescu's comment here can be read as a useful summary of the epistemology of Jungian arts-based research. It makes knowledge through materializing psychic creativity in symbols that can be collectively apprehended through the traditions of the arts.

An example of Jungian alchemical arts-based methodology

Below are a few extracts from an essay by playwright Cheri Steinkellner as she embraced the methodology of Jungian alchemical arts-based research. The result is her beautiful play, *Prima Materia* (2019), which focuses on the final conversation between a dying mother and her adult daughter.

> When I began writing this play, I did not know I was embarking on an arts-based research project. When unconscious figures showed up to help

me write from a deeper place of knowing, I did not know I was engaging in *heuristic*, or intuitive and improvisational, learning. As a professional TV, film, animation, and theatre writer, I am well versed in the art and craft of creating a fictional world, concocting characters to populate it, putting words in said characters' mouths, and devising their narratives according to my sensibilities. Not so with *Prima Materia*. This process has been – and continues to be – a radical experiment in setting aside my authorial practices, expectations, and plans, and following Inspiration wherever she may lead ...

In *Anatomy of the Psyche: Alchemical Symbolism in Psychotherapy* (1990), Edward Edinger identifies calcination, or the process of intense heating, as the first stage in the alchemical order of operations. [My play concerned] my own burning – and frustrated – desire to connect with my mother, Carole, who died in a medicated coma in 2003 ... If I couldn't fix my mom and me, it felt like the next best thing. I didn't realize it was the first step in the process of recognizing my unconscious desire, and solidifying it in the *calcination*...

Solutio

Just as *calcination* pertains to the element fire ... so *solutio* pertains to water ... The solid seems to disappear into the solvent as if it had been swallowed up. *Solutio* represents a return to the womb, the amniotic sea, the undifferentiated state that exists between the unborn baby and the mother growing and nourishing it, effortlessly and unconsciously in her body ...

As *solutio* follows *calcinatio*, so did rain follow fire. And so did dissolution into the initial writing of *Prima Materia* coincide with an epic 500-year rainstorm that came on the heels of the then biggest fire in California history ...

On January 8, 2018, evacuated from our home due to an impending storm, I awoke in the dark of night, in a downtown hotel room, with so many thoughts and images swirling in my head, I had to reach for my laptop and write. As the rain poured down, the words poured out. I wrote all night, dissolving into an imagined scenario that felt so vital and immediate as to not be imagined, but *entered*.

The play that woke me to write it on the night of that 500-year storm prompted the emergence of a new way of writing for me; a new engagement with creativity and psyche – and with my mother. But, as Edinger points out, "often *solutio* is experienced not as a containment, but rather as a fragmentation and dismemberment." Indeed, in the weeks following the rain and mud, I lost my creative way, and I did not know when or where – or if – I would find it again. It would be two months before I'd enter the next alchemical phase.

Coagulatio

As *calcinatio* is the alchemical operation associated with fire, and *solutio* is that of water, then *coagulatio* brings in the element of earth. Edinger equates *coagulatio* with the earthy desire for creation saying, "Not only is desirousness a characteristic of the flesh – the coagulated aspect of the psyche – but also desire is said to initiate the incarnating process" (p. 87)

In March of 2018, I was stuck in the mud ...

Disappointed and discouraged, I set *Prima Materia* aside and turned my attention to other work that felt less important, but more achievable. I did not realize I had entered the *coagulatio* phase .... Then I visited my mother's grave, for the first time, on her fifteenth *jahrzeit*, the anniversary of her passing. At her gravesite, I felt compelled to leave a meaningful gift. I buried a special red coin I had intended to use for another creative project in the earth beneath my mother's headstone. This burial symbolized my creative surrender. I gave my "control" to my mother, and thus began an unexpected collaboration .... On March 28, 2018, I opened a new document, dimmed my laptop screen all the way, shut my eyes, and asked my mom for help. She blasted in, opinionated, unapologetic, and ready to rumble. She had been waiting for this moment of *coagulatio*, for this invitation for mother and daughter to create together.

(extracts from an unpublished manuscript by Cheri Steinkellner 2019,
quoted with permission)

Aesthetics as epistemology

As explored in Chapter 1, Jung had problems with valuing the aesthetic capacities of the psyche because he felt that aesthetics was disconnected from value judgments and feeling. By complete contrast, recent arts-based research regards aesthetics as an epistemology and methodology that increase, not decrease, its ethical potential. Jung thought that pursuit of beauty or pleasing qualities in art by him would remove the work from "reality" and distract from ethical considerations with patients (Jung 1963/1983: 213). He gives this reason for putting aside *The Red Book* (ibid.). Other scholars of ABR disagree, as we shall see.

Arts-based research, ethics and aesthetic epistemology

In his *Arts-Based Research Primer*, Rolling Jnr. shows that for the Western tradition, the aesthetic was intimately linked to the scientific approach called "natural philosophy" (Rolling Jnr. 2013: 14). Dominant from the fourteenth to nineteenth centuries, natural philosophy aimed to describe and explain nature and the universe in the cause of benefiting humanity. The development of visual arts in the European Renaissance was intimately connected to the project of natural philosophy. Leonardo Da Vinci is its exemplary arts-based researcher. Rolling Jnr. also offers a valuable summary of the arts as knowing in other cultures.

> In non-Western worlds, art-making has also been an instrument of knowledge, whether making marks *upon* the world, making representation of symbolic models *of* the world, or making "special" aesthetic interventions that signal a person, object, artifact, action, event or phenomenon as uniquely valuable, sacred or life-sustaining – and thus *set apart* from the mundane and the ordinary within the world.
>
> (Rolling Jnr. 2013: 14)

Overall, Rolling Jnr. suggests that the arts have always served to provide knowing about what most matters to human beings. To the Western tradition, the arts have revealed what is lacking in the research of the subject/object split and experimental science. Now they return as arguably the core methodology of the successor culture, which Jungian arts-based research would locate in transdisciplinarity. Nicolescu is explicit that creative imagination is necessary to transdisciplinary knowing.

> The imaginary and the real complement each other *in a fruitful contradictory relationship*, revealing a deeper reality that that available to the sense organs.
>
> (Nicolescu 2014: 179; italics in original)

Evoking reality as including what can only be intuited via the imagination provides a wider context to Patricia Leavy's assertion of the epistemology of ABR as "*aesthetic knowing*" (Leavy 2015: 20, italics in original). She insists that ABR disrupts what is assumed to be true and fosters empathy through the aesthetic exploration (including critical analysis) of beauty. She quotes R. Dunlop to suggest that aesthetics extends to the beauty of constantly revising what is deemed to be true, and in growing more connected to the subject, persons or nature of the research (Dunlop 2004: 95). Here aesthetics is vitally linked to what Leavy calls "utility"; it is beautiful because it not only inspires love, it enacts loving connection to the other in the art-making itself (ibid.).

In this way art practice becomes aesthetics as ethical and feeling connections. In effect, Leavy depicts ABR aesthetics as Jungian Eros, which is appropriate because the mother of Greek God Eros is Aphrodite, she who bestows the beauty that inspires erotic love. Arts-based research could be said to restore Eros to modernity, just as Jung strived to do with his individuation restoring Eros to its central role in being. Leavy's aesthetic knowing explicitly embraces transdisciplinarity's multiple roots of aesthetics, in the pre-verbal image's sensory, bodily and imaginary modes. She implicitly embraces Jungian Eros, in re-orienting research from detached subject/object Logos ways of being to loving, creating and re-creating participation.

Barone and Eisner use the term "aesthetic vision" for their understanding of aesthetic epistemology (Barone and Eisner 2012: 37). In a powerful passage, they describe aesthetic vision as pursuing complexity with feeling, imagination and a valuing of the paradoxical. Aesthetic vision "adjusts the flow of time" because it seizes upon the potential for transformation in any moment and in any material, be it a block of wood or an actor's fleeting expression (ibid.). Always located and embodied in a specific point of view, aesthetic vision is relational. Barone and Eisner call it "personal and situational" (ibid.). In Jungian terms this aesthetic vision is human, and more than human, for taking intuition and sensation into tacit and creative knowing beyond the ego.

Also, without venturing into explicitly Jungian notions, Barone and Eisner's aesthetic vision includes archetypal energies by embracing spontaneity that manifests in patterns. These are a precursor to meaning.

> [Aesthetic vision looks] for patterns within disorder, for unity beneath superficial disruption, and for disruption beneath superficial unity. [It] construct[s] form and suggest[s] meanings.
>
> (ibid.)

With the focus on form as the structuring inherent in arts-based research, Barone and Eisner stick to their structuralist bases. A/r/tography, for example, aims to avoid form lest it congeal their primary fidelity to imaginal experience. Perhaps between these two positions is an ABR that accepts laws and structures when they emerge without consciously seeking them. What Barone and Eisner's aesthetic vision does contribute to Jungian ABR is a concept of the aesthetic that enacts what Jung called Eros, a relational feeling-directed and empathetic search for patterns and meaning. Again, Aphrodite is a silent partner, in bringing beauty indivisible from love. Eros and Aphrodite become epistemological energies in such Jungian arts-based research.

The most Jungian in the field of ABR theorists, Shaun McNiff (1998), fascinatingly, uses aesthetics as an epistemology to reconcile art and science. Feeling may drive the creative imagination, but is not necessarily personal idiosyncrasy. He points out that appreciation for beauty is often shared. Indeed, that is what art traditions do, share beauty among many audiences. Given that art is a testimony to centuries of aesthetic responses to the world, the collective priorities of science can be explored in the individual responses of the trained artist.

> Because this interplay between subjective and objective elements takes place all of the time within the creative process, it is foolish and limiting to set them as antagonists. The introspective feeling of beauty does not

have to be separated from the empirical conditions being experienced ... Art and science are integrated into every aspect of our disciplines.

(McNiff 1998: 58)

McNiff also combines ethics and aesthetics by arguing that, as in Jung's therapy practice of active imagination, how one interacts with a psychic image conditions what happens (McNiff: 185). Treating the image as autonomous, as having ethical being in its own right, enables greater and less predictable knowing. Indeed, in another book, McNiff describes how art psychotherapy creates a "third object" in the clinical relationship (McNiff 1981). Here McNiff's aesthetic knowing of the psychic image as materialized in art is an intimation of Nicolescu's hidden third, standing for the invisible and multiple realities. Arts-based research overcomes the subject/object split and enters transdisciplinarity in McNiff's recognition that art and science both stem from the (Jungian) imagination.

These ABR theorists share the conviction that aesthetic knowing is intrinsically relational, ethical, feeling-rich and interventional in the moment. Such aesthetic knowing is in play whether making art as research is conducted with other people or not. Such ethical aesthetic knowing includes working with dynamic images that could be visual, verbal, aural or bodily where the artist is the only human being present. These epistemologies in ABR are what Jung called Eros knowing, and invoke Aphrodite by extending the field of beauty-inspiring love to the nonhuman, including nature and the cosmos. Jungian ABR is here reliant upon the ensouled body as organ of intuition and sensation, as inseparable from feeling and empathy. Jungian ABR disagrees with Jung on ethics in art.

It takes a post-Jungian such as Shaun McNiff to show that ABR need not be confined to what Jung called Eros. It can be Logos knowing of separation and discrimination, because of its access to historical collective forms and ideas of beauty. Put another way, Jungian arts-based research can embrace the ecstatic energies of Dionysus, making the artist into Ariadne, and/or see the resulting art as a gestalt, or an image of a whole that is more than a sum of the parts (see below), as Barone and Eisner suggest. Jungian ABR may be structuralist or poststructuralist, Eros-focused for Aphrodite, or Logos-oriented to knowledges where other gods roam. In fact, all these epistemological principles may be reconciled in transdisciplinarity.

Ariadne, Dionysus and gestalt: transdisciplinary ABR

Epistemology is ways of knowing and how we justify knowing. Jung offers ABR knowing as primarily unfixed and dynamic. For him, knowing comes through psychological disintegration and re-integration in the lifelong process of individuation. By contrast, the very concept of arts-based research might seem to imply that the artwork is a finished, relatively static artefact. Like all research projects, it is subject to endpoints such as publication, and sometimes academic assessment. Here the structures of the academy in what it means to embark on research would seem to favor Barone and Eisner's predilection for form. However, I want to argue that their addition of gestalt as an aesthetic epistemology expands the functionality of the artwork. Now it can be both object that materializes knowing, and subject that continues to generate it.

Barone and Eisner see the notion of gestalt as crucial to art-making as research as well as to the eventual response, including assessment, of the work. They suggest that the ability of art to make a world shows the gestalt creating "new psychological landscapes," or an "as *if* world" (Barone and Eisner 2012: 22). "As if" takes arts-based research into the field of metaphor. Following on, they argue for the empiricism of such ABR in the careful observation, including participation, of the ABR artist. Here they claim again a significant overlap with mainstream science (ibid.: 46). Gestalt is therefore the world-making capacity of art that also transforms the artist through the creation of new psychic spaces.

Calling this gestalt process "crystallization," Barone and Eisner emphasize that arts-based subjects the artist to her own gestalt disintegration and reformation (ibid.: 50). They explicitly draw on gestalt psychology's law of *pragnanz*, referring to the constituent parts in an intricate assemblage relating to each other. Looking for the internal coherence of the work enables assessment of the art as both aesthetic form and organ of knowing (ibid.: 151). Additionally, *pragnanz* can be applied to the artist as well as the work. During the art-making both are entangled.

Barone and Eisner's use of gestalt and its psychology closely resembles Jung on individuation. Both depict the breaking up of established attitudes in favor of new psychological relationships. Both rely on inner psychic images being generated in conjunction with material, emotional and empirical relationships outside the person. Where gestalt and individuation differ is in the gestalt suggestion of achieving viable complexity in form, whereas Jungian individuation tends to be a continuous ongoing process. On the other hand, Jung's notion of the self is of an intimated greater totality that simultaneously produces orientation and meaning within, and potential union with the cosmos, or *unus mundus* without. This could be argued as a very ambitious gestalt.

Either way, it is Dionysus who adds to classic Jungian individuation the importance of the collective, of art being potent for the world beyond the artist. Like Ariadne, the arts-based researcher is skillful navigating the labyrinth, and enables what is monstrous to be defeated. Yet she is abandoned by the hero, Theseus, on an island. Perhaps Ariadne's lesson for the researcher is that enabling the hero is not the proper role of her art. Far more transformational is her wooing by Dionysus, and eventual marriage, leading to her ascent into the heavens.

Ariadne's artist thread leads to the death of her half-brother, the Minotaur, which ends his terrible reign of human sacrifices. She then is dismembered, in the sense of being abandoned, only to discover an entirely different mode of knowing and being in love, one that embraces the *unus mundus*.

The gestalt that Ariadne offers is of Dionysian collective transformation. So too does transdisciplinarity. As noted earlier, James Hillman memorably shows that Dionysian consciousness is bodily, instinctual and reliant upon parts as being conscious that they are *parts* of a whole, a *unus mundus* never to be fully conscious.

> Rather the crucial experience would be the awareness of the parts *as parts* distinct from each other, dismembered, each with its own light, a state in which the body becomes conscious of itself as a composite of differences. The scintillae and fishes' eyes of which Jung speaks … may be experienced as embedded in physical expressions. The distribution of Dionysus through matter may be compared with the distribution of consciousness through members, organs, and zones.
>
> (Hillman 1972: 28)

So too does transdisciplinarity argue for the body of knowledge to be re-membered in this Dionysian fashion. For in transdisciplinarity disciplines become parts that know themselves to be parts of multiple realities; some invisible, denoted by all other disciplines, and some ways of knowing as yet unfounded. Transdisciplinarity is divine Dionysus because it is the dismembered re-membering body of knowing and being that is both manyness and oneness, esoteric Tradition and all possible academic disciplines.

Arts-based research in its gestalts, individuation or migration of the psychic image produces in each work conscious and unconscious images of the *unus mundus* (its gestalt). In doing so, it remembers and re-members its partiality in emerging from a particular time, place, artist-researcher, its tacit acceptance of partiality or manyness. Arts-based research epistemology concerns the migration of the psychic image into a Dionysian aesthetics, because it dismembers and re-members the world and how we inhabit it.

Jung suggested, or at least inferred, much of the potential of ABR in his essays on art. He also intuited ABR in composing what was published in 2009 as *The Red Book*. As prototype to Dionysian arts-based research, this remarkable volume is the subject of the following chapter.

References

Baring, A. and J. Cashford. (1991) *The Myth of the Goddess: Evolution of an Image.* New York and London: Vintage.

Barone, T. and E. W. Eisner. (2012) *Arts Based Research.* Los Angeles, CA and London: Sage Publications.

Dunlop, R. (2004) 'Scar Tissue, Testimony, Beauty: Notebooks on Theory', in A. L. Cole, L. Neilsen, J. G. Knowles and T. C. Luciani, eds. *Provoked by Art: Theorizing Arts-Informed Research*, pp. 84–99. Ontario: Backalong Books, Toronto.

Edinger, E. (1990) *Anatomy of the Psyche: Alchemical Symbolism in Psychotherapy*. New York: Open Court Publishing.

Hillman, J. (1972) 'Dionysus in Jung's Writings', *Spring: A Journal of Archetype and Culture*, 1972, in J. Hillman, ed. *Mythic Figures: Uniform Edition of the Writings of James Hillman, Volume 6.1*. Putnam, CT: Spring Publications Inc., 2007, pp. 15–30.

Jung, C. G. (1921) 'Definitions', in *Collected Works, Volume 6, Psychological Types*, pp. 408–486.

Jung, C. G. (1922) 'On the Relation of Analytical Psychology to Poetry', in *Collected Works, Volume 15: The Spirit in Man, Art and Literature*, pp. 65–83.

Jung, C. G. (1930) 'Psychology and Literature', in *Collected Works, Volume 15: The Spirit in Man, Art and Literature*, pp. 109–134.

Jung, C. G. (1932) '"Ulysses": A Monologue', in *Collected Works, Volume 15: The Spirit in Man, Art and Literature*, pp. 127–154.

Jung, C. G. (1933/2001) *Modern Man in Search of a Soul*. London and New York: Routledge.

Jung, C. G. (1935) 'The Tavistock Lectures', in *Collected Works, Volume 18: The Symbolic Life*, pp. 5–182.

Jung, C. G. (1951) 'Aion: Studies in the Phenomenology of the Self', in *Collected Works, Volume 9, Part 2*.

Jung, C. G. (1952) 'Synchronicity: An Acausal Connecting Principle', in *Collected Works, Volume 8: The Structure and Dynamics of the Psyche*, pp. 417–532.

Jung, C. G. (1954) 'Archetypes of the Collective Unconscious', in *Collected Works, Volume 12: The Archetypes and the Collective Unconscious*, pp. 3–41.

Jung, C. G. (1963/1983) *Memories, Dreams, Reflections*. recorded and edited by Aniela Jaffe. London: Fontana.

Jung, C. G. (1968) *The Tavistock Lectures*. London: Ark Paperbacks.

Jung, C. G. (2009) *The Red Book: Liber Novus*. ed. S. Shamdasani, trans. M. Kyburz, J. Peck and S. Shamdasani. New York: W.W. Norton & Co.

Leavy, P. (2015) *Method Meets Art: Arts-Based Research Practice*. 2nd edition. New York and London: The Guilford Press.

Leavy, P. ed. (2018) *Handbook of Arts-Based Research*. New York and London: The Guilford Press.

McNiff, S. (1981) *The Arts and Psychotherapy*. Springfield, MO: Charles C Thomas Pub Ltd.

McNiff, S. (1998) *Art-Based Research*. London and Philadelphia, PA: Jessica Kingsley Publishers.

Nicolescu, B. (2014) *From Modernity to Cosmodernity: Science, Culture and Spirituality*. New York: SUNY.

Paris, G. (1998) *Pagan Grace: Dionysus, Hermes and Goddess Memory in Daily Life*. Woodstock, CT: Spring Publications Inc.

Polyani, M. (1967) *The Tacit Dimension*. London: Routledge & Kegan Paul.

Rolling Jnr., J. H. (2013) *Arts-Based Research Primer*. New York: Peter Lang.

Rowland, S. (2017) *Remembering Dionysus: Revisioning Psychology and Literature in C. G. Jung and James Hillman*. Hove and New York: Routledge.

Samuels, A., B. Shorter and F. Plaut. (1986) *A Critical Dictionary of Jungian Analysis*. London and New York: Routledge.

Shakespeare, W. (1611/2004) *The Tempest*. Folger Shakespeare Library. New York: Simon & Schuster.

Shelley, M. (1816/1996) *Frankenstein*. Norton Critical Edition. New York: W. W. Norton & Co.

Shlain, L. (1991) *Art & Physics: Parallel Visions in Space, Time and Light*. New York: Morrow.

Steinkellner, C. (2019) 'On Writing *Prima Materia*', Unpublished Manuscript.

Jung's *The Red Book* as arts-based research

Introduction

Chapter 4 explores *The Red Book* as arts-based research. Not authorized for publication by Jung himself, *The Red Book* was also not defined by him according to the new paradigm of ABR. On the other hand, in the *Handbook of Arts-Based Research* Jung, along with Sigmund Freud, is recognized as a founder (Malchiodi in Leavy 2018: 73). In it, *The Red Book* is called "personal arts-based research" and a "seminal example of art-based inquiry" (ibid.). Without reference to Jung's own conflicts over *The Red Book*, the work is cited as a pioneering example.

Coming from one of the two early providers of the ontology and epistemology of the psychic image, *The Red Book* enters the lineage of ABR. Both Freud and Jung positioned the psychic image as the core of being and knowing. Although neither foregrounded art as a source of such psychic imagery, both saw artistic creation as stemming from the psychic material that they worked on directly with patients. It is indicative of the transdisciplinary nature of ABR that depth *psychology* becomes re-framed in the new methodological paradigm of arts-based research in the previous chapters of this book.

The Red Book occurs again in the *Handbook* in the context of Jung's particular gift of active imagination to arts-based research. Researching with children through drawing and painting, Barbara J. Fish cites *The Red Book*, and quotes Jung on the value of the experiences upon which his book was based (Fish 2018: 352–3). Jung calls those experiences *"prima materia* for a lifetime's work," using the alchemical term for the prime matter of fertile, dark, painful stuff from which alchemical transformations can be made (Jung 1963/1983: 199).

Some of the psychic images from these *prima materia* experiences are reworked in *The Red Book*. However, at the time, Jung decided that *The Red Book* did not represent the kind of research he wished to pursue. He abandoned it, and did not allow its publication in his lifetime. Jung may have been a founder of ABR, but if he was a practitioner it was something he also rejected, at least for himself.

> In the Red Book I tried an aesthetic elaboration of my fantasies ... There-
> fore, I gave up this aestheticizing tendency in good time, in favour of
> a rigorous process of *understanding*... For me, reality meant scientific
> comprehension.
>
> (Jung 1963/1983: 213)

Chapter 1 considered Tjeu van den Berk's invaluable study of Jung's distrust
of aesthetics (Berk 2012: 57–60). Jung regarded the appreciation of beauty to
be derived from the sensation function alone. It meant that essential thinking
and feeling were not innate to the effects of beauty in art and elsewhere.
Hence aesthetics is not ethical. It risks removing artist and audience from
genuine empathetic engagement. Chapter 3 saw that arts-based research today
wholly rejects this notion. For ABR, the aesthetic dimension is wedded to art's
ability to immerse the artist into matter, shaping it to what most matters. What
matters most is a path to a valuing of the other, including other people.

Earlier chapters of this book show that Jung had a number of opportunities to go beyond his distrust of the aesthetic, for example, his cultural
notion of visionary art, also in sensing the artistic side of alchemy, and even
in his transpersonal synchronicity. These latter two aspects of Jung's work
suggest an innate patterning or organization in the cosmos that could ultimately reconcile Jung's famous dispute with the woman inside him (Jung
1963/1983: 210–11).

At a moment of crisis, an inner feminine voice asserts that his visions and
fantasies amount to art. He replies that, no, they are nature, and proceeds to
strenuously deny any idea that he could be an artist. Yet in alchemy and synchronicity Jung discovers the ancient unity of art and science as enquiries into
what is the nature of reality. This, Jung does not pursue. Although he comes to
recognize the presence of the collective unconscious in "visionary art," and the
potentially valid psychology of his "psychological art," the language of beauty
and genre is not for him (Jung 1930, CW15: para. 139).

Fortunately, Jung's own psychology encourages us to separate the work
from the man. To confine *The Red Book* to what Jung said it was, or could be,
is to prioritize the artist or maker over the work, something Jung explicitly
refused to do in his essays (see previous chapters). He insisted that trying to
understand a creative entity by the creator's conscious intention is to privilege
the ego over the limitless possibilities of the archetypal unconscious. Such
a move is not Jungian.

Therefore, I suggest that *The Red Book* should be saved from Jung's anxieties, just as Jung should not be judged or limited by the unfinished work he
chose not to publish (see my *Remembering Dionysus* Chapters 3 and 4). For
this reason, this chapter will use arts-based research as a lens by which to read
The Red Book anew for the twenty-first century. It will conclude by suggesting
that Jung's actual published writing, *The Collected Works*, can more effectively
be understood as arts-based research. After all, since creativity is fundamental

to Jungian psychology, it is not surprising that this trickster writer provides a poetic inquiry.

First of all, *The Red Book*, a peculiarly Dionysian text of dismembering and re-membering, can be understood via the four categories of ABR proposed by Rolling Jnr.: analytic, synthetic, critical-activist and improvisatory (Rolling Jnr. 2013: 51–8). Of course, no single chapter study of this rich work can cover everything pertinent. I pay tribute to recent essay collections and cultural research by Stanford Drob, Murray Stein, James Hillman, John Beebe, editor, Sonu Shamdasani, Tom Kirsch and many more studies by Jungian scholars and analysts. What follows is an attempt to offer a different perspective from this life-enhancing new paradigm of arts-based research.

The Red Book as analytic: thinking in materials

Although *The Red Book* is crafted as a medieval manuscript, it is in no way a straightforward imitation. Artist and researcher Jill Mellick has shown how Jung was indeed thinking in materials in the construction of the text (Mellick 2018). She shows that, in totality, Jung was an artist in pencil, pen, ink, pastel, gouache, watercolor, clay, wood, stone and mixed media (Mellick 2018: 217). Jung begins *The Red Book* confidently in parchment, yet chooses paints specifically designed for wall painting because of their intense brightness. Unfortunately, the parchment proves too transparent for use on both sides. Moreover, the wall paint flakes. His second section is more successfully inscribed on vellum, also used in the medieval period. Jung even discovers how to apply a varnish that limits the peeling of the paint.

Also, medieval book manufacture relied upon four specialists: the scribe, rubricator, illustrator and illuminator. By contrast, Jung performed all four of these functions (Mellick 2018: 219–20). Crucially, Mellick reveals the extent to which the composition of *The Red Book* combined the meticulous and the free-flowing, as she puts it, "disciplined spontaneity" (ibid.: 220). Jung testified to involuntary visions and long active imaginations as origin of *The Red Book*. This psychic work was recorded elsewhere in his Black Books. *The Red Book* is noted for its aesthetic arrangement. To get to the final pages, Jung experimented, planned, carefully wrote and spent countless hours on paintings that were structured to demand minute brushstrokes. *The Red Book* is active imagination combined with conscious, deliberate self-discipline.

As part of that discipline, Mellick notes four stylistic patterns in the paintings: that of mutating shapes, of size according to the layout of the page, of color, and finally the use of outlining to create different effects (Mellick 2018: 224). Overall in the paintings Jung emphasizes mosaic as a strong patterning influence, with every cell made of only one color. However, he moved from transparent and opaque ways of daubing (ibid.: 225). In short, Mellick reveals the unusual focus on Jung's sensation function because it is so extensively disciplined by conscious striving with matter, paint, parchment, ink and vellum.

Jung married his intimate understanding – of the characteristics of each pigment, each brush, the binding medium, the carrier, and the supports – to his skills and concentration. He perfected a confluence among eye, hand, paint, and surface: his tiny mosaic-like cells required perfectly bounded fields of color. Each cell was a discipline, an irrevocable commitment, a painting in itself.

(Mellick 2018: 223)

This extraordinary mobilization of matter extends to psychological designs on the viewer, she demonstrates (ibid.: 226–7). Put another way, Jung's thinking in matter is also experiments with sensation and feeling responses through visual imagery. While there are compositions that evoke calm and feed the spirit, one painting in particular, on page 115 of *The Red Book*, uses distortions and mixed perspectives to evoke a bodily unease and sensations of disorder and crisis. On the other hand, by coordinating the mixture of perspectives in the figure of Philemon with outstretched wings, the painting conveys deep integration (ibid.:154).

Here *The Red Book* is the material enactment of the Dionysian experience of dismembering and re-membering that Jung noted of his visionary experiences in *Memories, Dreams, Reflections* (Jung 1963/1983: 194–226). After his break with Freud, Jung was so afflicted by spontaneous eruptions from the deep psyche that he had do something drastic in order to carry on with everyday living. He was being torn apart by the unruly god who visits those who do not find a way to include their bodily, instinctual life. Fortunately, Jung does find a way to re-member and remember his Dionysian self by shaping overwhelming visions into active imagination. He even recognizes the collective nature of the god, by teaching active imagination to patients and publishing references to it for posterity.

Through evolving active imagination, Jung learned to value his unbidden images. Through the manufacture of *The Red Book*, Jung treasured his unruly psyche by turning it into treasure. Jung was no longer a mere recipient of visions, but rather an active participant in making them into something material. As the research of scholars such as Mellick demonstrates, *The Red Book* is a product of Jung's unconscious functions of sensation and intuition closely woven into physical being by thinking and, as we will see further, poised to evoke his function of feeling. After all, Jung had studied the history of using color to invoke emotions.

Color psychology and alchemy

In "C. G. Jung's Concepts of Color in the Context of Modern Art," Medea Hoch examines the history of color as evocative of human qualities (Hoch 2018). Jung found in alchemy stages of transformation via colors that he decided corresponded to his idea of individuation (Jung 1944: paras. 342–96).

Working with chemicals, extracts and precious metals, the alchemists were enraptured because they had unknowingly projected their psyches on to the matter in their fabulous glass devices. Changes in color for the alchemist marked stages on the route from *prima materia* or worthless dark matter to golden spirit, elixir or the most precious matter.

So colors represented the process that included the psyche of the alchemist: melanosis (blackening), leucosis (whitening), xanthosis (yellowing) and iosis (reddening) (Hoch 2018: 43). Moreover, in the medieval period adopted by Jung for *The Red Book*, colors were identified with the four elements. These were also elemental to human beings: four basic characteristics.

> In the work of alchemist Gerhard Dorn, Jung found the association of the alchemical colors with the temperaments: yellow with the choleric, red with the sanguine, white with the phlegmatic, and black with the melancholic.
>
> (Hoch 2018: 45)

Therefore, it is not surprising that Hoch records Jung aligning his four functions with colors in a lecture in 1934 (ibid.: 45). Thinking becomes blue because it can be ethereal, whereas feeling is substantiated in red. Intuition is white or yellow, while sensation is the color of the Swiss earth, green. Moreover, the psychological importance of color was not lost to art history after alchemy fell from favor in the eighteenth century.

A figure well known to Jung, the poet Johann Wolfgang Goethe, published in 1810 his *Theory of Colors*, strongly arguing for their capacity to evoke emotions (Hoch 2018: 33). Later, the modernist art of Jung's own time took up this tradition of color psychology, one notable practitioner being Wassily Kandinsky. Hoch describes Kandinsky's 1911 publication, *On the Spiritual in Art*, as drawing on Goethe and containing the almost Jungian utterance that: "color is a means of exercising direct influence on the soul" (Hoch 2018: 34).

Hoch shows that Jung was familiar with colorist modernist painters such as Giovanni Segantini, Odilon Redon, Augusto Giacometti and Paul Klee (Hoch 2018: 35). Also, his painter friend, Sophie Taeuber-Arp, published on color theory. Like a number of contemporary modernist works, *The Red Book* adopts medieval practices of flat, undifferentiated colors that are evocative rather than naturalistic. While Jung did not produce a formal color theory, *The Red Book* shows that he consciously drew on medieval colorism in ways that experimented with, rather than copied, the past. The paintings in *The Red Book* are not all styled from medieval books. Some take inspiration from the stained glass of the period; others borrow from early mosaics. *The Red Book* explores rather than imitates, in its thinking in paint and color.

Hoch makes a convincing case for Jung as actively pursuing an abiding interest in modernist art. Thomas Fischer and Bettina Kaufmann also show that Jung knew artists, visited exhibitions and collected books of art and also volumes of ethnographical studies that similarly fascinated the artists (Fischer and Kaufmann 2018: 28). Most influential for Jung amongst the modernist art theorists seems to have been Wilhelm Worringer, whose *Abstraction and Empathy* (1908/1953) he heavily annotated. Worringer proposed that the abstraction that haunted early-twentieth-century art as well as in ancient periods was not the result of some logical linear history of aesthetic representation. Rather art should be understood in the context of the society in which it was made (Fischer and Kaufmann 2018: 22). Times of confidence and security produced the realist art of empathy, whereas times of insecurity led art into abstraction.

Jung was able to absorb Worringer's thesis into his typological argument, calling empathetic art extrovert and abstract painting introvert (Hoch 2018: 47). What is fascinating is how Worringer provides a bridge followed by Jung from art style associated wholly with the artist, her choices in the context of aesthetics, to seeing art as more truly speaking to and of the entire era. Fischer and Kaufmann conclude that, despite Jung's abiding pre-occupation with art and literature, he was only truly engaged when it communicated human experience (Fischer and Kaufmann 2018: 28). In my view, this rather undersells Jung's speculative yet sophisticated sense of visionary art. Where the making of art is mysterious that is not directed by consciousness, it reveals what is unknown to the collective (see earlier chapters).

Like contemporary modernist painters, Jung could draw on a history of color as prime matter for psychology. So thinking in paint becomes also feeling in color as well as intuition and sensation coagulating into material being. In this context he could even see aesthetics as "applied psychology" (Jung 1921, CW6: para. 485). It is time to look at the other matter examined in *The Red Book*, the nature of words and their genres.

The Red Book: genres, thoughts, words, symbols, personifications, principles

The Red Book's writing is picaresque. It consists of a bundle of literary genres without an overt ordering structure. Through these changing styles and landscapes, an "I" figure wanders. He is not on a named quest nor a journey with a particular purpose. The written genres include lamentation, a stream of consciousness (not unlike that found in literary modernism), medieval mystery plays, novels, fairy tales and trickster-like mutations of characters into different figures, including from human to animal.

Within the generic hybridization is, however, a profound scrutiny of words as they relate to consciousness. In this sense of conducting an agonized experiment in language, *The Red Book* provides a structure suitably inhabited by ghosts towards the end. "I" begins painfully split between the spirit of the times and that of the depths. Such fragmentation shatters words, disperses meaning and makes the rational discourses of his science empty. "I" then meets figures who initiate him into nature, and force him to confront an aspect of his own nature in Ammonius, an unhappy hermit who is a religious ascetic tortured by words that cannot be confined to one meaning.

> You cry out for the word which has one meaning and no other … The God of words is cold and dead.
>
> (Jung 2012: 250–1)

However, it is not only in religion that words (of one meaning) are dead. When "I" encounters Izdubar, his scientific words of one meaning kill the ancient divine being with their literalism. Fortunately, "I" is starting to appreciate the psychic reality of his encounters. Having previously met Elijah and his startling erotic companion, Salome, he sees that psychic beings are real in the sense that his ego did not originate them. Like producing physical children, we "give birth to beings of thought which … live their own lives" (ibid.: 314).

Ultimately, these autonomous beings of thought are psychic images that stem from innate archetypes. They are nature in human nature, arriving in *The Red Book* to teach "I" that fostering their independent reality is essential to health. Archetypes are sources of religion and science, but cannot live in these homes if religion and science are squeezed into single meanings. Elijah mutates into the less human figure of Philemon. Spreading his kingfisher wings, Philemon helps "I" to hear the voices of the unsatisfied dead and a blue shade who may be Christ. Divine intimations meld with Jung's evolving psychology on the reality of these enactments of the soul. Of course the soul also speaks eloquently on her own behalf in *The Red Book*. Her tones and behavior criticize the schism within Christianity between flesh and spirit.

"I" learns in *The Red Book* of the necessity of symbols, of psychic images enfleshed in words, paint or other media that shimmer with multiplicity and the mystery of the deep unconscious. The characters of *The Red Book* are autonomous yet not separate from each other, nor from "I." Female figures such as the boring blonde heroine and the faithful fat cook in the hot kitchen suggest other aspects of "I"'s soul, while Salome is serpentine and sometimes actually becomes a snake. Elijah's problems are dramatized by the trials of the librarian, and the professor in the madhouse, before he finds his spiritual gravity in and as Philemon.

The Red Book helpfully includes Jung's own commentary emphasizing that Elijah and Salome are personifications of Logos and Eros as opposites necessary to each other (ibid.: 563–4). Suggestively, his definition of these powers in *The Red Book* is not as gendered nor as potentially divided as elsewhere. "Where Logos is ordering and insistence, Eros is dissolution and movement" is explicit that, if not allied, Eros will be craziness and Logos stuck and without liveliness (ibid.: 563). Put another way, Eros will be images in water where no meanings can stabilize, and Logos will be words with single meanings that literalize and deaden.

Jung insists that Logos and Eros are two rather than one entity. In thinking in materials, he has discovered the necessity of plurality of being. The gates of salvation are symbols because the symbol is a portal to unknown mysteries of a psyche that is real and so forms the bedrock of science and religion (ibid.: 392). Logos and Eros stand for *The Red Book* itself, with the dissolution of ego control in an active imagination that is followed by the disciplined spontaneity and ordering of writing and painting.

As an example of analytic ABR thinking in materials, *The Red Book* is a superb exploration of what matters in matter, in the media of paint and words. *The Red Book* discovers the significance of the psychic image. It requires manifesting in a Jungian symbol that invites the psyche into participation with mysteries. Moreover, *The Red Book* shows that the symbol is magnified by being multi-generic. Symbols are not just paint and words; they also inhere in mixing past genres and forms (also found in contemporary modernists). As we shall see later, *The Red Book*'s Logos and Eros engagement with the past makes it pertinent to other modes of arts-based research, as well as being itself a modernist characteristic.

The Red Book as synthetic arts-based research in discourses

According to critical theory, a discourse is a particular mode of knowledge that has material as well as textual form (Barry 2017: 69). For example, the dominant discourse of modern science is that of a scientific method with an absolute split between subject and object. The spread of this type of knowledge into creating powerful hierarchies and institutions of knowing and being has been criticized earlier in this book. Scientific method as a discourse has far-reaching historical, cultural and even psychological effects.

The Red Book explicitly counters the pre-eminence of the subject/object split, as we will see. Reading it as a synthesizing of discourses shows that re-orienting knowing (epistemology) creates a new understanding of being (ontology). In fact, changing knowing by weaving its discourses differently is an active re-creation of being. *The Red Book*'s experimental artistry produces a revolution of being by inviting the past into the present. Hence, synthesizing discourses is the essential framework of *The Red Book*: it is what it does to produce new knowing. For the modern reader, *The Red Book* re-makes the psyche through a picaresque excursion into time, science, religion and gender.

Discourses of above and below

The Red Book begins with the loss of joy and belief through a countering force to the spirit of the times, that of the spirit of the depths (Jung 2012: 119–20). Yet even here the spirit of the depths is not merely destructive of conventional attitudes. Rather the depths arise to combine reason and the irrational in such a way to make possible their eventual union. Such a potential uniting of consciousness and what it has suppressed will offer "the supreme meaning" (ibid.: 120).

Above and below can also be mapped religiously, and the "I" of *The Red Book* finds himself in the Christian dungeon of hell. He is in hell, and becomes hell. What must happen is that "I" accepts the hell within; he has to embrace the spirit of the depths. Such acceptance means that "I" plants a seed in the underworld that will grow to link heaven, earth and the infernal. It will be the Tree of Life (ibid.: 356). This organic union of above and below is framed in the discourse of Jung's symbol (ibid.: 392).

Symbols unite above and below. They do so because they are the material expression of psychic images from the depth that rise to potency in consciousness; they are effective, not fully comprehensible. Symbols embed mystery in conscious being. They are the mode of *The Red Book* in synthesizing discourses into a new framework for the psyche where above and below can be commingle. What further matter is entrusted to synthesizing symbols, why they *matter*, is considered below.

Synthesizing discourses of time and history

One signifying pathway for the discordant spirits of contemporary times and depths is motifs of time and history itself. John Beebe has insightfully shown the thematic relevance of *The Red Book* to the slaughter in the trenches of World War One (Beebe 2010). In *The Red Book*, the blond hero is killed early, leaving "I" to find a different way of relating to his world (Jung 2012: 151). The heroism of warrior conquest is explicitly disavowed. Today's reader is reminded that the impact of that war was devastating to more than soft human bodies. A whole culture of glory in battle was cut down by machine guns and the mud of Flanders.

So "I" is cut off from the kind of mindless conquering that engendered the war itself. Indeed, at times he is thrown into a past too ancient for the fallacies of modern history. From now on he encounters figures and landscapes that refuse to be accommodated by his modern persona. Explicitly or implicitly, what he finds will enable him to act or feel like a successful hero. Elijah and Salome first arrive to destabilize "I." He, Elijah, disconcerts "I" with his reality and venerable wisdom; she, Salome, tries to seduce our anti-hero.

Elijah and Salome recur in *The Red Book* until they are identified in the commentaries with Logos and Eros. These principles of ordering and dissolution have to be together. At the start, blind Salome's eroticism is overwhelming. She attempts to deify "I" as the Christ and then recovers her sight (ibid.: 197–8). As well as her sensual beauty, she can entice "I" by finding divine, or at least miraculous, powers in him. Perhaps it is significant that at this point, "I" decides that the spirit of the depths wants the war to be seen as that within "every man's own nature" (ibid.: 199).

The temptation to assume god-like invincibility was surely part of the blindness of the culture that led so many nations into war. That conflagration became the prolonged killing of a whole generation of young men. "I" might remember the fate of Christ when, later, his soul, previously Salome, induces him to taste the liver of a dead child in a grotesque parody of the mass.

However, there is a less aggrandizing incursion into discourses of history. "I" also meets characters from ordinary working life, such as the dying man and the fat cook. In "One of the Lowly," "I" meets a one-eyed man who tells him he enjoys the cinema (ibid.: 232–6). "I" reflects that the lowly man's penchant for marvels resembles the delight of an earlier age for tales of saints who could carry their heads under their arms. The unfortunate ex-prisoner dies in the presence of "I," who realizes that he has neglected to take account of such everyday pain. This man represents humanity's suffering animal nature. Later it is the dead who suffer because "they did not live their animal" (ibid.: 341).

One aspect of living the animal, we are told, is to love one's own kind. Living the animal is, in a sense, the reverse of the blond hero who finds validation in overcoming and killing his own kind. So "I" learns kinship with those for whom his life in the spirit of the times places him above. As a rich European male, poor men, prisoners, madhouse occupants and working women like the devout cook live lives far removed. To a certain extent, "I" will even confront his patriarchal superiority to the feminine. His gender other ranges in form from serpent to novel heroine to a divinizing, slippery Salome.

Finally, "I" falls into deep time and meets a myth, the part-god, part-human Izdubar. This personage, together with Philemon, is one of the few who appears in a painting. Moreover, Izdubar is that figure of pastness beloved by modernism, a pre-history that is also distinctively new. For Izdubar is better known as Gilgamesh. The man-god is the protagonist of an epic journey that suggestively tempers masculine fighting bravado with the erotic feminine. It too ends with coming to accept one's animal mortality (Mitchell 2004). Gilgamesh's story was unknown until the middle of the nineteenth century, when the Sumerian tablets were uncovered (Mitchell: 2–7). First known as Izdubar, Gilgamesh later proved to be the more accurate translation.

Gilgamesh is one of the oldest extant works of literature (Mitchell 2004). It tells the story of how ruler Gilgamesh is too riotously troublesome for his city of Uruk. Therefore, a sacred prostitute is dispatched to the forest to civilize a wild man, Enkidu, with the arts of love. Enkidu becomes the constant companion of Gilgamesh, and it is his death that spurs the over-ambitious hero to go on a quest for immortality. This quest fails in procuring eternal life, yet succeeds in teaching Gilgamesh to accept his animal quality of mortality. At last he becomes a good and beloved king.

For *The Red Book*, Izdubar provides "I" with another confrontation with a personified past that radically challenges his modern psychic biases. While the rational logic of "I" defeats mythical power, so that Izdubar dwindles in the face of "I's" toxic ideas, this is no heroic triumph. In fact, "I" learns that he can and must preserve this divine–human hybrid within. For the psyche needs its depths, including Deep Time and the stories that embed it as history and myth. It is time to look more closely at the science that threatened to extinguish Izdubar. Just how restricted to the spirit of the times are the science and psychology proffered by the increasingly hapless "I"?

Synthesizing discourses of science and/as psychology

Early in *The Red Book*, "I" laments that he has made his soul into an object for his science through judging her (ibid.: 128). The subject/object split of rational science has infected his relationship with his psyche, or soul. For does not psychology, the logos of psyche, require that the psyche be observed objectively, in effect making it an object? And yet this object is so cut off that it has no life. In despair, "I" decides that this so-called object cannot be his soul, for it is now a "dead system" (ibid.: 129).

Showing that the conventional subject/object structures of science are deathly to the soul is made most evident when "I" encounters the man-god, Izdubar. Huge, stupendously powerful and invincible, Izdubar does not crush "I." He does not fight as a warrior, although he obviously could (ibid.: 277–96). Rather, Izdubar and "I" engage in conversation. The man-god makes the fatal mistake in being interested in this creature from another world. Through an attempt at mutual understanding, they realize that they each possess different kinds of truth.

Izdubar's world relies upon truth sensed inwardly. Although his people also cannot see their gods, they believe in them because of what is real inside. By contrast, "I" rejects the immortality that Izdubar is seeking, and claims that the science of his era is built upon knowing outer reality. Here again the subject/object split structures the discourses that Izdubar and "I" are debating. For Izdubar, there is no inside versus outside truth. All reality, physical and psychological, is bathed in the blinding sun of his lands. There is no psychological, spiritual or physical reality because all is one reality.

Unfortunately, "I" is able to introduce Izdubar to the scientific method of structuring of reality, an absolute splitting between inside and outside. Such science declares the immortality that Izdubar seeks to be impossible. The mythical being is horrified and throws down his weapon. Hearing about modern science from "I," Izdubar points out the contrast between his style of being and that described by his verbal opponent. While Izdubar has lived like Dionysus rejoicing in *zoe* as endless instinctual life, "I" can only long for such psychological expansion in Izdubar's kind of truth (ibid.: 283).

It becomes evident that the encounter between Izdubar and "I" is changing both of them. Izdubar calls the discourse of science poison, and begins to weaken. "I" is unable to stop the devastating effect of his words on Izdubar. Put another way, Izdubar has fatally started to develop a personal consciousness.

Instead of ranging with unconscious wholeness that is the mind of a god, Izdubar begins to credit "I's" tall tales of science and a split between inside and outside truths. By doing so he begins splitting off into an ego's sense of meeting limits. The ego in him cannot find immortality. He realizes that creaturely life has an ending. Such rational ideas structure an ego's division from the unconscious identification with the cosmos. Instead of being in the mind of Dionysus, Izdubar is dismembered by beginning the process of individuation.

Izdubar has to undergo the full Dionysian dismembering and re-membering before he can become Ariadne, a human soul wedded to Dionysus/*zoe*, in touch with, not swallowed by, the instinctual god. This Izdubar achieves with the help of "I." Here in *The Red Book* we have an unusual psychotherapy case history. Both "I" and Izdubar undergo important stages of individuation while they also exist as parts of *one* psyche. In effect, *The Red Book* dramatizes individuation within one soul, and not only in the scenes with Izdubar and toxic science.

For "I" too has much to learn from the encounter. Telling Izdubar about objective science confirms that such rationality that incarnates the spirit of the times is deadly. The spirit of the times offers only words, whereas Izdubar possesses, and is possessed by, a cosmos. "I" cannot simply switch to Izdubar's way of being, yet he notices that even his rejection is a kind of engagement (ibid.: 284). That which is denied is still part of the psyche; the shadow is also real.

With the rhetoric of a heroic egoic conquest put aside, there is a touching scene between "I" and a physical specimen beyond the reach of any ordinary man. It is the latter who is almost destroyed by words. The fatal epithets are the scientific attitude, which is poison to him. "I" is not David triumphing over beating the giant Goliath. Rather, "I" is horrified by Izdubar's rapid decline. He realizes that Logos alone is poison to everyone, himself included. Science in Logos mode is deadly. It is most pernicious when it has denied any connection to Eros, so forcing that relationship into darkness and deception.

> Some have their reason in thinking, others in feeling. Both are servants of Logos, and in secret become worshippers of the serpent.
>
> (ibid.: 287)

Eros is serpent-like and devilish when denied and made a secret component of the psyche. Fortunately, just as Izdubar is losing his vital connection to the vitality of archetypes by becoming conscious, "I" experiences a reverse move in his growing *feeling* for Izdubar. "I" is discovering the creative power that science has locked away in the subject/object split. Put another way, by overcoming his separation from Izdubar by empathy, "I" can help him as an archetype because he knows him anew as *his* archetype.

The dismembering of Izdubar's sacred being can be re-membered by "I" realizing, that is, making real, the divine being as a fantasy. Izdubar is now carried in an egg before being reborn. He has had his Dionysian initiation: "[w]here was I? I was completely sun" (ibid.: 307). It seems that the synthesis of discourses around science in *The Red Book* insists that Logos and Eros are related. Indeed, the recurrence of the personified pair throughout the book, Elijah and Salome, plus their avatars, is the main thematic motif of the picaresque series of encounters. Denial of intimacy between Logos and Eros in the spirit of the times has provoked this eruption from the spirit of the depths.

Izdubar's attitude could be classed as pre-scientific. Yet the encounter clearly shows that science, or Logos without Eros, is deadly to modern as well as ancient psyches. Healing the discursive split that characterizes mainstream science, "I" and Izdubar mutually individuate each other. Within the narrative of *The Red Book* they are two characters who change each other (as many of the encounters do), and also constituent parts of one psyche. In the story, Izdubar and "I" become friends. By extension, the dialogue between them is designed to overcome those fierce divides between rationality and imagination, science and the sacred, ego and archetypal unconscious. It is time to consider how discourses of religion fare in the artistic re-weaving of Logos and Eros that is *The Red Book*.

Synthesizing discourses of religion

While Izdubar comes from an ancient and little-known religion, godliness in *The Red Book* typically concerns the Christian era. These religious encounters range from early days of saints in the desert to a modern domestic cook discussing Thomas à Kempis's *The Imitation of Christ*, or an inmate in a madhouse proclaiming his divinity. In particular, "I" takes an active and transformational role in religious encounters and landscapes. We have already encountered hell as the depths that "I" has to visit and to become. "I" also becomes a leaf daimon sprouting leaves when coming across a devil avatar in The Red One (ibid.: 216–18).

In fact a major narrative thread of *The Red Book* proves to be that religion itself needs saving from its own splitting into the spirit of the times and the depths. Or, put another way, Logos and Eros are both essential energies in religion where spirit (Logos) has become severed from soul (Eros). The result is that hell itself has become death. No wonder that later in *The Red Book* the dead return crying out for blood from both "I" and Philemon. They return because they have had only part of life in a world that has severed Logos from Eros. Elijah's first appearance in *The Red Book* is to insist that blind Salome is his daughter and his wisdom. Time and time again "I" enters the drama of discovering the fundamental relationship between Logos and Eros.

In this sense, *The Red Book* is a work devoted to synthesizing discourses that make up various dimensions of Logos and Eros energies. Ultimately, the synthesis is psychological: "I" can unite ordering Logos with wayward Eros by accepting their integral home in his own being. For religion, "I" undergoes initiations designed to reincorporate nature, flesh, sexuality, the demonic, the mysterious and simple devotion into religious practice. For example, he becomes a flourishing green daimon confronting a lively red devil who speaks of dancing; also, he will acknowledge Salome as his soul, and will be embraced by her as a serpent.

Of course when Salome insists that "I" is Christ, and he acquires a lion head, this is far from Christian orthodoxy. By Jung, the lion head is associated with the religion of Mithras, who was worshipped underground by soldiers in Roman times. Sonu Shamdasani, *The Red Book*'s editor, quotes extensively from Jung identifying the episode as a Mithraic deification mystery (Shamdasani 2009: 197). Here figures from Christian and Jewish traditions, Elijah and Salome, merge with a religion that competed with Christianity in the Roman Empire. That which was repressed as Christianity developed, the animal and the body, is here re-embraced.

"I" goes on to meet less vivid versions of Elijah and Salome, in an episode in a castle surrounded by a forest. By identifying the old man and the boring heroine with earlier characters, "I" grows his awareness of how religious structures color his mindset. The spirit of the times is heavily influenced by conventional religion, *The Red Book* shows. Meeting Ammonius is to discover that Logos reliance on words of order; that is, words that give order because they have only one meaning. Such words are empty. They invite hell as death to flood the land and make it into desert. The depths rise up and "I" is both hell and inside hell.

Fortunately, Logos as Elijah, and later, more holistically, as Philemon, has a lot yet to teach "I." Moreover Eros as Salome, the serpent and various females, does not abandon him either. Elijah initiates the theme of the independence of thoughts that eventually will become the magic of symbols. Thoughts born as children have their own being, as "I" learns from the divine vulnerability of Izdubar. Words of science are poison because, like the words persecuting Ammonius, they have been severed from Eros. By having one, literal, meaning, such words enact ordering, not being.

If, on the other hand, the severed word can unite with an autonomous being of thought, then words can be a home for images. They become symbols. The magic of symbols *works* because they unite Time and Depth, Logos and Eros. Symbols even conjoin heaven and hell, as the seed that grows in the depths to be the uniting Tree of Life (see above). Philemon teaches this magic. He comes alone to "I," and yet is associated mythologically with his wife, Baucis.

Philemon and Baucis are a devoted elderly couple who entertain the gods unawares and find favor. Given the majestic splendor of Philemon's painting in *The Red Book*, and especially given his kingfisher wings associating him with birds rather than angels, I suggest Philemon is redolent of a more integrated Logos–Eros.

Philemon also introduces "I" to a blue shade we are told is probably the Christ (Jung 2012: 551–3). A character from Greek myth, Philemon is comfortable in the Christianized atmosphere and figuring of *The Red Book*. He has the wings of the feminine soul, and is both serpent and bird in *The Red Book*. So on the one hand Philemon happily represents what Jung in his psychology will call the self image, the greater whole that is largely mysterious and androgynous. On the other hand, his discourse of the dead who call for blood, and need sermons to be put back in their *place*, recalls the most gruesome aspect of religion in *The Red Book*.

Jung meets his soul as a woman by a pile of dead bodies. She is a girl with red-gold hair who has driven the hook of a fishing rod through the eye of the devil. Not content with this cruelty, she induces "I" to taste the flesh of a dead female child. This tabooed action is a reverse of the Christian mass, in which bread and wine stand for the flesh and blood of a living god. Still somewhat horrified by this rite, "I" concludes that he wants to be reasonable, rather than divine (ibid.: 325).

Fortunately, the soul's bloodthirsty behavior, echoed later in the dead calling for blood, is only one part of who she is. "I" meets another kind of fleshly appetite and spiritual yearning in the fat cook who, like him, knows the book, *The Imitation of Christ*. In one sense, learning to imitate Christ is the story of "I" in *The Red Book*. However, there is a major difference here from conventional Christianity. "I" should imitate Christ, not the spirit of the times, but in those ways impelled by the depths.

In scripture, Christ met devils (casting them out); suffered in the desert the temptation of doubt; had significant encounters with women, including at least one who represented sexual unruliness; was crucified, his flesh and blood symbolically eaten and drunk in the Mass. In *The Red Book*, the fat cook is evidently successful in sustaining the body; she is a bit lost about the spirit. On the other hand, she is devout and trusting in the mystery as represented in the book.

Throughout *The Red Book*, "I" learns to value feeling as well as thinking. He feels for the lowly, such as the one-eyed man and the fat cook. While his sexuality is aroused by the erotic modes of the soul, he also begins to integrate his four functions of thinking, feeling, sensation and intuition by the time the fat cook turns up. *The Red Book* stops when "I" meets with the blue shade, identified as Christ in the Black Books, as a note mentions (ibid.: 551–3). *The Red Book* stops rather than ends because Jung acknowledges its incompletion later. However, "I," Philemon and the blue shade speak of beauty, love and suffering. While a being called a shade suggests a lack of fleshly appetites, Philemon asks him to accept that he too has the nature of the serpent (ibid.: 553).

This final note appears to sum up the synthesizing or religious discourse in *The Red Book*. Hapless anti-hero "I" is guided by magnificent transmogrified Philemon who has taken in nature as a bird-feminine. They come to the blue shade that is the essence of Christianity. United, this trinity shows that that so-called opposites cannot be configured as separate if destruction is to be avoided or halted. Soul as serpent is nature; it is also the feminine, also the erotic woman, or the one who attends to, or represents, the body. She is Eros who is part of Logos if Logos is to live. He is Logos who is part of Eros if we are not to materialize hell as a pile of tangled bodies. Christianity must embrace all it has demonized as serpent, feminine, body, nature, and even the devil. For if the psychological self archetype does not encompass all of these, then neither religion nor science can help the suffering world.

Synthesizing discourses by means of gender

As is evident from the above synthesizing discourses of science and religion, a major structuring role is played by gender. The identification of Logos and Eros as masculine and feminine is in Jung's later psychology linked, unhelpfully, to bodily sex. He even says that Eros is actually the true nature of women (Jung 1951, CW9ii: para. 29). Here lies Jung's complicated essentializing of gender while in the midst of simultaneously taking it apart. On the one hand, Jung believed that woman and men had fundamentally different temperaments because of their bodily differences. On the other hand, his entire psychology is devoted to undoing such polarization in the project of individuation (see Chapter 1).

The Red Book both exhibits and undoes Jung's gender essentialism. Its project of synthesizing discourses is to understand feminine as masculine as components of the soul or psyche that need each other in order to live their fullness. Without the feminine as Eros, the spirit is stuck in dead systems; Logos is order and not life. Without the tempering of masculine Logos, Eros is cannibalistic and crazy; that is, Eros is fluidity to the point of chaos. *The Red Book* actually demonstrates weakness of the gender essentializing that Jung slips into when forced to consider actual women. He much preferred the feminine as Eros.

The Red Book as critical-activist arts-based research

It may seem perverse to consider *The Red Book* as critical-activist ABR when it was never published by its author. A more usual critical-activist arts-based enquiry involves the artist co-creating with marginalized groups or using art to draw public attention to some grave injustice. Such art would expose alleged social wrongs, or propose various reforms. By definition, critical-activist ABR is both *critical* of the status quo and *active* in attempting to engage with a view to real change.

On the other hand, ABR stalwarts Leavy and Barone and Eisner insist upon a radical reconsideration of empathy in the epistemology of creativity as a means to knowing. Arts-based research is not limited to supplying questions that must be answered in the project. Research requiring answers conceives of the enterprise as discovering a pre-existing stable reality. Such a framing often presupposes the subject/object split that ABR deliberately critiques and goes beyond. So, in this sense, all arts-based research is critical-activist because it dismantles the presumed superiority of scientific subject/object enquiry. Arts-based research is paradigmatically critical-activist.

Of course another objection to *The Red Book* as critical-activist is that C. G. Jung was far from a progressive thinker who sought social change. Furthermore, as a wealthy white European male in a patriarchal and colonial era, he exhibited many of the associated biases that I have written about previously (Rowland 1996, 2002, 2005). In fact, there is a wealth of recent scholarship on Jung's racism from Fanny Brewster and Andrew Samuels, among others (Brewster 2017; Samuels 1993) Also material that challenges Jung's gender assumptions (from early women Jungian analysts such as Emma Jung) has been valuably studied by Claire Douglas in *The Woman in the Mirror* (1989/2000).

However, I suggest that it remains helpful to look at *The Red Book* through a critical-activist lens because, as has been shown in this chapter, it is both critical and active. *The Red Book* was generated from a rupture in Jung's psyche. That rupture leads to visions that develop a profound criticism of Western modernity's split psyche. As the previous section on synthesizing discourses shows, these criticisms focus on war, religion, science and gender. It reveals these areas to be entangled and lacking. Ironically, perhaps, war, religion, science and gender all lack the sense of absence that would begin to give them a bond to mystery, or to the other.

Jung's breakdown roughly coincided with the outbreak of what was called "the war to end wars." *The Red Book* goes further than those unfulfilled hopes. It suggests that warring armies are connected to an unacknowledged inner war. Splitting across Europe is a direct consequence of blind unconsciousness, of psychic splitting. The subject/object division has spiraled into losing sight of the other as indigenous to being. Rather, war is when the subject/object is enacted by subject soldiers fighting an enemy that has been turned into an object.

In this way, *The Red Book* can be seen as a radical attempt to examine the problem of war in the microcosm of one's soul. Critical of the splitting within, the work is *active* in providing a process by which it can be avoided.

Moreover, *The Red Book* is critical of religion, in its damning examination of what has been left out of mainstream Christianity by the privileging of rationality. Splitting the nature of the divine from the body, feminine, imagination and nature, results in a divorce of heaven and hell. On the one hand, there is the abandonment to hell of the mad and the creaturely. On the other, there are those like the unsatisfied dead who did not live their animal self (Jung 2012: 341). Jung's avatar, "I," has to learn empathy for the animal, or bodily, nature in people. Crucially, he has to learn compassion in social terms, in feeling for the lowly man and the cook.

For science, *The Red Book* shows that a psychology of reason that requires words stick to one meaning is empty; it is a dead system. After all, in *The Red Book* the dead return because they have never fully lived. Jung's science has no life until he stumbles upon the power of the imagination by saving Izdubar. By empathizing with the sinking man-god instead of trying to suppress him, "I" discovers that he has the power to save Izdubar into a different kind of animation. "I" saves Izdubar by forging a permanent connection to him as a symbol, words full of mystery. Science in *The Red Book* is converted from rational empty words that poison both divine and human to a discourse of symbols. The psychic image finds a home in words that function as portals to deeper mysteries.

Similarly, gender is criticized and actively changing in *The Red Book*. Gender literally trans-forms and is transformational. It is worth arguing that gender in *The Red Book* is a major signifying power that dismembers and re-members the "I" figure. Both feminine and masculine are stripped of their conventions. Masculinity is diverted from war-making and as epistemological authority in religion and science by the dethroning of rationality as sufficient. Of course it must be acknowledged that *The Red Book* continues to associate the masculine with Logos and the feminine with Eros. This persistence will result in binary language elsewhere in Jung's writing, as noted earlier.

Yet, *The Red Book* was composed by one man who finds an extraordinary range of gender position not only possible but necessary to find psychological life. Gender is dramatized in scenes that do not limit it to the human, that borrow from the theater of religion, expose its pervasive quality in science, and expose its variances in other cultures. Above all, gender flexibility is required to put faith in imagination and connect to the mysterious at the heart of being.

Finally, I suggest that the analytical qualities of *The Red Book* considered above should also count as critical-activist. For examining the capacity of the material aspects of Jung's use of paint along with language to re-present the psyche contributes to *The Red Book* as a modernist work of art. Modernism was a revolution in arts and culture that by definition extended to critical-activism in domains not limited to the aesthetic (Butler 2010). Moving from word to symbol, for example, from word as the basic unit of reason to it as home for the whole psyche, this too is critical of modernity's privileging of the rational that has led to the repression of so much that is other. Perhaps this elemental core to *The Red Book* enables the work to be a contribution to ABR as improvisatory.

The Red Book as improvisatory arts-based research

In *A Taste for Chaos*, Randy Fertel describes Jung as achieving the essential paradox of improvisation (2015: 368–82). For by embracing spontaneity, aiming to become the mere instrument of what wants to be, the improviser will discover limits and patterns that interrupt the embrace of chaos.

Improvisation is often undervalued or ignored in the literary tradition that Fertel examines. So too is its dialectical shadow, its relation to craft. In discovering improvisation's road to patterns, the improvisatory artist realizes, as in making real, the need for craft to shape something recognizable and distinct. Out of the collision of psychic fluidity with what Jung would call archetypes, Eros and Logos unite again in improvisatory art, as Fertel demonstrates.

> [F]or Jung the source of our actions and our health lay beyond us and within us in a Self over which we have no conscious control. Enriched by relation with the unconscious, man's consciousness fulfills the teleology of the universe, the *unus mundus* or one world in which everything is related by becoming conscious.
>
> (Fertel 2015: 370)

Fertel also points to the usefulness of Jung's two artistic categories, the psychological and the visionary. By making the latter the art of spontaneity, in allowing the archetypal energies the maximum freedom to make the art, Jung tacitly adopts improvisation as an artistic process. By generating this notion together with the psychological art of conscious workmanship, it could be argued that Jung implicitly endorses of the necessity of linking improvisation with craft. This link is what Fertel's book proposes (ibid.: 371).

Undoubtedly *The Red Book* stems from improvisation. Active imagination as the originating method of composition places *The Red Book* as a specialized improvisation, one with a specific method devised by Jung. Whereas improvisation can be defined as a surrender to spontaneity, active imagination is a discipline of relating to a psychic image allowed *its* spontaneity. Instead of the artist's whole being embracing the potential of chaos, active imagination deliberately invites chaos as the psychic "other." To do so means a relaxing ego control, a move that could be regarded as a discipline.

Here again is the paradox of improvisation; that it has rules in order for spontaneity to be realized, or made real. The rule of improvised theater, that each actor must react to whatever comes up positively with "yes, and," is necessary for the flow. Each must follow, and no one should assert control. Only with this rule is spontaneity free to dance among the participants. With active imagination the ego must follow, not manage. The ego follows the other's lead so that the images become fully alive in their own spontaneity.

Reading *The Red Book* is to taste those disciplined free-flowing eruptions. Some are so powerful as to almost drown the ego. Visions of blood and frost give way to a sense of being overwhelmed by the reality of the unconscious depths. Even the soul conceives by the violation of a virgin (Jung 2012: 171). Less painful experiences of the unconscious arrive in the sense of thoughts growing like a forest or being born into their own independent being. "I" is the hapless ego figure who is witness and participant in this theater of the archetypal psyche.

Like other improvisatory works, *The Red Book* discovers its pattern or limits. Patterning coalesces into theme, in the mutation of Eros and Logos. These beings morph from the initial strangeness of Elijah and Salome, through her attempt to deify "I," her recovery from blindness, their reappearance, and their eventual manifesting as Philemon with Baucis conveniently out of sight. They emerge at last in Jung's final summary Eros and Logos as essential psychic principles. Here too it is worth noting how Eros and Logos resemble the necessity of spontaneity and craft as allied, not antithetical.

Naturally, *The Red Book* has other notable figures and events in the journey of "I" to his better comprehension of his masculine personification of Logos and feminine of Eros. *The Red Book* is a testimony to the multiplicity of the psyche and to its innate improvisatory propensities. In fact, one could argue that as improvisatory arts-based research *The Red Book* discovers that individuation requires improvisation *and* craft. Just as Elijah and Salome are necessarily together, so too must the psyche live its animal, embrace the spontaneity of its nature as nature. Yet also the psyche hankers for the ordering of a spirit that orients the person into the larger patterns of the cosmos as *unus mundus*.

"I" sprouts green leaves and views the unhappy Ammonius. The hermit is tortured by words forced into so much craft that spontaneity and flow are squeezed out. Only one meaning is permitted. "I" is also hunted by Salome, tempted by her, dragged into her own healing ritual, forced into cannibalism and shut in a madhouse. Unrestrained improvisatory instinctual desires are as dangerous as too much order is deadening. Fortunately, Philemon arrives with wings, suggesting a union of nature and God. He symbolically provides magic in the wedding of Eros and Logos.

The entry of Philemon transforms the atmosphere of *The Red Book* into a harmonious union of improvisation and craft. Philemon can even satisfy the lamenting dead. They have returned because they overdosed on Logos, and neglected Eros in not living their spontaneity in their animal natures.

The Red Book is additionally an extraordinary example of improvisatory arts-based research because it discovers something about improvisation itself. It discovers the necessity of spontaneity for a person to be fully alive, so validating improvisation to an age that has largely discounted it. It also discovers something intrinsic to Jung's psychology and arguably to the whole profession of psychotherapy; that within the free-flowing unconscious psyche are ordering forces themselves that require the relaxation of consciousness in order to be supportive of being.

In a real sense, *The Red Book* shows Jungian individuation to be an art of improvisation. After all, the alchemy that Jung recognized as proto-individuation called itself an art. It too allowed for improvisation, hence the acknowledgment that there was no one set of procedures, nor an unvarying order. Within these arts that embrace improvisation and immediacy, looking for *what happens*, is the further realization of patterns and principles that connect us to all that is. Surely such a realization qualifies it for ABR, whatever Jung's qualms about its publication.

It is time to look further at C. G. Jung's penchant for spontaneity and immediacy in his published writing. Might his *Collected Works* prove to be a modernist work of improvisatory arts-based research?

Jung's *Collected Works* as arts-based research

Matthew Spano has persuasively argued that *The Red Book* closely resembles literary modernism in its experimental form (Spano 2010), while *The Art of C. G. Jung* demonstrates Jung's fascination with, and participation in, styles of modernist painting, as detailed above (Hoerni et al. 2018). Moreover, *The Red Book* proves to resemble in theme and structure modernist texts such as T. S. Eliot's poem, "The Wasteland," with its multiple voices, figures from contemporary life and antiquity, spiritual yearning, problematic feminine and desert location for psychological distress (Eliot 1922/2002).

Another contemporary poet with a similar concern for images and symbols is W. B. Yeats. Like Jung, Yeats finds a need to turn to what has been ignored or repressed in modernity.

> Those masterful images because complete
> Grew in pure mind, but out of what began?
> A mound of refuse or the sweepings of a street,
> Old kettles, old bottles, and a broken can,
> Old iron, old bones, old rags, that raving slut
> Who keeps the till. Now that my ladder's gone,
> I must lie down where all the ladders start,
> In the foul rag-and-bone-shop of the heart.
> (Yeats 1979)

In this late poem, "The Circus Animals' Desertion," Yeats seeks rhythmic integration of what modernity has repressed as other: the feminine, sexuality, poverty, the body, dirt and the debris of the city (Yeats 1979: 391–2). Modernism in Yeats, Eliot and *The Red Book* breaks up those very forms of exclusion, to allow what has been repressed to speak. Breaking with earlier conventions by bringing back the medieval illumination of paint and word, the reflexive nature of the work, its bricolage or juxtaposition of diverse materials and many sources, by use of myth, fragmentation of consciousness, and in the explicit revolt against modern consciousness, *The Red Book* is profoundly modernist.

In fact, placing artistic modernism in this chapter's examination of *The Red Book* is to uncover modernism's legacy within arts-based research. It could be argued that all four of Rolling Jnr.'s four categories of arts-based research have their antecedents in modernism. The analytic exploration of materials, not what we perceive but how we perceive it, is the essence of the modernist break with, and interrogation of, past artistic forms. Previously taken for granted, artistic forms are now examined and challenged because of a perceived sense of crisis about what is real and how to represent it.

Secondly, the synthesizing of discourses to make new meanings began in modernist bricolage. In addition, the critical stance of so much modernist art is taken further in the activism of the research methodology of ABR. Finally, modernism began the radical embrace of improvisation in arts such as jazz. All four categories of arts-based research stem from modernist experimentation.

Such a crucial development of modernism into a research methodology and paradigm is not surprising given how far modernist artists were the arts-based researchers of their age. The recent writing about ABR in the academy changes how we construe modernism, I suggest. Here *The Red Book* is an outstanding example. Artists of the modernist era (1890–1939) imagined into the split subject of modernity and saw vistas of what had been excluded from dominant genres of art and of knowledge. If these artists were engaging in what we now recognize as research, might there be a response from science? Might a psychologist who wanted to be considered a scientist also be doing arts-based research even though he rejected the term art?

After all, Jung admits that to claim absolute knowledge of the psyche is to mistake its very nature. To take the existence of the unconscious seriously one must accept that all knowledge is incomplete to an unknown extent (Jung 1947, CW8: para. 358). It follows that Jung's intention, his conscious disciplinary sense, is not unquestionable. As noted before, if we take Jung's disavowal of art too seriously with regard to his whole oeuvre, then we would be privileging his ego, not what he considers most significant in the psyche.

In addition, taking Jung's disavowal of art too seriously would place everything Jung wrote into his art category of the psychological. All would be carefully worked out, reeking of conscious, ego control. Such an attitude to *The Collected Works* would be untrue to his psychology, which asks us to restore, even to re-story, what has been excluded, to re-connect with the unknown and transgressive. Individuation itself is a counter-argument to reading for ego intention.

The question remains, does Jung's writing invite the individuating reader? Does he ever adopt the visionary mode in work authorized by him for publication? To answer this query, it is worth taking the four types of arts-based research and briefly applying them to Jung's *The Collected Works*.

Analytic, synthetic, critical-activist and improvisatory ABR in *The Collected Works*

Given that I have argued for the artistic nature of *The Collected Works* in previous books, I simply mention the analytic ABR aspect of Jung's publications for their experiments with language (Rowland 2005). Jung's essays weave and juxtapose an astonishing variety of expressive tropes. Among these are

a liberal use of humor, a discursive tone that ranges from the poetic to collo-
quial, the invocation of other disciplines, bricolage, circling spiral structures to
argument, a tricky relation to the reader, an emphasis on rhetorical modes, an
embroidering by mythic and non-ego voices, and the *figuring* of his psychology by notion of the model and the net. All these are explored in in *Jung as
a Writer* (2005).

It is worth pausing on the figures of model and net.

> It is not a question of … asserting anything, but of constructing a *model*
> which opens up a promising and useful field of enquiry. A model … simply
> illustrates a particular mode of observation.
>
> (Jung 1947, CW8: para. 381)

> I fancied I was working along the best scientific lines … only to discover
> in the end that I had involved myself in a net of reflections … into the
> fields of philosophy, theology, comparative religion, and the human sci-
> ences in general.
>
> (ibid.: para. 421)

A net of reflections and a model are presented as discoveries that remove
psychology from any fidelity to the traditional science of the subject/object
split. They also invoke other disciplines. Above all, the model and the net of
reflections are frames for what has been undervalued in Jung: psychic mystery
in the writing manifested in words, as symbol. We recall from earlier chapters
that the symbol can be engendered by the attitude of the reader. Moreover, to
Jung symbols are the true language of science that it is open to what is not yet
known (Jung 1921, CW6: 817–18).

Again and again, *The Collected Works* assert that the psyche is a living mystery not to be adequately or completely captured in conceptual language.
Indeed, a very different type of language is more true and precise to what the
psyche is.

> Therefore, in describing the living processes of the psyche, I deliberately
> and consciously give preference to a dramatic, mythological way of think-
> ing and speaking, because this is not only more expressive *but also more
> exact* than an abstract scientific terminology.
>
> (Jung 1921, CW 9ii, para. 25, italics added)

"More exact" would appear to be the outcome of Jung's analytic arts-based
research into writing down the imaginal truth of the psyche. A net or a model
of word symbols is the genre that *The Collected Works* evolves over twenty
volumes.

Turning to synthetic arts-based research of multiple discourses, we can see
that Jung's writing requires that the mysteries of the psyche be invoked in

a transdisciplinary manner (see Chapters 2 and 3). In volumes such as *Psychology and Alchemy* CW12 (1944), Jung creates a tissue of voices, or bricolage, by substantial quotation from alchemy texts of other eras. These mysterious recipes for material and spiritual transformation are also placed liminally. They are neither quite inside because the alchemists did not fully grasp their individuation, nor wholly outside, because alchemy remains proto-Jungian psychology.

The alchemical discourses are also both distanced and brought closer when Jung admits differences of worldview, and speculates that his new research into synchronicity might be bringing psychology to a very similar perspective. Speculation is a major trope in *The Collected Works*, along with the notion of differences, this persistence of *otherness*, whether it be of gender, culture, era or disciplinary otherness. The other stands for that mystery that cannot be fully captured in rational argument. Jung even makes that point an ecology of Logos.

> The moment one forms an idea of a thing … One has taken possession of it, and it has become an inalienable piece of property, like a slain creature of the wild that can no longer run away.
>
> (Jung 1947, CW8: para. 356)

Forming a fixed idea and surrendering it wholly to Jung's Logos is to kill the psyche, as learned in *The Red Book*. Eros as fluidity and relationship is necessary. Together Eros and Logos can engender symbols in writing that are more exact in openness to the mystery. Jung's bricolage becomes critical-activist in a recognizable manner when, for example, discussing the psyche of non-Western peoples. While displaying many racist and colonial assumptions, an essay such as "Archaic Man" additionally deconstructs such assumptions (Jung 1933/2002: 127–54). Beginning with colonial condescension towards the "primitive," the essay ends by contrasting the well-adapted tribal person with the primitive habits of Europeans with their Easter eggs and Christmas trees.

Even more indigenous to *The Collected Works* is the way the writing acts as psychology itself. Jung's spiral, symbol-rich, mythologically animated bricolage is a treatment of the reader's psyche. Its multiple voices evoke multiplicity in the imagination. We individuate in the act of making sense of the ideas while the word symbols connect us to other, less conscious parts of being. *The Collected Works* are critical-activist arts-based research into the psychology of attitudes and presuppositions about the other. Again, this other takes on a cultural as well as poetic and spiritual reference. *The Collected Works* are activist, opening the psyche to be critical of, and remake, our conventional being.

Suggestion of the improvisatory ABR nature of *The Collected Works* confirms the synthesizing of discourses with critical-activist possibilities. I have quoted these three sentences many times, for their apparent misogyny conceals a trick.

The anima has an erotic, emotional character, the animus a rationalizing one. Hence most of what men say about feminine eroticism, and particularly about the emotional life of women, is derived from their own anima projections and distorted accordingly. On the other hand, the astonishing assumptions and fantasies that women make about men come from the activity of the animus, who produces an inexhaustible supply of illogical arguments and false explanations.

(Jung 1925, CW17: para. 338)

On several occasions in *The Collected Works*, colloquialisms spill into irritation with what to Jung is a woman's masculine potential or the animus. Part of this attitude stems from his flawed gender essentialism. By assuming that all men naturally possess Logos in their consciousness, he infers that women have it in the unconscious, where the ordering spirituality of Logos becomes disputatious and opinionated. However, what appears here as crude prejudice is also a trick that simultaneously invokes improvisatory arts-based research. For if we follow the logic of these three sentences the overwrought speaker of the third is not the writer's ego, but his anima.

In a nice unpacking of the subject/object paradigm, the passage starts by insisting that neither gender can be wholly objective about the other. Men are not objective about women because their inner feminine gets in the way. Immediately this situation occurs when the irrational voice of the anima (because the previous sentence said so) takes over the writer's pen. Is this an improvisatory discovery made by letting the writing flow? Or is it rather a plot, a trick to see if the reader is paying attention? We cannot know, with the undecidability an opportunity for the reader's capacity to evolve (individuate) a response.

However the reader may feel about Jung as a trickster writer, as I contend he is, *The Collected Works* are a testimony to the spontaneity of the psyche with the flavor of improvisatory arts-based research. With such a precedent in arts-based research as the work of C. G. Jung, it is time to turn to another formidable achievement: *The Nuclear Enchantment of New Mexico* by Joel Weishaus.

References

Barry, P. (2017) *Beginning Theory: An Introduction to Literary and Cultural Theory.* 4th edition. Manchester, UK: Manchester University Press.

Beebe, J. (2010) '*The Red Book* as a Work of Conscience; Notes from a Seminar Given for the 35th Annual Jungian Conference, C.G. Jung Club of Orange County, April 10th 2010', *Quadrant, XXXX* (2) (Summer 2010), 41–58.

Berk, T. V. D. (2012) *Jung on Art: The Autonomy of the Creative Drive.* New York and Hove: Routledge.

Brewster, F. (2017) *African Americans and Jungian Psychology: Leaving the Shadows.* Hove and New York: Routledge.

Butler, C. (2010) *Modernism: A Very Short Introduction.* Oxford and New York: Oxford University Press.

Douglas, C. (1989/2000) *The Woman in the Mirror: Analytical Psychology and the Feminine.* New York: iUniverse.

Eliot, T. S. (1922/2002) *Collected Poems 1909–1962.* London: Faber & Faber.

Fertel, R. (2015) *A Taste for Chaos: The Art of Literary Improvisation.* New Orleans: Spring Journal and Books.

Fischer, T. and B. Kaufmann. (2018) 'C. G. Jung and Modern Art', in U. Hoerni, T. Fischer and B. Kaufmann, eds. *The Art of C. G. Jung.* New York and London: W. W. Norton & Company, pp. 19–31.

Fish, B. J. (2018) 'Drawing and Painting Research', in P. Leavy, ed. *Handbook of Arts-Based Research.* New York and London: The Guilford Press, pp. 336–354.

Hoch, M. (2018) 'C. G. Jung' Concepts of Color in the Context of Modern Art', in U. Hoerni, T. Fischer and B. Kaufmann, eds. *The Art of C. G. Jung.* New York and London: W. W. Norton & Company, pp. 33–49.

Hoerni, U., T. Fischer and B. Kaufmann. (2018) *The Art of C. G. Jung.* New York and London: W. W. Norton & Company.

Jung, C. G. (1921) 'Definitions', in *Collected Works, Volume 6, Psychological Types*, pp. 408–486.

Jung, C. G. (1925) 'Marriage as a Psychological Relationship', in *Collected Works, Volume 17: The Development of Personality*, pp. 187–204.

Jung, C. G. (1930) 'Psychology and Literature', in *Collected Works, Volume 15: The Spirit in Man, Art and Literature*, pp. 109–134.

Jung, C. G. (1933/2002) 'Archaic Man', in *Modern Man in Search of a Soul.* London and New York: Routledge, pp. 127–154.

Jung, C. G. (1944) 'Individual Dream Symbolism in Relation to Alchemy', in *Collected Works, Volume 12: Psychology and Alchemy*, pp. 39–214.

Jung, C. G. (1947) 'On the Nature of the Psyche', in *Collected Works, Volume 8: The Structure and Dynamics of the Psyche*, pp. 159–234.

Jung, C. G. (1951) 'The Syzygy: Anima and Animus', in *Collected Works, Volume 9ii: Aion: Researches into the Phenomenology of the Self*, pp. 11–22.

Jung, C. G. (1963/1983) *Memories, Dreams, Reflections.* Recorded and edited by Aniela Jaffe. London: Fontana.

Jung, C. G. (2009) *The Red Book: Liber Novus.* ed. S. Shamdasani, trans. M. Kyburz, J. Peck and S. Shamdasani. New York: W.W. Norton & Company.

Jung, C. G. (2012) *The Red Book: A Reader's Edition.* New York: W. W. Norton & Company.

Leavy, P. ed. (2018) *Handbook of Arts-Based Research.* New York and London: The Guilford Press.

Malchiodi, C. A. (2018) 'Creative Arts Therapies and Arts-Based Research', in P. Leavy (2018), pp. 68–87.

Mellick, J. (2018) 'Matter and Methods in *the Red Book*: Selected Findings', in U. Hoerni, T. Fischer and B. Kaufmann, eds. *The Art of C. G. Jung.* New York and London: W. W. Norton & Company, pp. 217–231.

Mitchell, S. (2004) *Gilgamesh: A New English Version.* New York: Simon & Schuster.

Rolling Jnr., J. H. (2013) *Arts-Based Research Primer.* New York: Peter Lang.

Rowland, S. (1996) *C. G. Jung and Literary Theory: The Challenge from Fiction.* London and New York: Palgrave.

Rowland, S. (2002) *Jung: A Feminist Revision.* Oxford: Polity.

Rowland, S. (2005) *Jung as a Writer.* Hove and New York: Routledge.

Rowland, S. (2017) *Remembering Dionysus: Revisioning Psychology and Literature in C. G. Jung and James Hillman.* Hove and New York: Routledge.

Samuels, A. (1993) *The Political Psyche.* Hove and New York: Routledge.

Shamdasani, S. (2009) 'Introduction', in S. Shamdasani, ed. *The Red Book: Liber Novus, A Reader's Edition.* trans. M. Kyburz, J. Peck and S. Shamdasani. New York: W.W. Norton & Company, pp. 1–95.

Spano, M. V. (2010) '*Modern(-ist) Man in Search of a Soul: Jung's **Red Book** as Modernist Visionary Literature,*' *cgjungpage*: www.cgjungpage.org/index.php?option=com_content&task=view&id=934&Itemid=1 (Accessed 27th September 2012).

Worringer, W. (1908/1953) *Abstraction and Empathy; A Contribution to the Psychology of Style.* trans. M. Bullock. New York: International Universities Press.

Yeats, W. B. (1979) 'The Circus Animals' Desertion', in *Collected Poems of W.B. Yeats.* London: Macmillan, p. 392.

Chapter 5

The Nuclear Enchantment of New Mexico as Jungian arts-based research

Introduction

Poetic inquiry

The Nuclear Enchantment of New Mexico (hereafter *Nuclear Enchantment*) belongs to that branch of arts-based research known as poetic inquiry. In *Poetic Inquiry: Enchantment of Place*, one of the editors, Kedrick James, produces an admirably comprehensive definition.

> Thus, poetic inquiry is understood as the act of writing poetry with greater purpose and intent than solely for self-expression.
>
> (James 2017: 25)

Yet, it is possible to query this definition. Poetic self-expression might meet the criteria for arts-based research should it be addressed to knowing in ways that transform or alter what is conventional. Surely poetic inquiry is even more distinguished by its challenge to art as an object rather than as a subject of being in the world. After all, James cites the ancient tradition of perceiving the world through poetry, and also points to a suggestive first use of the term in modern times: "that great spirit of poetic inquiry that was Milton's and Browning's" (1921 anon, quoted in James 2017: 24).

Here poetic inquiry is germane to poetry itself. To Milton, poetry was the best way of exploring the depths of his religion. Similarly, before the era of printing enabled reading to become a largely private affair, poetry was the best medium for everything from storytelling to historical annals, to recording the capricious ways of the gods. Only in modernity did the expansion of the subject/object division come to be seen as fundamental to understanding reality (as considered in Chapter 2). Poetry that calls for imaginative participation in the world was to this version of knowledge a mere distraction. Poetry became diminished while styles of prose developed that were capable of imitating so-called scientific objectivity.

In imaginative terms, prose took from poetry techniques that developed into the novel as a genre of social examination. Metaphors, symbols and words as potent spells were less welcome in new writing modes for academic disciplines. Once knowledge was split into the pursuit of different ontological versions of reality, these fundamental assumptions demanded that language honor their relatively fixed versions of truth. As explored in earlier chapters of this book, for too long scientific disciplines pretended that language can be reduced to a transparent membrane for a reality consisting of stable objects "out there." Poetic inquiry knows different.

> What makes Poetic Inquiry so useful is its capaciousness of expression ... It admits to the fallibility of a singular expression of truths about something – poetry's capaciousness comes from the inherent polyvalence of poetic expression, to see in many directions at once through the multiple lenses of language ... in any particular field the language we use ... might have a big influence in the knowledge we generate ... if the language used in our own work is unduly generic and predictable, it might just be that our research will also turn out to be generic and predictable.
>
> (James 2017: 23)

When no longer ideologically wedded to the subject/object split as the foundation for all knowing and being, words of research become the research. Language is not a neutral medium through which objects represent truth or reality. Rather, language is part of knowing and being. Such insight drives *Nuclear Enchantment*. The language of nuclear weapons is part of their construction as a cultural event as well as a military enterprise.

Arguably *only* poetic inquiry can evoke the sublime horrors of nuclear weapons technology. For, whereas a nuclear bomb is modernity's addiction to splitting taken to an insane extreme, in dividing the very grains of being itself, poetic inquiry re-members that human beings depend upon complex webs of bones and blood, oxygen and food from the land, communities of animals, humans and cosmic entities. Poetry is inherently multifaceted. Poetry is language as plural, as rooting unknown unconscious being to conscious discourses. Poetry connects.

As *Nuclear Enchantment* reveals, only by re-connecting this devastating knowing to multiple resources of being can we overcome where subject/object splitting has taken this culture. For nuclear weapons, predicated on splitting atoms, are the ultimate magical beans that make everything into an object targeted for destruction. The poetic inquiry of *Nuclear Enchantment* dis-enchants the magic beans by re-weaving the cosmos that produced us and them. Since the entirety of *The Nuclear Enchantment of New Mexico* is printed in this book, references will be to sections rather than page numbers.

Joel Weishaus on the Jungian frame

In his introduction, the poet refers to the presence of Jung in the work in the context of a Native American myth of destruction by the sun.

I was drawn to the trip C. G. Jung famously made in 1925 to Taos Pueblo, about 60 miles north of Santa Fe, because of a Jicarilla Apache myth in which the center of the Earth is near Taos, and that, "Some time ... that place will start to burn ... That fire will spread all over the world."

(Weishaus "Introduction" 2019, Chapter 6 this book)

In Jung's own account of his visit to Taos there is also a focus on the sun. Ochwiay Biano, whom Jung also calls Mountain Lake, informs his visitor that his religion has rituals to the sun. These are necessary to the continuation of life on Earth.

If we were to cease practicing our religion, in ten years the sun would no longer rise. Then it would be night forever.

(Jung 1963/1983: 280)

Impressed by the dignity granted by discussion of the sacred, Jung speculates that these rituals are intended as a participatory rite. The action of the ritual invokes a reciprocal response from the god as sun. Here I suggest Jung intimates what *Nuclear Enchantment* as arts-based research will later develop. This chapter will show that Weishaus' poetic inquiry is a parallel cultural endeavor to the indigenous religion; both seek to support the life-giving function of the star. For the nuclear era, we will need rituals to contain the power of fission, of splitting. We all have to participate in holding back weapons that appear as bright as the sun and employ its nuclear fission.

Weishaus points also to Jung in the psychological dimension of the ABR of *Nuclear Enchantment*; that nuclear weapons exist as "an *autonomous* complex ... a split-off portion of the psyche, which leads a life of its own outside the hierarchy of consciousness" (Jung 1922, CW15: para. 115; italics in original). He refers to the Jungian precept that the psyche is not fully controlled by the ego, but rather is populated by energies that can be mysterious and potentially overwhelming. Complexes form when someone is ignorant of their dark side. Once a complex exists, it can erupt without warning. This can happen to groups and nations as well.

The Cultural Complex (2004), edited by Jungians Tom Singer and Samuel L. Kimbles, develops the notion of the collective cultural complex. A society can form irrational nodes of energy around events or ideas with painful histories. If not addressed by society and brought into a relationship with consciousness, cultural complexes can swallow up rational responses. In naming nuclear weapons as a complex within the modern psyche, Weishaus allies his *Nuclear Enchantment* with the project of psychotherapy: it is psychotherapy for the entire culture of modernity.

Finally, in his introduction Weishaus describes the mythical quality of nuclear fission. By dismembering atoms, a terrifying Dionysian chaos is unleashed. God of dismembering and re-membering, Dionysus is also the god of comedy and tragedy. His myth is another evocative frame for *Nuclear Enchantment*. Can art re-member the collective psyche that built nuclear weapons? Such an ambitious aim drives *Nuclear Enchantment*. Here poetic inquiry will dismember the rhetoric and assumptions from which the terrifying technology emerged, and re-member them. Such re-integration will restore, by re-storying nuclear potential as a culture that is also an ethnography and an ecology.

As examined in Chapter 3 of this book, Dionysian re-membering is a necessary ingredient of arts-based research. It transforms knowing into being as connected, not divided. *Nuclear Enchantment* does far more than re-member what nuclear weapons are. The work rehearses the stories the weapons enact as well as those they suppress, in the colonization of New Mexico and beyond. This revolutionary new poetry is a chalice for containing the darkest darkness of modernity; all that which has been split off and demonized as other.

The exaggerated fear of the other materializes in the weapons we produce. Jung wrote that Ochwiay Biano made him see the white colonials as part of a race of pirates (Jung 1963/1983: 277). *Nuclear Enchantment* enables us to face the psyche locked into weapons of mass destruction. If we can re-member the complex, then we can learn not to be consumed by it.

Nuclear Enchantment will be examined in the rest of this chapter using Rolling Jnr.'s four genres of arts-based research: analytic, synthetic, critical-activist and improvisatory (Rolling Jnr. 2013: 51–8).

Nuclear Enchantment as analytic arts-based research: poetic inquiry trans-forming

Poetic inquiry of form

As Rolling Jnr. describes, analytic arts-based research is thinking in materials (Rolling Jnr.: 79). The material of *Nuclear Enchantment* is words wrought in their artistic form as poetry and prose. Just as nuclear weapons have changed war by unraveling the very ingredients of materiality, so *Nuclear Enchantment* trans-forms the ingredients of conventional assumptions about poetry, prose and knowing. Nuclear fission grew from the dismembering science of the subject/object split, and is arguably part of the assault on modernity in the period of 1890–1945. Here, *Nuclear Enchantment* belongs to modernist and postmodernist literary revolutions.

For the form of *Nuclear Enchantment* exposes radical splitting. Open any page and a list of notes appears in impeccable traditional scholarship on the left, with corresponding poetry on the right. Implicitly the poetry is privileged because in book form the eye glances to the right first, and because English is read left to right. On the other hand, having notes on the prior left page presents a challenge to the reader: which to read first? Normally "notes" are placed after the main text and are meant to be an expansion of core ideas; or, most usually, a precise list of sources. Such notes are not innate parts of the work.

This is why Weishaus calls his notes a paratext. Belonging in a new way to the poetry, the notes are both supplementary and integral to the work. *Nuclear Enchantment* is not poetry with notes, it is scholarly prose and poetic prose juxtaposed into an organic and multiple relationship. The paratexts are inside the work and also a liminal border to the work. They frame in their left page position, but they also belong to writing and research elsewhere as many are attributed quotations. Paratexts bring other voices into a dialogical relationship with the poetry.

For example, "yellowcake" is raw uranium ore. Additionally in the poetry of "Homestake Mining" it becomes the dung of the Golden Calf of the Israelites, as well as the sinister milk of a goddess leading to Death's twins. The paratext explains nuclear yellowcake and the mythical attributions such as that the goddess Isis could not find the penis of Osiris when seeking to regenerate him. It quotes a 1988 text by the German artist Anselm Kiefer that a nuclear pile is a kind of penis, seeking a regenerative effect from utter destruction.

The note for Death's twins also quotes a scholar on the Navajo myth that says these twins could kill with their eyes. The resonant juxtaposition of paratext on the left, poetry on the right challenges the reader to become more conscious of cultural strategies around reading and making meaning. Does the reader obey the tacit rules and attend to the left-hand page of scholarly sources before diving into the poems? Or is she fascinated first by the evocative and invocative poetry before returning to writing that obeys modernity's conventions of what knowledge is?

In short, the form of *Nuclear Enchantment* is a stark depiction of, and alternative to, the hierarchies of knowing based on the subject/object split. The paratexts visually enact the splitting into different disciplines by separating the notes and drawing attention to that separation by references to sources. By contrast, the poetry combines. Together, the two types of writing conjoin in the reader.

These choices about reading force us to be conscious of alternative ways of knowing. In this way, the work is dialogical as the philosopher M. M. Bakhtin defined it as a constant circulation and exchange of meaning (Bakhtin 1981: 10–13; 426; 428). Put in Bakhtin's terms, the ABR of poetic inquiry and analytic *Nuclear Enchantment* breaks down knowledge hierarchies to create dialogical heteroglossia.

> At any given time, in any given place, there will be a set of conditions – social, historical, meteorological, physiological – that will insure that a word uttered in that place and at that time will have a meaning different than it would have under any other conditions; all utterances are heteroglot

in that they are functions of a matric of forces practically impossible to recoup, and therefore impossible to resolve.

(ibid.: 428)

Another sense in which *Nuclear Enchantment* is dialogical is its interrogation of Jung's alternatives over the psyche in words. By dividing language between signs and symbols (as explored previously), Jung noted the predilection of collective, *disciplined* consciousness for stable singular meanings as signs, while symbols lead the reader into the wilderness of the unconscious. As earlier chapters of this book have shown, separating humans from the subject of knowledge (the subject/object split) has led to all kinds of other splitting, including dividing consciousness from the unknown psyche. Symbols are language to heal such splits.

It would not be correct to say of *Nuclear Enchantment* that Jung's signs only occur in the paratext and symbols in the poetry. Rather, the work of *Nuclear Enchantment* reveals something even more insidious and dangerous in what nuclear weapons do to language. To begin with, *Nuclear Enchantment* reveals that the psyche of such weapons is so bound up with splitting that words lose even their sign-making capacities. Words die first. *Nuclear Enchantment* shows that the weapons are made from a denial of rational meaning (signs) and an obliteration of unconscious generativity that is required for symbols.

Such splitting of words from their desire to breed more meaning degrades language. Nuclear fission does not only occur with words as the vehicle of a psyche split off from emotions, but also splitting between actions and consequences, between indigenous and colonizing cultures, splitting from the land, the environment and, as we will see, a detonation of language that cannot support the devasting reality. First I will look at the exploration of language decay around the weapons in *Nuclear Enchantment*, then how arts-based research offers healing through a poetic inquiry that fosters symbols.

Weapons against words; symbolic restoration

Rockeyes, snakeyes, bull pups, sidewinders, snark, minuteman, star wars, BONZO, WIMP, HOPE, aardvark: all words used by the military-industrial complex that produces and maintains nuclear weapons. These words are both familiar and wholly estranged from familiar contexts. In effect, nuclear weapons culture wrenches words out of context in ways that permit a distancing from what they actually refer to in this new, deadly use. Rockeyes, snakeyes, bull pups and sidewinders are types of bombs or missiles, as is snark, taken from a Lewis Carroll poem for children. Star wars is a defense system that was never meant to work as the public believed; and, of course, it invoked the famous film about success in war. Aardvark was a plane that failed to deliver its lethal bombs.

The acronyms, of which there are many more, disguise in plain sight the reality of the weapons' research and manufacture. BONZO stands for Bulwark Order Negating Zealous Offense. WIMP is Western Intercontinental Missile Protection, while HOPE is Hostile Projection Elimination. These are acronyms as euphemism magnified because neither the abbreviation nor the full version conveys any real sense of nuclear war. Such acronyms and borrowings are not Jung's signs as rational straightforward meaning; nor are they symbols evoking the mysteries of the deep psyche.

Rather, the use of aggressive animals, such as the sidewinder snake, and cozy acronyms drain language of meaning and psyche. A nuclear warhead killing masses of life-forms is not accurately named after a predator whose life depends upon the continued existence of his prey. Such misrepresentation of nature suggests something very wrong with human nature that can, uniquely among the planet's species, destroy all life.

Indeed, *Nuclear Enchantment* includes the philosopher Jacques Derrida on the coining of "biodegradable" as a recent unstable artefact made from Greek and Latin ("Kwahu Kachina") while the poem suggests "life biodegrades into molecular mud," pointing to the lack of real understanding of how humans are caught up in heterogeneous processes of life and death. A word made by splicing different languages signifies carelessness in the making of other kinds. Neither plastic nor plutonium is biodegradable in ways that foster life on the planet.

Nuclear Enchantment is ABR demonstrating that nuclear weapons use language that separates psyche from meaning. Neither sign nor symbol, it is euphemistic, sentimental and mystifying. "Broken arrows" are failed weapons with at least thirty-two accidents and six completely lost, the paratext of "Accidental H-Bomb" records. Here is *Nuclear Enchantment* as a critical (in both senses) investigation of language in poetic inquiry.

In 1954, the Matador became the first plutonium armed cruise missile. Designed to be broken into seven parts for convenient shipping, its macho name bestows and destroys meaning. The brave bull-fighting matador of elegance, performance and vulnerability belies the true function of the Matador missile to kill more people than the bombs dropped on Japan ("Alamogordo Chamber of Commerce").

Nuclear Enchantment offers a straightforward account of deadly history of the Matador in the paratext. Across the open page is poetry of the seven deadly sins sealed into the Matador's seven parts. This poem ends with grim humor about endings.

> What would you say if you knew that the world was about to end?
> Who would you phone?
> I'd dial the Chamber of Commerce and say:
> *I'm open for business.*
> *Wait for the tone.*

The paratext framing this poem also records the huge sums of money spent by tourists to White Sands National Monument. Some of the land became dedicated to the weapons industry. Tourism supports 307 local jobs, while a dial tone was used to signal the dropping of the atomic bomb on Hiroshima. I suggest that what *Nuclear Enchantment* here achieves is more than just exposing the attack on language that is part of such weapons of mass destruction. Rather, the technique of multiple juxtaposition and rhythm in the quotation above is a project of restoration: the restoration of the degraded psyche through seeding new possible meanings.

The poetry contains multiple voices made from an astonishing range of references. This particular text, "Alamogordo Chamber of Commerce," has a paratext covering the economic and military history of White Sands, New Mexico, as well as research on zombies in Haiti, while the poetry combines what the paratext shows separately. Paychecks and matadors precede the manufacture of the Seven Deadly Sins in the cruise missile and the question of what to do if the world ends. "Open for business" is the state of the weapons industry, a euphemism for preparing planet-encompassing disaster.

Humor and irony are often generated by paradox and the failure of words to *work* to absorb the psyche. "Rocket Lounge" also exhibits rueful humor at the business of mass annihilation. Located also in Alamagordo NM, its serving of prime ribs is likened in the paratext to the choicest offering going to the gods because a critic commented that, given the proximity to the site of testing the first bomb, Alamagordo could be the altar for the entire planet as a burnt offering. The same text includes "Desire's fantasy" and "love gasoline," referring both to the American love affair with speed, and Marcel Duchamp's famous glass artwork, another splitting in flight from grounding responsibility. The automobile and the rocket to the moon are American technology shared with nuclear bombs in the worship of power at all costs.

Nuclear Enchantment does not provide single meanings to replace the hollowing out of meaning in the nuclear project. Rather, it uses plural referential language to activate the reading psyche. Such activation exposes the degrading of meaning in the euphemistic byways of the weapons industry. It also sparks, fertilizes and potentially regenerates the reader's psyche. In Jungian terms, the extreme splitting of weapons language from meaning in the repression of the reality of what these weapons actually do, such splitting further divides the psyche as we repress the literally unspeakable truth. By contrast, the poetic inquiry of *Nuclear Enchantment*'s core strategy of many voices and juxtaposition stimulates the multiple capacities that Jung noted in the psyche.

Ultimately, Weishaus' project is in the business of restoring language to psychic wholeness by creating symbols where they have been detonated out of being. The Matador missile is an incomprehensible term because a once graceful warrior is linked to the potential murder of millions. By suggesting that the missile is composed of the Seven Deadly Sins of medieval Christianity in the midst of revealing the complicity of commerce with the nuclear weapons industry, a symbol is constructed out of the very destruction of meaning. In calling a deadly missile a matador, the history of trying to tame the destructive capability of humans is repressed. Fortunately, history can be recalled in multiple languages, including that of religion and black humor.

Jungian symbols unite meaning and being in ways that include mystery. *Nuclear Enchantment* makes such symbols by putting together fragments of language from history and culture. The work evokes what military language denies: the potential reality of weapons' use creates; in zombies, for example. Summoning the cultural referent and horror of zombies adopts the Jungian symbol for the project of connecting meaning to being. The aim in this analytic ABR is to discover if poetry and research can contain our ability to unleash the ultimate destructive power we've also invented.

The sublime stands for that which cannot be fully put into words (Shaw 2006). Crucially, the mystery evoked by Weishaus' symbols is not just the sublime reality of mass devastation. The mystery is also evoked by the juxtaposition of cultural resources from many cultures and many disciplines, and this source of the sublime is generative. *Nuclear Enchantment* makes Jungian symbols out of each text; each text which is paratext and poetry *together* works as a symbol. As a symbol, it conjures both the sublime of nuclear weapons, so restoring meaning and psyche to language, and the sublime of the psyche itself, in an unknown potential for making meaning.

Therefore, after considering the language of fissile splitting, it is time look more closely at the language of fusion, of joining and connecting. For *Nuclear Enchantment* offers an eco-logic of words, psyche and land, as well as the deep resonance of Jung's favored language of connecting: myth.

Restoration in language, ecology and myth

The connecting language of *Nuclear Enchantment* is the bedrock of the entire form that prompts the reader to reconnect what has been split, without privileging any particular meaning. The *work* is the work of Jungian symbols. It includes a substantial eco-logic because one fundamental divorce excavated by *Nuclear Enchantment* is that of a modernity riven from the land.

Hence, from "sagebrush mentalities" to the "ominous mound" of a uranium mine, to the "little mounds" that are the remains of "*hibakusha* children" (those living and dying from the atomic bombs dropped in Japan), *The Nuclear Enchantment of New Mexico* does not remain in New Mexico, just as radiation does not stop at the border. Bombs made in New Mexico were ignited far away, and so too the work unites the elements mined in the American state to the dying bodies in foreign lands.

Here, of course, connecting New Mexico and Japan as nuclear bombs have done is again both revealing and attempting to remedy the radical splitting that occurs in the collective psyche over weapons manufacture. What happens in

New Mexico does not stay in New Mexico, where "fissionable seeds" produced the Fat Man bomb ("Atomic Wrecking"). Seeds here is not a metaphor but rather an apt term for what is dug from the earth to become something productive of devasting energy.

"Laguna with Fish" links Christian fish iconography with the Laguna legend of a monstrous fish which vomited water all over the island, so drowning the people. Also, a Japanese boys' festival celebrates with fish for those who "survived the contaminant," evoking both radiation in Japan and the contaminated Native American lands in New Mexico. The same text includes "Mother's cloaked lap, adding stories to stories," referring to yet another tradition of the divine feminine in the earth.

Above all, the ecopoetry of *Nuclear Enchantment* is precise: it combines utmost precision from scrupulous research into nuclear weapons history, technology and culture with the mysteries of connecting in language. So the "carping voices" in "Laguna with Fish" play on a conventional use of carping for pointless negative attacking with the actual use of carp, the fish in the boys' festival. What makes this meticulous research into Jungian symbols is the daring connecting of what has been previously split. Loss of meaning in radioactive modernity is restored by re-storying in the poetic inquiry. Such connecting sparks the psyche into being; the psyche that Jung believed was innately attuned to meaning making if individuation was not prevented by complexes (the nuclear complex) or repression (of the shadow).

The eco-logic of *Nuclear Enchantment* also extends backwards in time as well as across the globe. Connecting in this ABR work is almost as limitless as the capacity of the weapons to destroy. "Sandia Dinosaurs" explores the fascination with extinction that hovers around these beasts while portraying the land of the Sandia Mountains as "a nervous system" with dinosaur-like potential to smash "disjunctive" or disconnected lives. Here the dinosaurs found in the Sandia range are long dead and also very much alive. They shudder the fluid potency of the land already bisected by "Hell's Canyon," and also persist in the reptilian extinction-obsessed mindset of weapons technology.

The paratext points out that children playing with toy dinosaurs may be learning to fixate on extinction, reviving language that has been stunted of meaning by the nuclear cultural complex. Its eco-logic is profound and a source of its protean mutability in the reader. This is eco-logic as cosmological, for it sifts contaminated sand in New Mexico into the immeasurably long history it contains. One key ingredient of the cosmology of this ecopoetry is the use of myth from multicultural sources. The Laguna legend, Isis and Death's Twins have already appeared. Among those also populating *Nuclear Enchantment* are Tewa Creation myth, Hekate, Moloch, Cybele, Pan's pipes, Urania, Kali, Nike/Hercules, Athena and the Furies, and many more.

One mythical conclusion stands out. While Native American cultures have treasured their myths, including those of destruction, the refusal of Western modernity to value its mythic heritage of the underworld and hellish capacities of the psyche is a refusal to face the real meaning of nuclear weapons. *Nuclear Enchantment* is clear that ignoring these myths is to reject stories of who we are, to connect with our own darkness. For example, Hekate, goddess of the dark side of the moon, is evoked in "red ochre moon ... between poles of manufactured beliefs" ("Fusion Reactor").

The note on the moon brings in Hekate as hope for renewal out of this darkness. She reveals the dark psyche in contrast to Apollo, whose tripod appears in the opening "Accidental H-Bomb" as sponsor of the blinding light that burns the retina, an effect of nuclear detonation. Here the paratext records James Hillman's warning that Apollo is too prominent in the Western psyche, providing blinding radiant light. He has been severed from the understanding represented by Hekate.

It is impossible to show all the threads of reference, mutual critique, contrast, juxtaposition, dark humor, idiom, irony that animate the mythical texture of *Nuclear Enchantment.* It is similarly impossible for a single reading to encompass all its mythical threads. That is the point of *Nuclear Enchantment*, to show that more meaning is always to be fathomed; to offer sublime potential for a psyche to hold the unspeakable. On the other hand, Hekate and Apollo offer myths providing a critique of the overwhelming fascination of nuclear fission.

Apollo is the sun god who rides the sky, tempting humans into flight disdainful of the earth, heedless of limitations of the human body. By contrast, dark magical Hekate is repressed in the desire to forget, or not to know, how she sponsors the journey to hell on earth that is nuclear war. If we might know Hekate within what we are and what we do, then, as Weishaus' note on her regenerative potential suggests, we might learn how to benefit from psychic darkness, rather than inflict it on others.

Myth in Jungian arts-based research is the narrative that gives shape to the psyche, simultaneously discovering and re-making its stories. As a way of traversing the liminal realm between known and unknown within, it also pervades culture consciously and unconsciously. *Nuclear Enchantment* shows that nuclear weapons do have buried myths that reveal, as well as the crude use of mystifying euphemisms that conceal.

Part of its achievement is to educate the reader on the willed unknowing of the nuclear complex. Such willed unknowing is psychic, as in the possession by Apollo and repression of Hekate. It is also found in other feminine deities, such as Persephone. For, in "Rocket Lounge" she is dragged down into the underworld, as the bomb threatens to drag humanity into hell.

Yet here myth is not confined to the psyche, because nothing is confined or compartmentalized in this work. Myth regenerates meaning through the project of connecting, re-weaving a cosmos divided by the subject/object split and detonated by its weapons of mass destruction. Unsurprisingly, *Nuclear Enchantment* is full of narratives, often fragmented by the effect of the complex or its repression. Myth is used as a potent narrative of revelation and restoration. So, Rio Lethe, a river of Hades and forgetting, resurfaces to link the contamination flowing on Indian land and suburbia alike ("Laguna Cracked").

What *Nuclear Enchantment* shows in depicting Native American myths is that, unlike that of their non-native neighbors, such myths are a living belief system and a series of practices that embed the people in the land. These stories are not only retold today, but also lived in ritual and ceremony. Very significantly, they include tales of devastation, such as the vomiting giant fish, or stories of the inevitability of death. Their creation myths include humans within an ecosystem, not as masters of it. By living their stories that include devastation, they rehearse the capacities of nature that includes human nature. They know the dark from their myth; Western modernity in repressing myth has become possessed by it.

For example, "Nike/Hercules" is the name of a text and a surface-to-air missile system with a nuclear warhead. Notes from Hillman again record Nike to be a child of the river Styx, or hate. She is the ego gripped by righteous destruction of all that is other in order to maintain her impregnability. Hercules, according to Hillman, is the hero, seeking for a fight to give him identity. Hence Nike/Hercules is a warrior of righteous hate.

> In what have we come to believe?
> A rocket flying like the Holy Ghost,
> a mechanical bird of prey,

Hercules fought the many-headed Hydra, so presaging the MIRVS (Multiple, Independently targetable Reentry Vehicles), or many bombs from one missile, and attempts at mechanical birds were the earliest prototypes of flying machines. Western culture learns something from nature and from myth, but there is a fatal disconnection in the new Holy Ghost of rockets for killing. Nike, now a well-known shoe brand, and Hercules, vaguely known as a strong heroic fighter, serve here more as euphemism than as meaning because the culture of the nuclear complex is one that refers to myth rather than engages with it.

Nuclear Enchantment is analytical arts-based poetic inquiry in a supremely important way because it shows how language is the very material of the nuclear complex in its divorce from the innately regenerative individuating psyche. The nuclear complex degrades life by poisoning the living land and people and by the threat to destroy the planet. To continue to do so, it has to petrify the psyche, turn part of it to stone (from fear) and so words fail to mean because meaning is psychic life.

To combat the nuclear complex, *Nuclear Enchantment* excavates the petrified psyche *and* provides the means of recovery by converting words severed from meaning into signs and symbols. In the end, the entire work is a Jungian symbol that re-weaves the psyche into the many cultures, the diverse capacities represented by gods and myths, into time and into the cosmos.

The rest of this chapter will explore the consequences of *Nuclear Enchantment* dis-enchanting us from just what nuclear weapons are and how we can survive making them. For *Nuclear Enchantment* is research no longer irrationally possessed by the subject/object split that fostered such weapons in the first place.

Nuclear Enchantment as synthetic arts-based research

The transdisciplinary chalice of being

Synthetic ABR brings together different discourses, each made up of the language and practices of specific ways of knowing and being. Art splicing and recombining such discourses is *research* because the individuality of the artwork suggests new potentials within knowing and being. Put another way, synthetic ABR is intrinsically transdisciplinary in the broadest sense because it threads conventionally separated areas of research into a new whole that amounts to more than the sum of its parts (Nicolescu 2014).

In this sense, *Nuclear Enchantment* is an excellent example of synthetic arts-based research. As already shown, its form makes visible conventions separating disciplines as well as providing radical, protean recombinations of such discourses as nuclear technology, myths from many cultures and discourses of geology, economics, ecopoetics, idiomatic colloquialism, local government and much more.

However, *Nuclear Enchantment* can also be viewed as synthetic ABR in the lens of the transdisciplinarity developed by Basarab Nicolescu and introduced earlier in this book. In dethroning the presumed supremacy of the subject/object split in knowledge, Nicolescu points to two major resources of human understanding, one celebrated by Western modernity, the other largely ignored. These are what he calls the classical science of the subject/object split, regarded as so foundational that it has colonized all sorts of disciplines and cultural practices, and what he calls Tradition, the heritage of learning from religions, mythologies, somatic and shamanic practices and found in all cultures on the planet. Western modernity has disowned Tradition to its own detriment, not least because new sciences of the quantum domain sound more like Tradition than they do so-called "objectivity."

Nicolescu does not emphasize that one important source of Tradition is the arts, which cling to the notion of the individual work as immanent and meaningful. *Nuclear Enchantment* is therefore a transdisciplinary work that bridges the classical science that birthed the Bomb, and Tradition in the multiple sources of myth, religion and cultural practices also included in the prose poetry. In subject/object terms, the classical science of the Bomb is revealed as building something regarded as an object to destroy other objects (people) rather than a meaningful aspect of the subject, the culture making it. Hence the work of *Nuclear Enchantment* is transdisciplinary in revealing the cardinal error of separating science and Tradition, and also by remedying that mistake. Moreover, it is transdisciplinary in a further sense of removing disciplinary hierarchy.

Transdisciplinarity is a vision of learning as an interconnected living web, always growing, never complete. It accepts mystery and the sacred as intrinsic to knowledge for much the same reason as Jung did, because some knowing is beyond rational comprehension and the living mystery of the psyche means that humans need to go on making new ideas and connections. So too *Nuclear Enchantment* is multidimensional, radically incomplete and invites the reader to make something new with every reading.

In this way, *Nuclear Enchantment* embraces a further characteristic of Nicolescu's transdisciplinarity: the necessity of writing in symbols as Jung defined them. In fact, the poems expose what Nicolescu argued about the literal language used by the disciplines devoted to so-called objectivity, that such literalism degrades meaning, whereas symbols revivify meaning. Where the researcher is split off from the research, words are supposed to cement this split by repressing any "other" connotations. Words too become objects to be manipulated rather than malleable vehicles for a plural living psyche.

By synthesizing discourses, *Nuclear Enchantment* evokes symbols to restore the psyche. Here the work exemplifies Nicolescu's call for imagination as an integral part of all knowing.

> The imaginary and the real complement each other *in a fruitful contradictory relationship*, revealing a deeper reality than that available to the sense organs.
>
> (Nicolescu 2014: 179)

That deeper reality is of the knowing available to Tradition, in the body, esoteric practices, in myth, etc. Imagination in Jungian arts-based research is a release of images to become part of Nicolescu's living web of disciplines. These include all the researches covered by Tradition, such as the traditions of art in poetry.

Finally, on synthetic ABR as transdisciplinary in *Nuclear Enchantment*, it is worth noting how the three axioms discussed in Chapter 2 are structurally present. The ontological axiom of multiple levels of reality, some invisible, is apparent in the weaving of Tradition and the dominant scientific paradigm. The logical axiom that the subject/object split is traversed by the logic of the included middle is performed by *Nuclear Enchantment* in the symbols and mythical narratives that animate the reading psyche.

The huge irony that underpins both *Nuclear Enchantment* and its subject, nuclear weapons, is that the weapons themselves eradicate the dangerously overhyped paradigm of objectivity. Nothing can be insulated from even a "local" nuclear war. While objectivity is not always a mistake as a means of making some kinds of knowledge, the mistake is in its monotheistic supremacy that has resulted in the nuclear complex. Push the separation too far and it will detonate. A far more comprehensive and viable model of knowing and being is to be found in the third axiom, that of complexity.

Complexity theory posits reality as a web of mutually involved complex adaptive systems (CAS). In transdisciplinarity, complexity pertains to academic disciplines as well. *Nuclear Enchantment* performs such complexity.

> Tall, slim, Urania is the muse of astronomy and the renaissance of poetry
> programmed to travel a self-correcting course; while Kali wears skulls as
> a necklace, earrings of bodies immutably hung, a girdle of severed hands,
> and blood the color of her stunning eyes.
> In a vision of militant technology, BOMARC scars the separate visions we
> have of each other, with a MACE like a Viking's hatchet, or a spiked ball
> and chain.
>
> ("Atomic Muse")

Here is a complex recombination that points to the complexity rather than obscuring it. It spans the Greek goddess whose name was given to uranium; the far more ferocious Hindu goddess Kali, the BOMARC pilotless fighter that in 1960 scattered weapons grade plutonium in New Jersey; and the MACE upgraded Matador missile. Such recombining poetry is not just about overcoming the false splitting off from the reality of nuclear weapons. It activates being in knowing by showing the cultural, geographic, economic and catastrophic interconnections of this technology. Calling uranium after the muse of studying distant stars versus the more apt Kali reveals the complexity systems of language and culture at work in shaping technology and vice versa.

Further examples of complexity in the woven chalice that is *Nuclear Enchantment* will be explored later. For more consideration of the synthetic ABR nature of the work, I want to look at some examples that are fundamentally critical of, and seek to unravel, the nuclear weapons psychic complex. These are the aesthetics of the bomb, the effects of contracting and expanding history, colonization and the discourse of ecocritical poetics.

Synthesizing aesthetics, history, colonization and ecology

As mentioned previously, the making of nuclear weapons is predicated on the subject/object split, which is not only about repressing the consequences of weapon use but also splitting off part of the psyche that might independently resist the rationalized work. In *Nuclear Enchantment* the aesthetics provided by the Bomb is divided between a mystifying naturalism and a fantasy cleanliness of laboratories and welcoming museums.

We have already encountered the sidewinders, snakeyes and broken arrows of false naturalism. *Nuclear Enchantment* does not indulge the clean white labs of the cultural complex of the cultivation destruction. While nuclear technology boasts sterile laboratories, *Nuclear Enchantment* records some of the actual incidents of contamination in those labs and victims "[s]anitized of hair" in "Atomic Muse." Furthermore, this synthetic ABR reveals a second, more apt nuclear aesthetics in the nuclear repression of meaning. This could be understood as a grotesque Gothic aesthetics (Botting 1990).

Gothic is a movement dedicated to uncovering what has been concealed or forgotten in modernity in the irrational exaltation of reason and consequent splitting off from the other. Hence Gothic violates conventional boundaries that kept rational meanings secure. Typical boundaries broken in Gothic writing include those between life and death, culture and nature, reason and madness and, of course, subject and object. Erupting in eighteenth-century novels of ghosts, tyrants and pacts with the devil, Gothic bred Mary Shelley's 1816 novel, *Frankenstein or the Modern Prometheus*. This work introduced the modern specter of the scientist who goes too far and conceives a monster he cannot control. It goes without saying that the creature made out of dead bodies and electricity resembles a nuclear holocaust victim.

Typically, Gothic in *Nuclear Enchantment* is "Bat Cave" where actual weapons projects are given the context of their historical antecedents in cruelty. Today is not the first time when culture was prepared to inflict suffering without empathy.

> A shadowy nation hangs upside down, mothers folding infants clinging
> with hooked thumbs ...
> Comic masks conform to facts that can't be faced: an aviator's fingers
>   poised with brutally ancient intent ...
> Prey is devoured –
> even as memories dawn
> of ancestors crucified
> on civilized doors.
>
> ("Bat Cave")

"Ancestors crucified on civilized doors" crosses the dividing of Western culture between animal and human, the profane and the sacred. The reference to Christ in "crucified" also recalls the dismembering of Dionysus in the lack of human/animal differentiation. Here *Nuclear Enchantment* Gothically associates Christian and pagan bodily dismembering. The aviator's fingers about to release an atom bomb are supposed to be like the bats with bombs, merely a machine for killing. Here the Gothic monstrosity of nuclear weapons is alluded to because by repressing the horror of these machines, we become these machines. The supposed boundary between machine and human is eliminated, making us into posthuman Frankensteins.

Here, also, "the shadowy nation" does, like the crucified St. Peter, hang upside down, caught in a Gothic aesthetics of desire and repression.

Discourses of contracting and expanding history

History is intimate and visceral in *Nuclear Enchantment.* And it is immeasurably vast in going way beyond the tiny moment of humanity. It is intimate, for example, in the thread of children, from the little mounds of burials, to children hiding under desks in Goddard High to practice futile sheltering from nuclear bombs, to the *hibakusha* children of Japan who survived the immediate impact of the weapons only to suffer cancers and lingering death. (For example, see "Wings over Trinity.")

Alongside such bitter ironies in meager scraps of the historical record are the counter-perspectives of geologic time. New Mexico has prehistoric roads, such as those fanning out from Chaco Canyon, that were suddenly abandoned, testifying to civilizations lost in eons of time.

Yet the intimate and vast discourses of time and history collide in nuclear hubris.

> As seen from a distance, history is …
> … corridors braced with six million cubic feet of noxious debris.
> Here someday will be unearthed
> the deadly remains of a civilization
> that sacrificed future generations to
> the radiant God of unlimited Power.
>
> ("Waste Isolation")

Built to last at least 10,000 years, the Waste Isolation Pilot Plant opened in 1999 only to begin failing in just fifteen. Just as synthetic arts-based research combines discourses, so nuclear waste itself resists isolation. It leaks and contaminates. The poison is psychological as well as physical; the repressed nuclear complex poisons the collective. Weapons of mass destruction are deadly offerings to the unappeasable desire for unlimited power over the other, a desire that poisons body and psyche.

Perhaps equally revealing is the way *Nuclear Enchantment* shows New Mexico itself as a history text. The land is inscribed by peoples and their stories as well as geologic events. Those prehistoric roads of vanished cultures traversed by brutal Spanish conquistadors, only to be followed centuries later by PhDs eager to work on a hellish bomb. All humanity is descended from Paleolithic hunters; indigenous people and invaders cannot be wholly divided from each other in ancestry and impulses. The paratext of "LAMPF" suggests that the terrifying violence humans are capable of today stems from spending the longest period of our evolution as hunters, to which our DNA is still tuned. On the other hand, the joining of shards of discourses in *Nuclear Enchantment* does not wipe out the sharp colonial contrasts, another theme of this synthetic work.

De/Colonization

The impact of nuclear weapons on three communities is explored in *Nuclear Enchantment*: the American inventors of the self-inflicted nuclear complex, the Japanese people who suffered two atomic bombings and the Native American peoples of New Mexico whose land was polluted by mining and its wastes. Also present are what's absent. The Chaco ruins are a potent reminder of how timely cultural extinction is. History and colonization overlap with the brutal invasion of the conquistadors, followed by the deceptively discreet and sudden arrival to northern New Mexico of the nuclear industrial complex.

Nuclear Enchantment explores the technology of the Bomb as a layer of colonization. For example, "Homestake Mining" explains that a sacred mountain of the Navajo holds "the nation's largest single deposit of high-grade uranium ore."

> Twenty million tons of uranium mill tailings piled 100 ft. high is looked down to by the image of a man hung between worlds, announcing the arrival of Death's twins –

Death's Twins are indigenous myth made horribly tangible in the toxic waste of the euphemistically named Homestake Mining Company. The paratext records that, after starting operations in in 1958, the milling of uranium here contaminated 245 acres and the groundwater "in the San Mateo alluvium and the upper Chinle aquifer," with names conveying layers of colonial imposition from Spanish to Anglo-American. Again, native cultures have myths to bring such horrors as mass death into consciousness. Yet in the same text the resemblance of the weapons to the dismembering and re-membering of Isis and Osiris is repressed in the culture of the Bomb.

Here *Nuclear Enchantment*, by synthesizing discourses of many communities with unequal power, is an act of de-colonization. It de-colonizes by stripping away the willed unconsciousness of the nuclear complex to expose the myths and fantasies simultaneously enacted and repressed. This is de-colonization in several levels. There is the re-membering of history in the bringing together of records of death and contamination, whether of thousands of Japanese, or a single child dying in a hospital, or the toxic land of local communities breeding cancers.

Then there is the de-colonization by bringing back awareness of the successive invasive cultures of New Mexico by supplying stories, myths and the sacred to eat through the euphemistic mystifying of the deadly weapons. Finally, there is the psychic de-colonization. *Nuclear Enchantment* digs out the nuclear complex of our collective world by synthesizing discourses, by rejoining what has been severed. It de-colonizes because this synthesizing of discourses restores meaning and makes new meaning from the lifting of repressive colonial power inside and outside the psyche.

"One bite of an apple may embody all the symbols of consciousness," so says Weishaus in "Manzano," an allusion to one of the many myths ignored by the nuclear complex that links imperfect knowledge to disastrous action. Eve eating the apple and encouraging Adam to do so becomes mountains emerging from fire, the Manzanos, just outside the city of Albuquerque, that ironically store weapons "as if apples ready to be baked and burned to their core." The paratext here records a witness to the nuclear detonation of Nagasaki that left the city looking like a baked apple. Manzano is also a type of apple grown in the enchanted land of New Mexico.

Discourses of myths of consciousness in Eden, the land of the Manzano Mountains, and the horror of a burned city the other side of the world are synthesized in meaning that is both tangible and sublime. It is sublime because we cannot truly imagine the horror of thousands of lives that expired in a moment. Bringing the context of Eve and Adam's apple into this devastating act of disconnection, or the colonial imposition of death, shows the reader that the destruction of Nagasaki belongs to those who claim the myth of Eden while also forgetting it. In synthesizing discourses, *Nuclear Enchantment* detonates the nuclear complex, because it demonstrates that the responsibility for these weapons belong to us and to our myths.

Ecocriticism

When considering *Nuclear Enchantment* as analytic ABR, the ecopoetics of the work was considered as the exploration of words in poetic inquiry. So here as a synthetic work of ABR it is worth noting that the poetics of *Nuclear Enchantment* provides a unique ecocriticism. Whereas the term "ecocriticism" covers a whole range of literary works and scholarship that challenge Western assumptions that downgrade, ignore or repress the natural world, the ecocriticism of synthesizing *Nuclear Enchantment* is particularly specific.

The yew tree of death becomes a yew green child. Dunes are militarized, the Sandia Mountains harbor dinosaurs that act out extinction fantasies, sparrows make suicidal nests in missiles, bats are made into bombs and it was hoped to use cockroaches to identify spies. The ecology of *Nuclear Enchantment* is where the discourses of nature and the nuclear complex collide to frustrate, ironize and re-make meaning in a raw mode. By raw I mean the unsentimental and lucid language of perversions and cruelties done *to* nature in recruiting bats as bombs, for example, that are additionally revealed as assaults on/with human nature.

The ecocriticism of *Nuclear Enchantment* reconnects human to nonhuman in ways that locate savagery in the human. Euphemistic disconnection from nature erupts in terms like "collateral damage," or "environmental adjustment" to signify total annihilation of life ("Mortandad Canyon"). "Lilith's ionized wings screech," as Lilith is a screech owl in a Hebrew prophecy of Yahweh's overwhelming vengeance. Lilith's wild heart beats in parallel with computers programmed to set off nuclear missiles. Here the ironizing discourse of *Nuclear Enchantment* is particularly bitter. Ecocriticism in this work is a synthesizing of the ironic disjunction between humans and nature, including human nature. It exposes the nuclear complex as a concentrated version of modernity's long war on nature and/as itself. Such focused and searching eco-criticism leads to the third type of ABR by its critical *action* in treating the nuclear complex.

Nuclear Enchantment as critical-activist arts-based research

Like Jung's *The Red Book* (Chapter 4 of this book), *Nuclear Enchantment* is not the kind of critical-activist ABR that paints murals on bombs, or plants a garden to reveal contaminated land. Also like *The Red Book*, I contend that critical-activism is a useful lens from a research perspective. After all, activism, even if narrowly defined as physical actions of intervention, requires knowledge. In fact, critical-activist ABR of any kind requires the exploration into materials of analytic ABR and the revelation of discourses in synthetic ABR.

So it is not surprising to see the overlaps building between these three categories when applied to the same work. In particular it is not surprising because *Nuclear Enchantment* is itself *active*. It activates and animates the psyche by re-weaving threads of knowing and being into the interconnected web that is trans-disciplinary. *Nuclear Enchantment* is a critical-activist poetic inquiry because it treats the American nuclear complex by reversing the repression of what nuclear weapons do. *Nuclear Enchantment* actively reconnects what has been most split off. It does so in four key areas: colliding communities, war, the activism of re-membering and above all, by disenchanting nuclear New Mexico.

Critical-activism in communities, about war and for re-membering

As a synthetic work of ABR, *Nuclear Enchantment* shows that nuclear technology continues political colonization and despoliation. Yet there is irony in the mention of a New Mexico river as Lethe, a river in the underworld signifying forgetting. For the nuclear complex obscures the understanding that it is not just Native Americans whose homes are poisoned.

> It is the witching hour, when Death jumps through hoops....
> the Rio Lethe systematically contaminating
> dusty Indian reservations, suburban watered lawns too.
> ("Laguna Cracked")

Communities collide like atoms when the Bomb is dropped on Japan. One culture also exploits the other in making the weapons on land tended by indigenous peoples. As part of that exploitation there is tremendous denial. It amounts to a willed dissociation of the psyche, a Lethe-like forgetting of the violence being manufactured. After all, Lethe flows in the underworld that is the psyche's collective unconscious.

Here two systems of myth meet without communicating. To Native Americans, witches die in dust storms, and jumping through hoops is for shapeshifting. These cultures nurture their stories of transformation and malice as a way of guarding against evil they might otherwise be unaware of. By contrast, the American nuclear complex includes forgetting its own myths that hide in dark and dangerous parts of the psyche.

Of course, communities collide most terribly in war. "Bradbury Museum" is a benign title for a text that collects the effects of nuclear weapons in the war with Japan. The thread of children is the most poignant and unbearable in *Nuclear Enchantment.* From children hiding under desks making "frail bony helmets" of fingers, to later in "Goddard High," we learn also that "the father of American rocketry," Robert Goddard, only got funding when war suggested a military use for his research. The children in Goddard High school are immeasurably more fortunate than the *hibakusha* children slowly dying from cancer in Japan. The fact that American children are crouching under a desk that will not protect them is evident throughout *Nuclear Enchantment.*

The paratext of "Bradbury Museum" gives a horrifying perspective on "Mother of Necessity." Throughout *Nuclear Enchantment*, mother stands for various divinities, including devouring mothers like Cybele and Nike. As mentioned earlier, James Hillman is quoted asserting that Nike's destruction is that of the righteous ego that must kill because it cannot bear anything that is other to itself. Inevitably, Nike/Hercules is also a nuclear weapon. Returning to "Mother of Necessity," we are told that this parent is the nuclear doctrine of Necessity that refers to third powers requiring weapons to "protect" against the mutual assured destruction (MAD) of the principal nuclear states.

Western modernity surrounds its reversion to the dark side of the mother archetype with the willed ignorance of unconsciousness in the nuclear complex. "University Reactor" exposes the war narrative woven into the other end of education from "Goddard High." Possessing a nuclear reactor since 1966, "superheated words" at the University of New Mexico have no experience teaching extinction. Here the nuclear reaction was demonstrated through ping pong balls on a table, just as if students were playing in a game in a lounge.

> Students highlighted calculations, the hard bodies of urchins modeled on masculine ideals …
>
> ("University Reactor")

War is constructed in the language of masculine heroism, mythically in Hercules, and pedagogically in calculating urchins, which are neutron sources for atomic weapons. Urchins are also unruly children, here to be disciplined into weapons of death. What results from the nuclear complex is not masculinity as a gender acknowledging others. After all, the divine figures (world destroying) of the Bomb are devoted to forgetting that they are one of many, and even that they are psychological. Nuclear war is so sublimely unthinkable that it severs a denatured psyche from unconscious archetypes. Rather, what emerges from the nuclear complex is a hypermasculinity toxic even to itself.

In "Trinity Site," "tongues of wires would be snaked like Medusa's hair growing from a doomsday device," and this new Medusa still freezes the hypermasculine nuclear war complex. Horrifyingly, the paratext records that on the explosion of the first atomic bomb at Trinity Site at 5.30 a.m. July 16th, 1945, physicist Enrico Fermi made a bet on whether it would set the air on fire; and if it did, would the conflagration encompass New Mexico or the entire planet? The bomb at this moment is Medusa, a gorgon, or winged female with snakes for hair who petrified, turned to stone, anyone who looked on her.

"Trinity Site" continues with the challenge to Dr. Robert Oppenheimer, the project director, to name it. Rather than recognize a polytheistic psyche of multiple capacities for love and hate, the physicist quotes seventeenth-century poet John Donne on the monotheistic "three-person'd God" at his most violent.

> *Batter my heart three-person'd God ...*
> *That I may rise, and stand, o'erthrow me, and bend*
> *Your force, to break, blow, burn, and make me new.*

Hence Trinity Site is to Oppenheimer the place of the three-personed God whose violence is *invited* by the poet as creation of being. There is a brutal irony of the "three-person'd" deity collapsed into literalness and singleness of meaning in the culture of the Bomb. Here too is the core of the nuclear war complex, the fantasy that extreme violence by itself is creation. It is a hypermasculine fantasy because it valorizes a single God as having no other, no nurturing feminine and no dark side. C. G. Jung recognized this fantasy as perilous and germane to nuclear weapons, as we will see later.

Of course *Nuclear Enchantment* as a whole is a critical-activist demystifying treatment of the war complex by re-membering, putting back what has been denied or lost, or forgotten. In this the work of arts-based research meets Jung in his encounter with Native Americans at Taos, New Mexico.

Critical-activist re-membering

As analytic and synthetic ABR, *Nuclear Enchantment* remembers how nuclear weapons technology got where it is today. The work includes detailed historical research that ranges from the eighteenth-century discovery of uranium to the experiments of the Curies that led to their deaths from radioactivity, to the bomb in New Mexico, its contaminating presence, its use in Japan and feverish spawning of ever more powerful missiles. However, as this chapter has shown, *Nuclear Enchantment* does far more than provide historical details. Rather, text and paratext connect to what the discourse of the cultural complex of weapons represses: the land, its diverse communities and a human psyche alienated from its own trackless nature.

Nuclear Enchantment re-members what has been repressed in the ignoring of indigenous communities, and of the suffering already inflected in Japan. It summons what has been unknown in the living being of the land, and what has been forgotten in the mythologies of the past that know of the capacity for unlimited hate, for endless violence. In "Missile Park," a pilgrim from Europe in the nineteenth century who lived as a hermit in New Mexico hears Pan's pipes. "[H]is fading world" is gone as Tewa sacred clowns dance like gods liberated from all fears "in the glaring light of a rocket's last stand."

While indigenous peoples embrace rituals and beliefs that expose extremes and contradictions, Christianity "unmasked" the ritual dancers. In fact, their masks revealed, rather than concealed, psychic wholeness. In this way, *Nuclear Enchantment* draws together in poetic inquiry a web of knowing and being out of a long history of violent severing. It re-members in a truly Dionysian mode what the forgetting of its own potential for evil by Western culture has dismembered. As discussed in Chapter 3 of this book, those who do not worship Dionysus perish by him. Rituals to honor a polytheistic psyche save society from blindly acting out dismembering fantasies; such acting out is possession by the archetype. The collective madness of nuclear weapons is an example of such possession.

Acknowledging Dionysus must be done collectively (Paris 1998). It means re-membering the body of the god that has been torn apart by repression, forgetting and the refusal to know and love other cultures, and the land. Therefore, *Nuclear Enchantment* is a critical-activist Dionysian rite. Reading it re-members us. Reading it treats the nuclear complex. Perhaps the most overt act of re-membering comes with the eagle in "United Nuclear," a bird sacred to many communities.

> The Black Eagle builds his nest in the Tree of Life,
> where even designers, makers and planners
> of nuclear weapons and wars
> may be healed.

The paratexts tells of a Navajo myth in which at night, eagles remove their feathers to reveal human forms in white suits, a vision uncannily able to morph into nuclear technicians. We learn also that Siberian nomads believe that the first shaman was born from a woman and an eagle, and that the black eagle in European alchemy was a synonym for the devil, according to Jung. In re-membering the psyche that produced nuclear weapons out of splitting, and is now split by the capacity to destroy the planet, *Nuclear Enchantment* is ABR as psychic and historical activism.

Fascinatingly, such activism of re-membering the psyche is anticipated by Jung's encounter with the Taos Pueblo chief, Mountain Lake (Jung 1963/1983: 280). Jung observes a ritual of prayer to help the sun rise, or so he is told. Without such rituals, the world would end. Jung does not understand that the people most in need of such a ritual are his own. Yet he does experience an image of white so-called civilization, the Aryan bird of prey, the eagle in its most vicious form. In an image later taken up by *Nuclear Enchantment*, Jung says: "[a]ll the eagles ... that adorn our coats of arms seem to me ... our true nature" (Jung 1963/1983: 277).

Ultimately, *Nuclear Enchantment* validates arts-based research as Dionysian re-membering. It does so because the public nature of art, its ability to have a life and being beyond the artist, gives it the necessary collective ritual quality. A final consideration of this work as critical-activist ABR should, of course, look at its title. With an early version completed fifteen years before Lee Bailey's book, *The Enchantments of Technology* (2005), discussed in Chapter 2, *The Nuclear Enchantment of New Mexico* pioneers a prescient mode of research as a vehicle for transformation.

Dis/Enchanting technology as nuclear weapons: Weishaus and C. G. Jung

Enchantment in *The Enchantments of Technology* pivots on Bailey's argument that the subject/object split, once a useful device in approaching the world, has become a mesmerizing fetish perverting modernity. In particular, the hegemony of the subject/object split in making knowledge has distorted culture in the matter of technology. In origin, Greek *techne* is allied to art and craft. Yet modern technology exists wholly in the fantasy that subjectivity is corralled in the human body facing a reality of discrete objects. In fact, as Jung came to see, the subject or psyche is not restricted to the body, as Bailey shows.

> The subject seems like a tight container but when we descend into the depths of the soul and the world, we find the notion of subjectivity to be bottomless. All the passions and images that the theory of projection attempts to separate into the objective psyche flow from endless mysterious, bottomless depths of existence itself, more primordial than the subject/object divide and its mechanical models.
>
> (Bailey 2005: 82)

The delusion about the psyche as entirely separated from any other is repeated in the fantasy that technology is merely a manipulation of objects. Such a fantasy is an enchantment because it seals up the psyche in unconsciousness. Technology is *the result and source* of this modern enchantment. Modernity is stuck in unconsciousness of the dangerous fantasies and myths propagated by such technology as guns, airplanes and space travel (Bailey 2005). Guns result from an outlook that is called "objective" and actually treats reality as objects to be subdued. With the enchanting pretense that technology is inert, fully under the control of a rational human subject, technology increases unaware-ness while perilous fantasies are hidden in plain sight.

What Bailey does not say is that the enchantments of technology he diagnoses are what Jungians Sam Kimbles and Tom Singer call "cultural complexes," after Jung's complexes (Singer and Kimbles 2004). Enchantment via technology is active in proliferating irrationality and autonomous unconsciousness concealing the bottomless subject to Bailey. Cultural complexes are active nodes of arche-typal (so potentially overwhelming) energy surrounding collective issues that seduce the rational psyche into fracturing and fantasies. Jung coined complexes to account for psychic fracturing when individual aspects of the psyche, such as actual parents, become archetypally possessed. In the language of Singer and Kimbles, Bailey's gun enchantment is a cultural complex.

Of course the very title of *The Nuclear Enchantment of New Mexico* unites the notion of a cultural complex with such enchantments. Nuclear weapons of world annihilation are a supreme example of enchanting in Bailey's sense. For such weapons imprison the psyche in the delusion that what they can do is not a psychic dimension of who we are. Through its arts-based research *Nuclear Enchantment* restores such technology to its ancient roots in arts and crafts. By doing so, it individuates, in a Jungian sense, the nuclear cultural complex; it unlocks the enchantment.

> Each inch of earth is a threshold,
> another step,
> another dream.
> ("Nike/Hercules")

Bringing back the enchantment of nuclear technology to art, here poetic inquiry *matters* because art is inspired or in-spirited matter. Art dis/enchants; that is, it explores, invites, shapes and invokes a conscious relation to enchantment, or the divine potencies of unconscious archetypes. Art, and in particular ABR, is disen-chanting because it individuates, makes a relationship between conscious and unconscious psychic energies. Psychotherapy also individuates. But art is a more collective mode of individuation. It follows that arts-based research, with its links to academic research paradigms, is a more collective mode of disenchantment from powerful delusions or autonomous cultural complexes.

Nuclear Enchantment is, therefore, an important model for arts-based research, tackling the most pernicious cultural complexes or technological enchantments. It shows that art disenchants by deconstructing enchantment, while not denying the magical and divine in the psyche. Deconstructing enchantment means stripping away its unconsciousness to reveal the archetypal myths that have been denied in the fantasy of making missiles of mass murder as neutral objects. It is being critical in a way that is both active and creative. Here *Nuclear Enchantment* as critical-activist ABR *holds* the terrible capacities incarnate in the weapons by revealing them to be mythological, to be *ours*.

Also, *Nuclear Enchantment* continues to deconstruct paralyzing enchantment by weaving a new web of being between New Mexico's earth, space and time, and the planetary tendrils of the nuclear project. In this way too *Nuclear Enchantment* is a chalice of arts-based research as psychic and social trans-formation, so that we might not "sacrifice[d] future generations to/the Radiant God of Unlimited Power" ("Waste Isolation").

Fascinatingly, *Nuclear Enchantment* unwittingly builds on Jung's own treatment of nuclear weapons technology. Without articulating the problem in the way Bailey does, Jung condemns the fantasy that psyche and weapons are somehow part of an absolute subject/object division.

> They believe only in physical facts, and must consequently come to the conclusion that either the uranium itself or the laboratory equipment created the atom bomb.
>
> (Jung 1952: para. 751)

On the bomb itself, Jung calls for something very like *Nuclear Enchantment* in coming to terms with the dark divine powers in the modern Western psyche.

> This involves man in a new responsibility ... for the dark God has slipped the atom bomb and chemical weapons into his hands and given him the power to empty out the apocalyptic vials of wrath ... he can no longer remain blind and unconscious.
>
> (Jung 1952: para. 747)

Of course, Jung omits what is also necessary to the twenty-first-century project of dis/enchantment: the voices of multiple others, such as in the indigenous communities, the suffering victims across the world and the land of New Mexico itself. However, in a real sense, *Nuclear Enchantment* continues Jung's research and treatment, leading to the fourth category of arts-based research, improvisatory.

Nuclear Enchantment as improvisatory arts-based research

At first glance, *Nuclear Enchantment* appears resistant to the free flow of improvisation given its form. The work is divided between the fluidity of the poetry and paratexts from academic, historical and cultural sources that are both inside and outside. Surely improvisatory ABR eschews disciplinary conventions? On the other hand, the most theorized variety of improvisatory ABR, a/r/tography, is capable of embracing dynamism that lingers within more traditional research. Pioneers Rita Irwin et al. describe evoking a flowing dimension within, and despite, the formal qualities of research, as shown in Chapter 2 of this book.

> [A/r/tography] is a dynamic force that is forever becoming entangled in the materiality of all things, human and nonhuman. To do so, it embraces the practices of artists, researchers and teachers/learners as a way to linger in this entanglement and to pursue the practice of living one's inquiry.
>
> (Irwin et al. 2018: 37)

I suggest that this summation of a/r/tography fits *Nuclear Enchantment*, which is dedicated to living the inquiry into the nuclear weapons complex and its roots in New Mexico. *Nuclear Enchantment* is a/r/tography in the entanglement it enacts between the improvisatory prose poetry and the traditional articulation of research in the paratexts. This is not to suggest that the poetry is simply improvised, but rather that it expresses the spontaneity of the psyche.

Irwin et al. describe the "living practice" of a/r/tography as not about discovery, because such a perception is a stepping back from reality, a trace of the subject/object split. Living inquiry, or a/r/tography, knows it is participating in what transdisciplinarity calls "the hidden third" between subject and object, abolishing their division (Nicolescu 2014: 117–19). It is by living the inquiry that a/r/tography constructs a new vitality (Irwin et al. 2018: 37–8).

Such a notion points to how *Nuclear Enchantment* treats the nuclear complex by its multiple entangling of poetry and research. The result is a partial lifting of the complex and a new vitality through the chalice of knowing and being that it offers the reader. True to a/r/tography, meaning in *Nuclear Enchantment* varies with every reading; it bristles with sparks of possible significances because of the a/r/tographical invoking of so many sources, cultures, myths, disciplines, historical moments, etc.

Therefore, as well as improvisation being part of the making of the poetry, it also liberates improvisatory qualities in reading, re-making the soul by a major source of modern dis/ease. It is an a/r/tographical work of multicultural and multidimensional entanglement. More insight into how this works can be gained from considering how improvisatory poetry focused on an autonomous cultural complex might connect with complexity theory.

Improvising complexes and complexity theory in *Nuclear Enchantment*

Related to transdisciplinarity, complexity theory suggests that reality, human and nonhuman, operates in a series of interweaving, mutually transmuting

CAS. Transdisciplinarity sees complexity as innate to what is, and posits that knowledge disciplines are also CAS wanting to creatively evolve.

Helene Shulman opened the door between complexity theory, stemming from computer science, and Jungian psychology in *Living at the Edge of Chaos* (1997). Just as nature evolves via the intersection of complex adaptive ecosystems, so do human groups, as well as our bodies and psyches.

> The conditions for complex systems arise spontaneously in the natural world anywhere that interconnected networks of multiple agents act in parallel. Under certain very specific circumstances of connectivity, these networks begin to generate autocatalytic structures, that is, growing creative patterns that have the capacity to reproduce themselves and adapt to changing conditions through feed forward models and feedback. They are able to make use of energy sources in their environment to sustain themselves as well as to grow and develop, so they do not move toward a state of entropy. Many natural phenomena can be modelled as complex systems: ant colonies, flocks of birds, molecules, DNA, immune systems, brains, cells, eco-logical niches, social systems, economies, or scientific communities. In complex systems, nothing is fixed, but all the agents are reaching to each other's actions in a constantly changing landscape.
>
> (Shulman 1997: 110)

Putting these ideas alongside *Nuclear Enchantment* offers two possibilities. Firstly, that the autonomous cultural complex of nuclear weapons poisons such a reality. Put another way, the *enchantment* depicted by Weishaus and theorized by Bailey petrifies the psyche to such an extent that nuclear weapons become locked off from the innate properties of complexity to change and grow as systems encounter each other. Secondly, I propose that *Nuclear Enchantment* is the antidote to the poison of the autonomous nuclear complex. The complex is poisonous because it is *autonomous* and resistant to, though not impermeable to, creative webs that might open it to the recuperative qualities of multiple CAS of culture and nature.

Computer scientist John Holland described seven characteristics of complexity, as follows (Holland 1994: 3–4). Found in culture as well as nature, CAS members have high capacity to function as a group, and such groups are non-linear, meaning that straightforward causes do not produce straightforward results. CAS are not determined by past events and so chance and creativity are possible. Fascinatingly, resources encountered through complexity will enliven a whole system: one change affects all. Complex systems are diverse and can learn from adjoining systems. They privilege certain patterns by tags or emblems, so possessing some sort of meaning-making capacity. Lastly, CAS will make internal models of the world.

Not mentioned in most sources on complexity theory is Nicolescu's argument that academic disciplines work in these ways, or will in the embrace of transdisciplinarity (Nicolescu 2014). Not fully explored by him is the resemblance of CAS to the arts, both the large contested category, "art," and as individual genres, subgenres, forms, down to the individual work. Language can be mapped as a CAS; so too can the languages of the arts, or any mode of creativity.

It is in this context that *Nuclear Enchantment* reveals itself as a CAS, in its non-linearity and multiple pathways towards meaning. *Nuclear Enchantment* is a CAS dedicated to exposing nuclear poisoning (because, generating heat, nuclear seals eventually leak!), to the transdisciplinary CAS of culture, history and nature. Like any CAS, *Nuclear Enchantment* models its world (the world of the nuclear complex) and, very importantly, is powerfully creative enough to *treat* it by also modeling the transdisciplinary web of inter-creative realities. For example, "Nuclear Sushi Museum" begins and ends with dragons.

> The taste that surfaced on Tibbet's tongue nine years later was deadly
> to a Lucky Dragon swallowing fish whose eyes cried poisoned tears ...
> Heaven cooks with thermonuclear heat, sautéing St. George's dragon
> and fried rice served with the soul of sailor and eyes of skeletal fish.

The work is a living CAS that changes with every reading, even while its complexity changes the reader's mind. However, the paratexts perhaps serve as the privileging patterns that Holland spoke of. *The Lucky Dragon* was an unfortunate Japanese trawler caught up in the Bikini Atoll nuclear tests. All the crew suffered radiation sickness; one died.

Ironically, dragons are thought to be a lucky omen in China and Japan.

A further irony was inflicted on the Utah town of St. George, where a nuclear accident caused massive fallout of radiation on the town. St. George defeated *his* dragon in legend to become the patron saint of England. "Fried rice" and "skeletal fish" refer to the destruction of Hiroshima. There, the paratext tells, someone saw the bomb blowing off the clothes from a Professor Takenaka, leaving him holding only a rice ball, which looked like "a symbol of the modest hope of human beings" ("Nuclear Sushi Museum").

From the taste of lead on a tongue, to the taste of fried rice anticipated by a victim whose nakedness emphasizes human vulnerability, *Nuclear Enchantment* is fired by the enlivening possibilities of CAS and transdisciplinarity. It is improvisatory arts-based research caught up in the webs of history, culture, politics and nature. It shows complexity at work within the work.

A final lens on *Nuclear Enchantment* as improvisatory ABR will include perspectives from alchemy, and the Borderland.

Alchemy and the borderland

Presented in the award-wining novel, *The Chymical Wedding*, is the notion that nuclear weapons are alchemy gone disastrously wrong (Clarke 1989). For the alchemy that C. G. Jung drew on had its own version of complexity theory. As noted in Chapter 3, alchemy operated in response to a network of correspondences that saw matter in-spirited. For the alchemists, the sun, moon and stars are included in elemental matter in their laboratories and in their souls. Alchemy was therefore an early arts-based research in that it fused science (investigating matter) and art (shaping matter). Here Jung's depiction of Native Americans praying to the rising sun makes them more truly alchemists than he, himself, with his theory of the projected psyche (see Chapter 3).

Nuclear Enchantment provides, like transdisciplinarity and complexity theory, another narrative arc for the dangerous story of classical science's subject/object split. For the cosmological web of alchemy was denied by dominant forces in Western modernity that elevated the subject/object split to an ideology, rather than a mere methodology. By cutting the psyche off from the other, Western modernity fell into the enchantments of technology depicted by Bailey, and into the autonomous nuclear complex depicted by Weishaus. Today, painfully, related movements of arts-based research, transdisciplinarity, even a revival of interest in alchemy, seek to heal the cosmological splitting. *Nuclear Enchantment* shows how and why it is necessary. It is a healing of classical science in itself.

> Red-beaked, red-eared mystic flowers bloom, petals flying
> in all directions; with a belt of ropes, shells, bells, and earth-
> bound agravic shoes.
>
> ("Kwahu Kachina")

From this poem's paratext we learn that the inventor of compasses was Talos, born from a mystic flower. Talos is also a long-range surface-to-air missile whose "rope" is electromagnetic reflectors. Yet rope is also strips of leather made by Native Americans for sacred butterflies. In this way *Nuclear Enchantment* works to heal the appalling nigredo (darkness, despair, deathliness) of nuclear weapons by connecting to myth and the land.

The poetry of *Nuclear Enchantment* enacts the *solve et coagula* that so impressed Jung. The process includes the dissolving of fixed meaning in a fluid of multiple references. It is a process leading to an eventual re-solving in a new substance of being, the coagulation. Here the poems' alchemy is improvisatory ABR because their profound moral purpose gives the work theme and grounding, fostering the fluidity and intuition of the psyche in writing and reading.

In this sense, too, *Nuclear Enchantment* is hospitable to the last perspective of this book on Jungian arts-based research, that of the borderland proposed by Jerome Bernstein in his powerful book, *Living in the Borderland* (2005). Without dealing with art or research, *Living in the Borderland* proposes that complexity theory can and must rapidly overcome the split within the Western psyche if the planet is to survive. Bernstein's particular contribution is the notion of living in the borderland, meaning psychologically connected to nonhuman, and more-than-human, nature in the ways that many indigenous peoples are. Borderland people are those who "hear" the voices of suffering that nature is presently bearing (Bernstein 2005: 6–14). They are not projecting; they are listening.

Bernstein suggests several portals to the borderland; one is trauma. He does not suggest art as a means of breaking out of the enchanted subject/object psyche, but I do. Jungian arts-based research could aspire to be a chalice, a grail in which the sacred energies of the other, including those of the earth, may be invoked, heard, shaped, *known*. Thus, Joel Weishaus and I offer as the next chapter of this book, *The Nuclear Enchantment of New Mexico*, to you, reader, as a portal into the borderland of Jungian arts-based research.

References

Bailey, L. W. (2005) *The Enchantments of Technology.* Urbana, IL: University of Illinois Press.

Bakhtin, M. M. (1981) *The Dialogic Imagination: Four Essays.* ed. M. Holquist, trans. C. Emerson and M. Holquist. Austin, TX: University of Texas Press.

Bernstein, J. (2005) *Living in the Borderland: The Evolution of Consciousness and the Challenge of Healing Trauma.* London and New York: Routledge.

Botting, F. (1990). *Gothic.* New Critical Idiom. London and New York: Routledge.

Clarke, L. (1989) *The Chymical Wedding.* London: Jonathan Cape.

Holland, J. (1994) 'Complexity Made Simple', *The Bulletin of the Santa Fe Institute, 9* (3), 3–4.

Irwin, R. L. N., J. Y. LeBlanc and R. G. Belliveau. (2018) 'A/r/tography as Living Inquiry', in P. Leavy, ed. *Handbook of Arts-Based Research.* New York and London: The Guilford Press, pp. 37–53.

James, K. (2017) 'What Lovely Words Might Also Mean', in P. Sameshima, A. Fidyk, K. James and C. Leggo, eds. *Poetic Inquiry: Enchantment of Place.* Wilmington, DE: Vernon Press, pp. 23–27.

Jung, C. G. (1922) 'On the Relation of Analytical Psychology to Poetry', in *Collected Works, Volume 15: The Spirit in Man, Art and Literature*, pp. 65–83.

Jung, C. G. (1952) 'Answer to Job', in *Collected Works, Volume 11: Psychology and Religion: West and East*, pp. 355–470.

Jung, C. G. (1963/1983) *Memories, Dreams, Reflections.* Recorded and edited by Aniela Jaffe. London: Fontana.

Nicolescu, B. (2014) *From Modernity to Cosmodernity: Science, Culture and Spirituality.* New York: SUNY.

Paris, G. (1998) *Pagan Grace: Dionysus, Hermes and Goddess Memory in Daily Life.* Woodstock, CT: Spring Publications Inc.

Rolling Jnr., J. H. (2013) *Arts-Based Research Primer.* New York: Peter Lang.

Shaw, P. (2006). *The Sublime.* New Critical Idiom. London and New York: Routledge.

Shelley, M. (1816/1996) *Frankenstein.* Norton Critical Edition. New York: W. W. Norton.

Shulman, H. (1997) *Living at the Edge of Chaos: Complex Systems in Culture and Psyche.* Zurich: Daimon Verlag.

Singer, T. and S. L. Kimbles. (2004) *The Cultural Complex.* Hove and New York: Routledge.

Chapter 6

The Nuclear Enchantment of New Mexico

CONTENTS

Acknowledgments

Bradbury Science Museum, Los Alamos National Laboratory.
Chamber of Commerce, Alamogordo, NM.
New Mexico of Natural History, Albuquerque.
New Mexico Environmental Improvement Division.
Public Affairs Office, White Sands Missile Range, NM.
Public Affairs Office, Cannon AFB, NM.
Sandia National Laboratories, Public Affairs Office, Albuquerque.
St. Joseph Hospital, Albuquerque.
U.S. Department of Energy, Albuquerque Operations Office.
U.S. Environmental Protection Agency, Dallas, TX.
U.S. Air Force Space Weapons Laboratory. Kirtland AFB.
U.S. Department of the Interior, National Park Service.
University of New Mexico, Center for Southwest Studies.
University of New Mexico, Nuclear Engineering Laboratory.
Westinghouse Electric Corporation, WIPP, Carlsbad, NM.
Witter Bynner Foundation for Poetry
Lee Bartlett
Miller Cravens
William L. Fox
George Hartley
Evelyn McConeghey
James Moore
David Morrissey
Patrick Nagatani
William Peterson
David H. Rosen
Debra Rosenthal
Susan Rowland
Kathleen Shields

And especially to Kevin and Adrian Campbell,
who were there in the darkest and brightest of times.

Preface
William L. Fox

Throughout the world there are only a handful of sites for the creation, testing and then eventual disposal of nuclear weapons and their waste materials. Nevada and New Mexico host the primary locations for one of the largest nuclear weapons programs in the world, programs which first manufacture and blow up weapons, then store and dispose of the remains (as well as the residue of commercial nuclear waste, in itself a not-so-indirect spin-off of the weapons program). While other areas in the United States host some weapons development, it's always the deserts that inherit the majority of the burden – the deserts because the majority of us incorrectly define them as empty, and because these thinly populated states lack the political weight necessary to fend off nuclear warfare practice and the disposal of radioactive waste.

Nuclear weapons are a threat most of us have grown up with; nuclear waste will remain a deadly factor in the life of the world for the next ten thousand years, even if all the weapons were dismantled this afternoon. These conditions, which breed anxiety and dread, anger and frustration, terror and even wonder, have been with us long enough that a significant body of art about nuclear weapons has been created. As important as some of these works are, not only for their subject matter, but also for their level of artistic achievement, only a few come close to creating an aesthetic capable of grasping the immense and profound role that nuclear weapons play in our conscious and unconsciousness lives. Part poetry, part essay, part encyclopedia, *The Nuclear Enchantment of New Mexico* by Joel Weishaus is one of them. The poetry by itself is a dense and almost impenetrable thicket of language, every image directed at the nuclear condition we have created for ourselves. The paratexts on facing pages not only explicate many of the images and allusions in the texts, but provide the elements toward a unique history of nuclear technology. Unlike a traditional encyclopedia, however, which is written to be as unambiguous and linear a reference work as possible, Weishaus encourages the reader to participate with him in the construction of the meaning, the "essay" formed from dialogue between the texts. The resulting interpretations, therefore, vary from reader to reader as each individual imagination assembles the elements.

Such deliberate indeterminacy is a hallmark of contemporary culture, which demands that art bring together disparate elements in unexpected ways, revealing previously hidden or unconscious truths – a technique refined throughout the twentieth century as one of the few sufficient to discover meaning in a world suffering from repetitive and meaningless military conflicts. This distinct aesthetic thread of disjunctive art, at times called "postmodern," has been further characterized by authors not attempting to hide from their readers, by making apparent the governing structural tenets of the text on the page, and by quoting from appropriate sources of any period. These are all strategies designed to push the text into a posture of ironic self-evaluation. So, in Weishaus' work, we find him juxtaposing the English philosopher Francis Bacon with Hopi creation myths and nuclear weapons nomenclature, and overtly facing prose to poetry, allowing the reader to freely associate fact-to-fact and fact-to-poetry. The reader's co-construction of the work. and subsequent decisions made in reading the text, are as revealing about the reader's psyche as the author's, a process Weishaus encourages us to bring into conscious range.

It has been said that the highest form of human concentration is play – that game rules are as complex an activity as higher mathematics, and that the attention, memory and various necessary skills engage us in greater neural effort than any other activity. Weishaus is asking us to play at a very high level in *The Nuclear Enchantment of New Mexico*. He sets us down in what is one of the most complicated playgrounds it is possible to publish, doing so in the belief that we better pay attention to and concentrate on this particular subject as a matter of survival. He does this with the devotion of a writer who believes that art can help save us, that it is in fact a necessary condition for saving ourselves.

Introduction

These forty texts and paratexts were originally written in response to forty photographs by Patrick Nagatani (1945–2017). At the time, I was a photography critic for *Artspace,* a quarterly journal of contemporary Southwest art (Weishaus 1989: 36–8).

While researching for a review of Nagatani's series of "Atomic Polaroids," I began to learn the extent of New Mexico's infrastructure for the research and production of nuclear weapons. With this in mind, Nagatani and I agreed to collaborate on a project based on what began with the making of the world's first nuclear device, in Los Alamos, NM, the testing of it in the desert of southern New Mexico, and continuing with the mining of uranium (much of it on Pueblo Indian land), and the research and designing of advanced nuclear devices, primarily by the two national laboratories located in the state.

On May 19, 1991, "The Nuclear Enchantment of New Mexico" opened at the Albuquerque Museum. My forty texts and Nagatani's forty photographs were hung across three rooms of the museum. (The paratexts were printed as handouts.) Two years later the show traveled to the Stanford University Museum of Art.

Nagatani exhibited, published and sold his pictures, while I digitized my texts for the then nascent World Wide Web, retitling them, "The Deeds and Sufferings of Light." Subsequently, over the years the texts continued to develop from the sight of Nagatani's pictures to the insight of my evolving poetics. This final version also returns the texts to their original title.

While updating the research for this book, I realized how indebted it is to Jungian scholarship, especially in the field of mythology. I was drawn to the trip C. G. Jung famously made in 1925 to Taos Pueblo, about 60 miles north of Santa Fe, because of a Jicarilla Apache myth in which the center of the Earth is near Taos, and that "Some time … that place will start to burn … That fire will spread to all over the world" (Opler 1969: 109–10).

Seeing "the exposed red faces of faraway mountains, from the brown waste-land" of Trinity Site, Koko Hayashi, a distinguished author and childhood survivor of the Nagasaki atomic bomb, wrote:

> Until now as I stand at the Trinity Site [where the first atomic bombs were tested], I have thought it was we humans who were the first atomic bomb victims on Earth. I was wrong. Here are my senior *hibakusha*. They are here but cannot cry or yell. Tears fill my eyes.

(Hayashi 2010: 50)

Planted in the psyche's darkest soil, thermonuclear technology continues to proliferate throughout a politically and psychologically unstable world. In 2017, the Nuclear Energy Institute reported that, "30 countries worldwide are operating 449 nuclear reactors for electricity generation and 60 new nuclear plants are under construction in 15 countries" (Report 2018). Electricity generated by each of these installations creates some 20 metric tons of radioactive waste every year, with no solution yet as to how to safely store it during its thousands of years of toxicity, or transubstantiate the radioactivity physicists unleashed during that fateful New Mexican summer in 1945, dramatically and lyrically shattering the nuclei of Gaia's body.

Meanwhile, the world's arsenal of over 13,000 nuclear weapons has become what Jung called "an *autonomous complex* … a split-off portion of the psyche, which leads a life of its own outside the hierarchy of consciousness" (Jung 1972: 75; italics in original).

The tragedy is Dionysian, and transdisciplinary, as the arts and sciences, after being riven apart for several hundred years, are beginning to reconnect their visions of reality, and the possibilities of human transformations. Perhaps T. S. Eliot was wrong, and the world won't end with a whimper. It may end in a tremendous *bang*. Or we may yet reanimate it, this time without the threat of a nuclear Armageddon.

–Joel Weishaus

References

Hayashi, K. (2010) *From Trinity to Trinity*. Barrytown, NY: Station Hill.

Jung, C. G. (1972) *The Spirit in Man, Art, and Literature*. Princeton, NJ: Princeton University Press.

Opler, M. E. (1969) *Myths and Tales of the Jicarilla Apache Indians*. New York: American Folklore Society.

Report. (2018) www.nei.org/Knowledge-Center/Nuclear-Statistics/World-Statistics (Accessed 8th February).

Weishaus, J. (1989) 'Patrick Nagatani & Andrée Tracey, "Atomic Polaroids"', *Artspace*, July–August.

broken arrows: "Since 1950, there have been 32 nuclear weapon accidents, known as 'Broken Arrows.' A Broken Arrow is defined as an unexpected event involving nuclear weapons that result in the accidental launching, firing, detonating, theft or loss of the weapon. To date, six nuclear weapons have been lost and never recovered." www.atomicarchive.com/Almanac/Brokenarrows_static.shtml (Accessed 20th April 2018)

chthonian inquiries: "Within the underworld perspective, the world does not fall into duality, needing balancing and bridges ... but the chthonic aspect in any archetypal pattern faces it away from external relations between things and the need for dyadic dialectics, turning it instead towards internal relations within things and imagistic explications" (Hillman 1979: 81).

boosting: "Boosting is a technology which scientists use in order to increase the efficiency of fission bombs by means of the introduction of a small amount of deuterium and tritium (typically this contains 2–3 g of tritium) inside the core." https://nuclear-knowledge.com/boosted.php (Accessed 18th April 2018)

Palomares/Thule: On January 17, 1966, a B-52G carrying four nuclear weapons collided in mid-air with a KC-135 tanker near Palomares, Spain, resulting in the falling of four MK28-type hydrogen bombs. On January 21, 1968, a B-52 crashed 7 miles southwest of Thule Air Base, Greenland, contaminating 237,000 cubic feet of biota with radioactivity. In both cases only high-explosive, non-nuclear materials, had detonated.

bombing New Mexico: The most serious reported accident in New Mexico took place about 4 miles south of Kirtland Air Force Base's (AFB's) control tower, on land owned by the University of New Mexico, when, on May 22, 1957, a B-36 "Peacemaker" released a Mark 17 thermonuclear bomb, "possibly the most powerful bomb we ever made."

retina: "the thermal radiation from a nuclear detonation causes more immediate damage at greater distance from the explosion than any other prompt catastrophic effect ... An example of this property is retinal burn ... which is in fact the most far-reaching, though not necessarily lethal, prompt pathogenic effect of the nuclear weapon" (Tsipis 1983: 49).

counterforce: "Counterforce doctrine, in nuclear strategy, the targeting of an opponent's military infrastructure with a nuclear strike, The counterforce doctrine is differentiated from the countervalue doctrine which targets enemy cities, destroying its civilian population and economic base. The counterforce doctrine asserts that a nuclear war can be limited and that it can be fought and won." www.britannica.com/topic/counterforce-doctrine (Accessed 8th May 2018)

tripod: The Pythian tripod stood in Apollo's temple at Delphi. "We do not realize the overwhelming power of Apollo ingrained in our mental set, and the blinding consequences of that light" (Hillman 2007: 325).

Accidental H-Bomb

With sparks of dry humor, vast spaces are enfolded into bureaucracies of sagebrush mentalities, broken arrows and chipped teeth, the desert vents chthonian inquiries shallowly rooted in I AM, boosting its way through science's circuitry.

Small thermonuclear cells light a land born on an altar of sintering fire, marshaling memories enchanted by the spaces they occupy, metamorphosing the inevitable into an image's parody of stability, clowning about its edges, staging pratfalls in Palomares and near Thule, bombing New Mexico caught in the heat of celebrity.

Flashbulbs burn the retina of History's blind eye;
dioramas held up as the land to avoid it fading away.

What resourcefulness!
What bravado!

A woman with a man's voice, bundled against the frost of dualities, mutters counterforce strategies atop a tripod, a nightmare of fire and dust to the terrified earth below.

Although nothing catastrophic occurred, the bombs made peace with the craters they created, by fulfilling light's epiphany:

I carry my ashes with me wherever I go.

paychecks: In 1906 President Herbert Hoover declared White Sands a national monument under the Antiquities Act of 1906, setting aside 142,987 acres about 16 miles southwest of Alamogordo, NM.

In 1942, after the attack by Japan on Pearl Harbor, President Roosevelt established the 1,243,000-acre Alamogordo Bombing and Gunnery Range. Presently the National Monument is surrounded by the missile range and Holloman AFB.

militarized dunes: White Sands includes the world's largest inland outcropping of pure gypsum stretches along the eastern portion of White Sands Missile Range, an area of about 100 by 40 miles used by the military for weapons testing. The range includes Trinity Site, where the first atomic detonation occurred in July 1945.

zombically In Haiti, writes C. H. Dewusm, "The Zombi is a dead person whom the sorcerer has taken from the tomb in order to make him, by means of magical powers, seem a living person, a walking cadaver. The soul of the corpse is sucked from the victim then blown into a bottle 'which (the sorcerer) immediately stops up'" (Tondriau and Villeneuve 1968: 241–2).

The Matador: In 1954 the TM-61A Matador became the Air Force's first operational cruise missile, or "pilotless bomber." It was armed with the W5 nuclear warhead, an improved version of the Fat Man plutonium bomb that was dropped on Nagasaki Japan.

teeth clenched: "The matador 'wants to get his teeth into the cause of social injustices in his region not in order to remedy them but to benefit from them himself in the spirit of revenge'" (Marvin 1988: 108–9).

suit of light: "someone dressed in the suit of light, a symbol of the 'truly male' male, that person of necessity is regarded as a man and the public's expectation of that person is that he is a man" (Ibid. 147).

paw: P(owered) A(ll) the W(ay).

Seven Deadly Sins: "Essentially the Matador missile is designed so that it can be broken into seven components to facilitate packing and shipping. Moreover, all these various sections are interchangeable" (Burgess 1957: 229).

beast: Slang for a missile.

the tone: Major Thomas Ferebee, bombardier who dropped the Atomic Bomb on Hiroshima, "mentioned to the radio operator to give the final warning. A continuous tone signal went out, telling (the escorts): 'In fifteen seconds she goes'" (Rhodes 1988: 709).

Alamogordo Chamber of Commerce

A blast of hot air lifts an array of government paychecks over militarized dunes, a sea of ancient brine burning competitive sarcomas into the feverish air of attaché cases strolling zombically toward bottlenecked boardrooms where spreadsheets guide missiles through nightmares of gilded dreams.

The Matador casts his body into a snorting bull market. Inertial data flows from insider tips, teeth clenched into snorting revenge: his suit of light, the red of his cape, man and machine paw blank checks of a collective fate.

The Seven Deadly Sins fabricated on an assembly line:

Lust fits snugly into its slot.
Pride's glued.
Gluttony's screwed.
Anger's arc welded.
A thick coat of Envy is sprayed on.
Greed is polished to a mirror.
Sloth takes a break from the beast whose shadow
faces its own demise.

What would you say if you knew the world was about to end?
Who would you phone?

I'd dial the Chamber of Commerce and say:

I'm open for business.
Wait for the tone.

nuclei: In the ion diode region of Sandia National Laboratory's Particle Beam Accelerator (PBFA II), intense heat will strip the nuclei of deuterium and tritium atoms of their electrons, creating a "plasma" (negatively charged free electrons and positively charged ions [bare nuclei and any electrons that remain bound to them]). The D and T nuclei will fuse and become helium, releasing energetic neutrons in the process and creating a sustained nuclear reaction.

plasma: Named by Irving Langmuir in 1929, referring to the phenomena he observed in heated gases to the "fluid portion of blood in which the particulate components are suspended."

Marxian: The PBFA II is encircled by thirty-six Marx generators, each of which stores, then delivers, a 95,000-volt charge lasting about one millionth of a second.

watery: The PBFA's water-insulated section, in which the process of pulse-forming begins, contains about 2000 tons of water.

moon: Among the numerous associations between rabbit and moon are the markings on the lunar surface called "The Mark of the Hare." Hekate, goddess of moon and magic, also gave hope for regeneration.

simulating: PBFA II will first be used to create miniature thermonuclear explosions in order to supplement the effects in weapons physics tests.

whirlwind: "This departing life has two components. One is called 'breath,' and it is this which leaves corpse via the sole of the foot in the form of a small whirlwind" (Opler 1936: 5).

Fusion Reactor

A neural chart bares nuclei,
stepped-up kilovolts ionizing negatives of molecular plasma,
pulse-forming lines,
as time floats by Marxian disprocketed flashes
filming shadows in acts of watery light---

>   Nothing is seen
>   that has not
>   been dreamed.

A red ochre moon tugs on blood, simulating an arc between poles
of manufactured beliefs.

Like breathing in a whirlwind,
                            scientists fuse
with their audience's applause.

this ominous mound: The Jackpile-Paguate Uranium Mine site is located at the Laguna Pueblo, about 40 miles west of Albuquerque. From 1952 to 1982 about 400 million tons of rocks were moved within the mine area, from which 25 million tons of uranium were extracted. It is presently a Superfund cleanup site. https://cumulis.epa.gov/supercpad/cursites/csitinfo.cfm?id=0607033 (Accessed 22nd May 2018).

unripe thoughts: In the Tewa creation myth, "the people were living in Sipo-fene beneath Sandy Place Lake far to the north." When a man was sent by the first mothers to explore the world above, he reported that it "was still ochu, 'green' or 'unripe'" (Ortiz 1969: 14).

witching hour: "When a suspected witch dies there is usually a severe dust storm within four days, which is the normal length of time it takes a soul to get into the underworld. This [storm] shows that the soul was rejected, and consequently ends its existence as dust and is completely forgotten." (Ibid: 140)

hoops: "Jumping through a hoop of yucca empowers us to make ourselves into dogs, cats, coyotes, hawks, crows, and owls, so that we pass quickly and unknown about the country" (Simmons 1980: 118).

protore: Ore that cannot be refined at a profit today but may be profitable in the future.

Rio Lethe: One of the five rivers of Hades. Lethe contains the waters of forgetfulness.

systematically: "Dirt (waste, tailings), then, is never a unique, isolated event. Where there is dirt there is system. Dirt is the byproduct of a systematic ordering and classification of matter, in so far as ordering involves rejecting inappropriate elements" (Douglas 1966: 44).

boomerang-like: "My Laguna informant said the boomerang-like stick was a *hachamuni* [usual word for feather-stick offering] for rabbits or jackrabbits, and that when offered it was painted and feathers were attached to it" (Parsons 1918: 385).

erratic loops: "One only discovers worlds through a long, broken flight" (Deleuze 1987: 36).

healing the rift: (Cheetham 2012: 19)

Laguna Cracked

Nature's poisonous snake is coiled,
warning of
this ominous mound.

Stars don't blink, but stare down to a dune,
a wind-sheared spectrum of lethal light,
a militant meteorology of unripe thoughts.

It is the witching hour, when Death jumps through hoops,
scooping up and topping off megatons of protore,
the Rio Lethe systematically contaminating
dusty Indian reservations, suburban watered lawns too.

Green is the color of a soul reflecting abalone shells and boomerang-
like feather stick offerings, pendants on long flights of erratic loops,
"healing the rift between thought and being,"
slowly reclaiming a poisoned land.

By the ruins: Chaco Culture National Historical Park is 137 miles northwest of Albuquerque, in the San Juan Basin. The park was established in 1907 as Chaco Canyon National Monument and was redesignated and renamed in 1980. It became a UNESCO World Heritage site in 1987. People began settling there around 500 C.E., developing a culture that reached its zenith between 1075 and 1130. Then by around 1250, the site was abandoned. DNA evidence is showing that "Today's Pueblo peoples claim, on fairly firm archaeological grounds, to be the direct descendants of the Chacoans; so do the Navajo, on whose land Chaco Canyon now sits" (Balter 2017).

like a plague: "Health officials in New Mexico have more experience with plague than many might expect: Every year for the last few years, a handful of people in New Mexico have come down with plague (Stack 2017: D2).

economy: "A new ranking of states based on their economic dependence on federal spending identifies New Mexico as the number one most dependent state, which is not altogether surprising given the presence of two national laboratories, four military bases and federal ownership of just over a quarter of the land in the state.

Other factors in the state's dependency on federal spending are likely the high rate of poverty, a growing elderly population, agricultural subsidies and the success of the congressional delegation in lobbying for federal dollars over the years" (Metcalf 2015).

Stealthy: The F-117A "stealth fighter" became operational October 1983. It is flown by the 37th Tactical Fighter Wing based at Holloman AFB, NM.

Beautiful Town: Pueblo Bonito, Spanish for "Beautiful Town," was the center of the Chacoan world. Occupied from the 800s to the 1200s, it was four stories tall and contained 600 rooms and forty kivas.

swept clean: The Chaco People "of the 12th century are indeed gone in flesh and blood, but … certain ruins appear so clean and fresh that I think to myself, 'If I wait just a little longer, they'll be back. I'm sure'" (Bensinger 1988: n.p.).

Changing Woman: "Here the decision-making power of the Navaho women is exercised by Changing Woman, the great Navaho earth goddess. Even for the great heroes, if she says no, it is no, they do not object" (Sandler 1991: 53).

roads engineered: "In prehistoric times, a great network of roadways radiated outward from Chaco Canyon National Monument. These once connected impressive sandstone citadels and large pueblo villages into a political and economic network worthy of the grandest feudal baron. Archaeologists refer to this as the Chaco Phenomenon, and it has received lavish publicity. For all that, few people realize just how vibrant, how brief, and how fragile was the world created by Chaco Anasazi farming peoples a millennium ago" (Stuart 2010: 77).

Chaco Ruins

By the ruins of a civilization that shimmered with skilled masonry,
dark shapes rise over lost conversations heaped like a plague of
phonemes dying under siege.

Tongues thicken from fantasies of future excavations---
the air
  holds its breath.

What signals a people to dream of a place that doesn't yet exist,
reshaping symbols that began a thousand years before Pythagoras
in the geometry of the dead; a vision that leaps synapses for the pleasure
of a thought?

Extinction is not a concept.
Erosion is a missing event in defense of economy and socialized tropes.

Stealthy figures reconnoiter a land whose parched lips peal
like an ancient bell in Beautiful Town...

swept clean by the presence of Changing Woman,
with roads engineered so true the visions of a people
                                      were misdirected.

Placed in: Sited 56 miles east of Farmington, NM, Gasbuggy was a project of the U.S. Atomic Energy Commission's Plowshare Program, and El Paso Natural Gas Company, as a way of fracking the earth. After 4 years of preparation, and 4.7 million dollars, the 26-kiloton explosion (larger than the bomb that destroyed Hiroshima) was detonated at 12:30 P.M., on December 10, 1967. https://aoghs.org/technology/project-gasbuggy (Accessed 18th May 2018)

fifteen miles away: The town of Dulce, NM, tribal headquarters of the Jicarilla Apache.

hactcin: "In the beginning, the Jicarilla believe, Black Sky and Earth Woman alone existed. From the union of these two were born certain anthropomorphic supernaturals called hactcin" (Opler 1936: 203).

blue mysterious glow: "One evening, sitting at the dinner table with a few guests, when the light was fading, [Pierre Curie] produced from his waistcoat pocket a tube of radium salt. It gave out its blue, mysterious glow over the table, and he turned to the young maid who was serving the meal and said, 'This is the light of the future!'" (Reid 1974: 109)

mudras: Symbolic, ritualistic hand gestures used in Buddhism.

nesting in palms: "Now we are speaking of the hand as healer, the flat of the hand, its palm, is the etymological root of our word feel" (Hillman 2013: 213).

enemy hiding: Knowing the location of one's enemy is said to be one of the powers some Apache shamans possess. "When a person dies, he goes underground to the world there. There is an opening in the ground and someone leads the dead person to it so they will not miss it. The hole is surrounded by tall grass to hide it and make it look natural" (Coffer 1981: 53).

wild plums: "The journey [to the underworld] lasts four days and terminates at the edge of the earth. Here a wild plum tree grows, the fruit of which is offered to the traveler. Should he refuse it he returns to his body and to life" (Opler 1936: 223).

weedy plot: "[Edgar] Anderson contends that the history of weeds is the history of man. We, like weeds, want to dominate not integrate; we too are 'nature's misfits'" (Schneidau 1977: 147).

hungry ghosts: In Buddhist theodicy, "hungry ghosts are beings with literally insatiable cravings and desires (they are often represented as having enormous stomachs and needle-like throats)" (LeFleur 1983: 28).

Gasbuggy

Placed in horizons of sandstone, a nuclear device pulverized walls
and telluric life, rattling windows fifteen miles away, where
hactcin run for cover.

A blue mysterious glow rises ... then vanishes into the rigors
of death's mudras.

What do cockroaches feel nesting in palms itchy with primeval fear?
At critical mass light squares scarabs etched at the height of prayer;
wild plums wither on their healthy limbs; hundred-headed *narkissos*
is plowed under; mushrooms become wet with perennial tears.

Where is the enemy hiding in this weedy plot?
Only the dead are innocent of war, with no sides to take anymore.

We are not even beings but the seeds of beings germinating hungry
ghosts choking on the odors of sophistic schemes, following the light
lost in shadows of eighteenth-century dreams.

children: "Remember the Child. See the world of nuclear devastation through the vision of the Child's presence; sense the wounded, dying innocence" (Perlman 1988: 116).

little mounds: "I crave so a small piece of earth, a testimony that I too had a mother, that this planet is mine too, so the salt of my tears on that little mound might make me part of the whole scheme of things" (Leitner 2018).

Moloch's: "Moloch whose mind is pure machinery! Moloch whose blood is running money! Moloch whose / fingers are ten armies! Moloch whose breast is a cannibal dynamo! Moloch whose ear is a / smoking tomb!" (A. Ginsberg. From, "Howl.")

blue flames: "The corpse lying on its back on the road had been killed immediately when the A-Bomb was dropped. Its head was lifted to the sky and the fingers were burning with blue flames … This hand must have embraced a child before" (Takakura 1977: 95).

inaccessible: "This is that prehistoric man did not consider the caverns as an edifice to be decorated: secret signs and figurations are placed in positions that are extremely difficult of access and at the uttermost end of the caves, where the walls narrow to a crack" (Giedion 1960: 80).

the museum's: Founded in 1963, in 1970 the Bradbury Museum and Science Hall was dedicated to the laboratory's second director, Norris E. Bradbury, who retired that year.

afterbodies: The tailward portion of a missile is its "afterbody."

digitized: "All cruise missiles have an internal guidance system, though the types vary. The Tomahawk cruise missile, which the U.S. Navy has deployed since 1984, uses a system called 'Terrain Contour Matching,' where an altimeter and an inertia detector plot the flight path against a pre-loaded terrain contour map. Later versions of the Tomahawk also use GPS, and there are other guidance systems that some cruise missiles use" (Atherton 2013).

Promethean: "Model-making is Promethean when it pretends to render the psyche in the form of dayworld objects such as maps, machines, houses, icebergs, [and nuclear weapons] … As the original interpreter of dreams, [Prometheus] represents that in us which seeks the measure of the immeasurable" (Hersh 1982: 153).

Necessity: "Nuclear engagement scenarios are not necessarily binary. Third countries may feel compelled to intervene in disputes between nuclear states or in conflicts involving weapons of mass destruction that could spill over into their territory or interests" (Younger 2000).

hibakusha: Japanese survivors of the atomic bombs.

Bradbury Museum

One hears no laughter from children who have not been given
but little mounds

> to mark their final resting place.

Another sacrifice embraced by Moloch's stench of smoking flesh
and leukemia-ridden bones lies in a crematorium lit by blue flames
flickering like torches in a Paleolithic cave, inaccessible and obscure.

This museum's graphics spell out ashes behind distorted reflections,
breaching "afterbodies" plotted to digitized targets with a mathematics
that counts the links on Promethean chains.

> Mother of Necessity,
> cradle these ghosts
> of *hibakusha* children.

rings of gold: "Then the snake coiled itself about my body and put its head close to my face. I saw that it had a crown upon its head and rings of gold around its body. I looked into the eyes of the snake and putting my arms about it I said: 'Serpent, you are beautiful to me'" (Jung 1997: 599).

Conquistadors: "The soldiers and adventurers gathering in Mexico, commanded by Francisco Vasquez de Coronado, were the first Europeans to organize an expedition to the American Southwest. Leaving from Culiacan in 1540, they went up the west coast of Mexico into modern Arizona, then east into New Mexico. The seven golden cities turned out to be the pueblos around Zuni, New Mexico, and not golden at all" (Christiansen 1972: 7).

deadly road: The Jornada del Muerto is an arid 90-mile stretch of high desert between Socorro and El Paso, 210 miles south of Los Alamos. It is now part of the White Sands Missile Range, on which Trinity Site is located.

emerald rocks: "Trinitite is the name given to the soil that was fused into glass-like objects by the heat from the Trinity atomic bomb test. Trinitite is typically a grayish or light olive green color, with a smooth fused top surface on one side and the irregular texture of the sandy desert surface on the other side" (Otake 2010: 46 n 35).

snaked: Medusa was "a snaky-haired, pig-tusked, long-tongued, wide-eyed visage that could petrify the viewer" (Eisner 1987: 57).

doomsday device: The first atomic device was exploded at Trinity Site at 5:30 A.M., on July 16, 1945, during a lull in a storm. While waiting for the explosion, the physicist Enrico Fermi wagered on whether it would ignite the atmosphere; and if it did, whether it would destroy New Mexico, or destroy the world.

tower: "It had been prefabricated of steel and shipped to the site in sections. Concrete footings poured through the hard desert caliche 20 feet in the earth supported its four legs, which were spaced 35 feet apart; braced with crossed struts it rose 100 feet into the air" (Rhodes 2012: 654).

Batter my heart: J. Donne. From, "Holy Sonnets, #14." When he was asked to name the test site, "Oppie [J. Robert Oppenheimer, 'the father of the atomic bomb'] turned to the opening lines of the holy sonnet he had just read" (Lamont 1965: 70).

Trinity Site

In the Sixteenth Century, sun-baked bricks glaring like rings of gold
on a serpent's crown were conjured by Conquistadors winding north
along the *Jornada del Muerto*, "The Journey of Death."

Four centuries later, a legion of Ph.D.s braved this deadly road,
carrying with them the madness of the Apollonian sun turned loose
from a workshop of calculating minds dreaming of this event centuries
ago in the flasks of alchemical labs, boiling up emerald rocks seen with
reverently shaded eyes.

Asked to name the site where long tongues of wires would be snaked like
Medusa's hair growing from a doomsday device winched up and hanging
between the thin legs of a steel tower, Dr. Oppenheimer thought:

> *Batter my heart, three-person'd God; for you*
> *As yet but knocke, breathe, shine, and seek to mend;*
> *That I may rise, and stand, o'erthrow me, and bend*
> *Your force, to break, blow, burn, and make me new.*

University Reactor: The AGN-201M has been a nuclear training reactor at the University of New Mexico since 1966, offering students on-hand training in nuclear engineering.

superheated words: "We are accustomed to teaching as a form of transmitting and possibly recasting knowledge. And in the service of that we form various narratives and interpretations of the information. But we have no experience teaching a narrative of potential extinction of ourselves as teachers and students, of our universities and schools, of our libraries and laboratories" (Lifton 1982: 1).

curdling: "Indra, the sky-god of Hindu mythology, was under an unknown curse. His strength began to diminish, and all the universe was losing its energy on the way to annihilation." The god Vishnu said, "I will restore your strength ... Cast into the Milky Sea some magic herbs, then take Mount Mandara for a churning-stick, the serpent Vasuki for a rope, and churn the ocean to obtain the Water of Life. To do this you will need the help of the Demons" (Mercatante 1974: 20).

pencils: On December 2, 1942, Enrico Fermi used stacks of graphite to achieve the world's first known controlled reaction of fissionable materials. "It was a familiar routine. The [control] rod was pulled out a bit, the counter was read to assess the intensity of neuron flux, and Fermi calculated with his pocket slide rule how far the next withdrawal should go. This day the flux mounted higher and higher until Fermi could announce, 'The pile has gone critical'" (Romer 1984: 519).

urchins: Neutron sources for the A-Bomb were called urchins.

Disneyfied: "The Disney example warns that in a technological culture sentimentality can very effectively simulate soul and ego-willfulness can be disguised in pseudo-imaginal animations. As we seek to develop an aesthetic sensitivity to the soul of things, including machines, we must not wish away the powerfully *anti*-aesthetic currents technology sets in motion'" (Noel 1988: 34).

ping-pong balls: This is an experiment that was set on a table at the University of New Mexico to demonstrate a chain reaction using ping-pong balls catapulted into the air from a tight formation of mouse traps.

University Reactor

Slurs of superheated words pointed toward a silent calamity stacked
in a room fitted for measuring interactions curdling in a core.

    Rod drop analyses, flux profiles, power calibrations,
    graphite pencils: spelling rods of neuronic linguistics.

Students highlighted calculations, the hard bodies of urchins modeled
on masculine ideals advanced in a society fitted with politicized solid state
organs, knee-jerk responses programmed into children as reality churned
in circuits of schemata downloading glitches.

Disneyfied whiffs of Chernobyl
are the illusion of sanguine
               humanoid mutations.

Publicized as peacekeeping atoms,
ping-pong balls were poised
on a university table.

Say Cheese! and they sprang
from mousetraps, blasting cause
into an orbit of lethal effects.

hyperphosphorescence: "The Curies first used the word radioactive to describe the behaviour of uranium-like substances. Silvanus Thompson's concoction of the same phenomenon, hyperphosphorescence, thankfully, never entered the English or any other language. But radioactivity had come to stay" (Reid 1974: 87).

luminous silhouettes: "At night [the Curies] would occasionally return to their workroom, stand in the centre of its cold, hard bituminous floor, and look around at the bottles of liquids and capsules of crystals. As their eyes became accustomed to the dark they would begin to see the feebly luminous silhouettes of the containers glowing from the tables and makeshift shelves. They stood together and watched, and felt themselves to have reached great heights" (Ibid. 97).

welling: "when you visualize it in a state where the outer senses are under restraint, you are shaken by such terror that you think you are about to die. And then, suddenly at the mouth of the well the extraordinary green light begins to shine" (Corbin 1971: 79).

yew-green: "The Yew is the central tree of death, associated with churchyards, where the Yew is said to root into the mouths of the dead and release their souls, and to absorb the odours of putrefaction, and the phosphorescence of the bodies" (Bleakley 1988: 111). The cancer drug Taxol is made from the bark of the Pacific yew tree.

pig: Slang for a container used to transport toxic materials, usually radioactive pharmaceuticals.

tangled growth: "The thicket is a Great Mother symbol, particularly in connexion with the boar hunt; there the boar turns at bay for its last self-defence before its death, and as such is commonly met with in classical literature. It is a tangled growth of an almost impenetrable complexity which can be a refuge for wild animals, but can also be a last stronghold from which they attack their pursuers" (Layard 1975: 72).

hell-dog: "The dog is often described mythologically as a healing and protecting escort into the Beyond. Thus the Egyptian dog-headed or jackal-headed god Anubis is the agent of resurrection; and among the Aztecs a yellow or red dog, Xolotl, brings the corpses in the kingdom of the dead back to life. In India, too, Shiva, the destroying god of death, is called Lord of the Dogs … And Virgil tells us in the Aeneid that the hell-dog Cerberus is actually the earth which devours corpses" (Von Franz 1998: 70).

heads blindly: "Death in the grassblade / a dull / substance, heading blindly / for the bone" (D. Levertov. From, "Three Meditations.")

Radium Springs

Reflecting the wild confusion of
                    "hyperphosphorescence,"
a sign of luminous silhouettes welling into the flora's
impressionistic pallor, millimicrocuries condensed
into a yew-green child.

All children are hybrids, transforming a sow
into a boar, raging like neutrons trapped in a
lead-lined pig.

While Mother's off bathing in the tangled growth,
a hell-dog heads "blindly
                    for the bone."

falling out: "The hair / comes out in patches. Teeth / break off like matchsticks / at the gumline but the loss / is painless ... Weeks later ... survivors must expel / day by day in little pisses / the membrane lining of their bladders ..." (M. Kumin. From, "How to Survive a Nuclear War.")

a museum: The National Atomic Museum was established by the Defense Nuclear Agency in 1969 to exhibit the shapes of unclassified nuclear weapons. The exhibits trace the evolution of nuclear weapons from the early 1940s on. Located on Kirtland AFB, Albuquerque, the facility was transferred to the Department of Energy in 1976.

Urania: Perhaps the daughter of Zeus and Mnemosyne, Urania is one of the nine muses. Her symbol is the globe and a pair of compasses. She is the muse of astronomy and poetry's measured lines.

Kali: The Hindu goddess who is "Cosmic Power, the totality of the universe, the harmonization of all the pairs of opposites, combining wonderfully the terror of absolute destruction with an impersonal motherly reassurance" (Campbell 2008: 95).

blood: "It is ghastly now to look around when blood-red clouds are gathering in the sky. The air is being dyed with the blood of men while the maidens of battle are singing" (Onians 1988: 356).

BOMARC: CIM-10 Bo(eing) M(ichigan) A(eronautical) R(esearch) C(enter). This was a cruise, or pilotless, fighter, built primarily to intercept bombers. The Bomarc saw service from 1960 until 1972. On June 7, 1960, at McGuire AFB, in New Jersey, a CIM-10 Bomarc nuclear warhead caught fire, scattering weapons grade plutonium. The site was covered with concrete and designated off-limits.

separate visions: "Other rabbis explain that Adam and Eve were created back to back, joined at their shoulders; then God separated them by a blow with a hatchet or by sawing them in half" (Reik 1973: 26).

MACE: The MGM-13 Mace was an improved version of the Matador cruise missile. The Mace was equipped with a Goodyear ATRAN (Automatic Terrain Recognition and Navigation) guidance system, and could deliver either a nuclear or high explosive warhead.

salt: "Here salt, arcane substance (the paradoxical 'lead of the air') the white dove *(Spiritus sapientiae)*, wisdom and femininity appear in one figure" (Jung 2003: 245).

balloons: Albuquerque is host to an annual international hot air balloon festival.

Atomic Muse

A new culture snakes its way through stockpiles of mummified nuclear devices drained of their poisons, delivery systems suited to curating souls and embalming toxic hearts.

Sanitized of hair, expelled bladder linings, teeth falling out,
victims burned alive---

> Who is the muse of a museum that exhibits
> Death as Memory in disguise?

Tall, slim, Urania is the muse of astronomy and the renaissance of poetry programmed to travel a self-correcting course; while Kali wears skulls as a necklace, earrings of bodies immutably hung, a girdle of severed hands, and blood the color of her stunning eyes.

In a vision of militant technology, BOMARC scars the separate visions we have of each other, with a MACE like a Viking's hatchet, or a spiked ball and chain.

Hidden behind black sunglasses, Urania's Geiger counter heart is clicking. Rockets become pillars of salt; backs unfold wings, buttocks bloat into hot air balloons.

a tree: Robert Hutchings Goddard has been called "the father of American rocketry." "On October 19, 1899, a day that became his 'Anniversary Day,' he climbed a cherry tree in his backyard and 'imagined how wonderful it would be to make some device which had even the *possibility* of ascending to Mars ... when I descended the tree,' he wrote in his diary, 'existence at last seemed very purposive'" (Lehman and Lehman 2016).

threat clouds: A flight of incoming enemy missiles. "The earth we would depart from is also the earth we have wired for destruction. Thus the death we would escape comes back to haunt us in the shape of the nuclear clouds of annihilation" (Romanyshyn 1989: 30).

the test: "War sets hard problems, affords the investigator opportunities to test his results in actual practice, is not niggardly with funds; therefore it is not to be wondered at that war gets results from laboratories" (Gray 1943: 40).

education: Robert H. Goddard Senior High School is located in Roswell, NM, near where Dr. Goddard had his workshop from 1930 to 1932, and again, from 1934 until 1942, when the Navy moved him to Annapolis.

nervous Nell: All of Goddard's rocket tests were named "Nell," after a student of his said, "They ain't done right by our Nell"; meaning the press had blown the dangers of a test out of proportion. Nell, here, also refers to "nervous Nellys," which is what President Lyndon Johnson called protestors against the Vietnam War.

normalcy: The normal "both sustains and kills, like a god. It is the ordinary made beautiful; it is also the average made lethal" (Shaffer 2005: 62).

Lathed: A lathe was loaned to the Roswell team by the Smithsonian. It had belonged to Samuel Pierpond Langley, who had used it to fabricate "Langley's Folly," an airplane that failed to gain flight.

ashes: "By the time he graduated [from high school], he had, he said, 'a set of models which would not work and a number of suggestions which, from the physics I had learned, I now knew were erroneous.' He gathered up all his models and his carefully catalogued notes and burned them" (Goddard 1968: 6).

smiles: "Behind every smile lurks a Hiroshima" (I. M. Panayotopoulos. From, "The World's Window.")

old adherences: A text that "always interweaves roots endlessly, bending them to send down roots among roots, to pass through the same points again, to redouble old adherences" (Derrida 1977: 102).

Goddard High

Sitting in a tree, following Time's puckish arrow as it leaves a faint trail
of vapor behind, when archetypes are traced as phrenology,
threat clouds appear in the blue of an angel's eyes wanting to know why
our fate is carried inside and out.

Here we are put to the test.

Each weapon is a triumph of perverted education, a nervous Nell passing
the point of no return, sustaining the look of normalcy while worshipping
a god who arcs across the sky on his disinterested route back to the stars.

Lathed in secrecy, inner institutions fume. Immolated corpses of
misbegotten lives aspire to ashes, twisting sheaves into clusters of
deracinated smiles stemming from old adherences

> slithering down
> and
> coiling around.

Kirtland AFB: Begun in late 1939 on 2000 acres adjacent to what is now Albuquerque International Airport, "In December 2014, the Air Force announced plans to realign the 377th Air Base Wing under Air Force Global Strike Command and to restructure the Air Force Nuclear Weapons Center to improve the effectiveness of and support for the Air Force's Nuclear Enterprise." www.mybaseguide.com/air_force/117-3313-20566/kirtland_afb_history (Accessed 21st May 2018)

yoked mind: An indication of viral hepatitis. (Yoke, here, is the alternate spelling for yolk.) "The disease was especially common among the military and was called 'campaign jaundice'" (Hollinger and Martin 2013: 550).

blood gland: "The liver was, in fact, supposed by early peoples to be the fountain of the blood supply and therefore of life itself" (Spence 2005: 269).
    "Priests, examining the entrails of birds, / Found the heart misplaced, and seeds / As black as death, emitting a strange odor" (L. Simpson. From "The Inner Part.")

Rockeyes: Cluster bombs that break out hundreds of fragmentation bomblets.

Snakeyes: High-drag bombs with pedal airbrakes and a laser head.

Walleyes: Unpowered glide bombs with TV guidance.

HARMS: Anti-radiation missiles that home in on radar and other electronic systems.

Bullpups: Self-powered missiles with radio guidance. The Air Force calls this missile, "the pooch with a punch."

Sidewinders: The AIM-9 Sidewinder is a short-range air-to-air missile. A sidewinder is also a poisonous snake found in the U.S. Southwest.

Sparrows: "Starlings and sparrows are very persistent once they choose a nesting site. If they happen to select your airplane as a place to call home, expect that the nest builders will return even if you completely remove all nesting materials while the nest is being built" (Kight 2005).

Enchilada Air Force: The 150th Tactical Fighter Group, New Mexico Air National Guard. Based at Kirtland AFB, in 1979 it was one of the two Air National Guard units to be chosen for the U.S.'s anti-terrorist Rapid Deployment Force.

captain's machine gun: On June 7, 1912, Capt. Charles Chandler fired the first machine gun mounted on an airplane. The plane was piloted by Col. (then Lt.) Roy C. Kirtland, for whom, on January 13, 1948, Kirtland AFB was named.

Kirtland AFB

A pilot's yoked mind is force-fed oxygen behind a dark visor,
a huge blood gland pumping bile through computerized circuits
of an unbroken chain of command.

Rockeyes are explosive motes in Snakeyes' ruby optics.
Walleyes seek new targets in black & white visions from the past.
HARMS hunger for microwave ovens.
Bullpups pull up short to Sidewinders' hearts pumping cold neutrons.

Sparrows build suicidal nests.
One bird evolves into a family of feral hunters
for odors of The Enchilada Air Force,
as a captain's machine gun slices through
a jaundiced sky.

Yellowcake: The output of a uranium mine is called "yellowcake" because of its appearance. "Yellowcake is a compound of uranium oxide with either ammonium or sodium; its exact composition varies but it usually contains 80 to 85 percent U3O8" (Lamperti 1982: 399).

Dung: "It occurs frequently in sagas that animal dung … is changed into gold as, inversely, gold sent by evil spirits is easily turned (again) into dung" (Silberer 1971: 322).

This Goddess: Isis "was the Crescent, crowned with the headdress of cow horns, the Horned Goddess, the Cow, and as such was identified with Hathor the Cow-Goddess who preceded her. Osiris [her husband], too, was a horned deity, known as the bull god" (Harding 1971: 184). "The Isis and Osiris story is about regeneration, which is what I think the theme of the nuclear story is. It is woman's story. Isis, you may recall, couldn't find the penis. The nuclear pile is a kind of penis. It is a constructive use of potentially destructive power. It is full of connotations of regeneration of power" (Kiefer 1988: 87).

uranium mill: The Homestake Mining Company (HMC) site is located near the village of Milan, and the city of Grants, New Mexico. Milling operations began in 1958. Wastes were disposed of in two tailing piles next to the mill, covering approximately 245 acres, impacting ground water in the San Mateo alluvium and the upper Chinle aquifer. In 1983 the HMC mill was placed on the National Priorities List of hazardous waste sites eligible for remedial action under the Superfund program. See United States Environmental Protection Agency Fact Sheet, November 2016. https://cumulis.epa.gov/supercpad/cur sites/csitinfo.cfm?id=0600816 (Accessed 21st May 2018)

Death's twins: "Roundish and tapered at one end, [Eye Killers] had no limbs or heads, but were provided with depressions somewhat like eyes. They could, however, kill by staring at their victims without winking. As they did so, their rudimentary eyes grew into the eyes of those they were killing" (Reichard 1974: 434).

Tongue Mountain: (*Tsodzil,* Navajo) Mount Taylor, 11,389 ft., is northeast of Grants, NM. It is the highest point of the San Mateo Mountains. Sacred to Native Americans of the region, the mountains also hold the nation's largest single deposit of high-grade uranium ore.

Homestake Mining

Yellowcake dollops.
Radioactive cow pies.
Dung of the Golden Calf.

Spidery black scrap-iron cadavers are mooned over by a cow searching
for her old man's bullish parts. But his phallus, having lost its luster,
had already been devoured by metastasizing light.

This Goddess, her underside revealing distended teats from which a
sinister milk was drained by the lubricous sleights of corporate hands,
fashioned as a dildo from uncollected myths. She conceived a son whose
wings spread out like the golden horns of a god.

Twenty million tons of uranium mill tailings piled 100 ft. high is looked
down to by the image of a man hung between worlds, announcing the
arrival of Death's twins---

> the lengths to which
> we are willing to go.

A hazy gray cloud drifts over Tongue Mountain:

> sick from
> the taste of
> humanity's waste

apple: Manzano: apple tree (Sp, NM.) "In any case, the paradox is no worse than the Creator's whimsical notion of enlivening his peaceful, innocent paradise with the presence of an obviously rather dangerous tree-snake, 'accidentally' located on the very same tree as the forbidden apples" (Jung 2014: 241).

the broil: (Kafka 1999: 294).

born of fire: The Manzano Mountains are located at the southeast corner of the City of Albuquerque. Although uplifted during the late Neogene Period after the great volcanic eruptions in this region, there still must have been volcanic activity all around and beneath these mountains.

storing nuclear devices: Located in Albuquerque, "Kirtland Air Force Base has become an important nuclear weapons complex. It hosts the Air Force's Nuclear Weapons Center, Sandia National Laboratories, and what is probably the nation's (and perhaps the world's) largest repository of nuclear weapons, estimated at up to 2,500 warheads." https://nukewatch.org/Kirtland.html (Accessed 25th May 2018)

apples … baked: "When I walked out of Nagasaki's roofless railroad station, I saw a city frizzled like a baked apple, crusted black at the open core" (Weller 1982: 3).

Cooking: Fire "is cookery and it is apocalypse" (Bachelard 1968: 7).

Falcons: The General Dynamics F-16 "Fighting Falcon" is a. single-engine, highly maneuverable, supersonic, tactical fighter. It went into service August 1978, and remains in service. Upgrades of the F-16 remain in service.

eyes red: Re is the ancient Egyptian solar god. He was a falcon-headed man, an "anthropozoomorph" who wore a coiled cobra, representing instantaneous death, and a sun disk.

delicate biota: "With the bullet brow / Of burying himself headfirst and ahead / Of his delicate bones, into the target / Collision" (T. Hughes. From, "And the Falcon Came.")

militant bones: "(I)n the Mabinogion tale called Branwen Daughter of Llyr, [there is] mention of a 'cauldron of rebirth' into which dead bodies were cast and next day arose 'as good fighting men as before, save they were not able to speak'" (Layard 1975: 153).

Manzano

One bite of an apple may embody all the symbols of consciousness.
One turn on evolution's spit and embers of a national dream
smolder in "the broil of earthly life."

Smoke curls and a flag of flames salutes the irony of a mountain
born of fire storing nuclear devices as if apples ready to be baked
and burned to their core.

Cooking in the brain's crucible broiling in the shadow of Falcons
flying toward the speed of light, all earthly beings transmuted
into birds with eyes red a New Mexican setting sun.

A fence is an illusion of its own linkage, ignoring sand blowing
between its teeth, while middleclass patios are stained with ashes
of delicate biota and the silence of militant bones.

victim's: "In Latin, the word is *victima* and refers to the sacrificial beast. Paradoxically, this word comes from the older roots (veg- and vio-) meaning 'increase' and 'growth.' It is remarkable how frequently the word growth is used in relation to cancer and tumorous enlargement" (Lockhart 1977: 5).

resurrecting: "the death of vegetation often appears as an image of human death and, at the same time, as a symbol of resurrection" (Von Franz 1987: 24).

Vesalius: Andreas Vesalius (1514–64) was a Flemish anatomist. Among other accomplishments, he was the first to dissect a human hand.

laughter: "Straining so hard against the strength of night, / they fling their tiny voices on the laughter / that will not burn." (R. M. Rilke. From, "Untitled.")

crabs' legs: "The connection between cancer and crab is not accidental and carries symbolic significance. The crab is an animal hidden from view, shrinking back, yet holding tenaciously to what it seizes" (Lockhart 1977: 2).

saliva: Located near the ear, the parotid gland is a source for the secretion of saliva.

grid: "The electrons are accelerated linearly along a wavegrid consisting of a series of copper cavities. The electrons are carried through the cavities by a radio frequency wave whose phase velocity increases along the tube, which is designed so that the wave and the electrons carried by it remain in phase. The electrons are grouped in bunches so that the accelerated electrons emerge from the window in pulses" (Almond 1976: 9).

bleaching: "the X-ray could 'bleach' its way through the upper atmosphere, and detonate, destroying any satellite within its potentially long range and line of sight" (Carter 1985: 178).

St. Peregrine: Peregrinus Lazios (1260–1345), canonized in 1780.

Radiation Therapy

Seeking out darkness in diseased tissue behind a quarter-ton door,
green is black curled into itself, a pathology of subcutaneous growth
pitted against its victim's fluorescent cells...

> resurrecting the loneliness of this nightmare field,
> an aporia too strong for physicians to prescribe.

Vesalius' skilled fingers could only perform a macabre dance,
his moist palms pressing against hips, knees raised to flatten back,
eyes gazing into faceless machinery, ears licked by the bane of laughter,
swollen veins radiating crabs' legs in warm saliva boiling over copper
cauldrons...

> a grid of phased electrons stepped up to blocks of Lipowitz metal,
> bombarded through a window of neutral vulnerability, or slowed

X-rays bleaching sea-green air in line of sight
with an aquaplast mask.

> St. Peregrine, patron saint of cancer,
> crossed his shadow, to the wholeness
> of his being.

Fat Man: Name of the plutonium bomb that, on August 9, 1945, was dropped on Nagasaki, Japan.

homunculus: "Soon something else emerged. I began to see on the front face, in the natural structure of the stone, a small circle, a sort of eye, which looked at me. I chiseled it into the stone, and in the centre made a tiny homunculus" (Jung 1965: 227).

never before seen: "Plutonium was the first man-made element produced in a quantity large enough to see" (McPhee 2000: 35).

lighting smokes: "Fifteen seconds after the nuclear device [at Trinity Site] flashed, Ted [Taylor] reached down to the parabolic mirror beside him and took from behind it a smoldering Pall Mall. He drew in a long pleasing draught of smoke. He had lit a cigarette with an atomic bomb" (Ibid: 94–5).

safe-secure trailer: SSTs hold up to three TRUPACT-II (TRU = transuranic) containers. Each TRUPACT holds up to fourteen 55-gallon drums of combustible trash and transuranic waste. In August 1989 the Nuclear Regulatory Commission (NRC) approved TRUPACT-II for hauling nuclear waste to the Waste Isolation Pilot Plant (WIPP) 26 miles southeast of Carlsbad from temporary storage sites around the country. (Shortly after NRC approval 74 welding defects to the containers were identified.)

window: "We are given the opportunity to discover that the bomb, for example, is a way of seeing, that it is not just an event in our world but also, and more fundamentally, the incarnation of an attitude or disposition toward the world, a way in which we have practiced being a self with distant vision behind a window" (Romanyshyn 1989: 67).

mirror: "Behold – In the window there is glass and in the mirror there is glass. But in the mirror the glass is covered with a little silver; and no sooner is the silver added than you cease to see others and see only yourself" (Ansky 1971: 65).

MAD: "Constant technological improvements in the scape and versatility of nuclear weapons and missile systems ultimately enabled a global achievement of 'mutual assured destruction' (or MAD) – a technoscientific belief system that promised immediate retaliatory nuclear strikes for any nuclear aggression" (Masco 2006: 8).

don't breathe: "Three workers at Los Alamos National Laboratory were contaminated on the job last month when an accident released radioactive material into the air and sent it spreading through a wing of the lab's plutonium facility. It was the second time in four weeks that lab workers were exposed to radioactive particles at the facility, and the same crew was involved in both events, according to a weekly report from the Defense Nuclear Facilities Safety Board, an independent adviser to the U.S. Department of Energy" (Moss 2017).

Atomic Wrecking

Conceived in a tube of fissionable seeds, a Fat Man, a fully grown homunculus of a type never before seen, was born to proud physicist fathers lighting smokes in the flare of their shaded eyes.

Decades later, in a shotgun wedding between Logic and Chance, a brand new truck was hitched to a "safe-secure trailer" balancing a trio of TRUPACT containers proudly standing ten feet tall---

> *cinches snapped...*
> > *canisters leaked...*

It's a window, not a mirror, reflecting eyes gone MAD as a truck skids around a bend to

> ATOMIC WRECKING---

> When you see this sign,
> don't breathe, *just drive!*

Christian Fish: "Symbologically, [Ichthys] is actually the hook or bait on God's fishing rod with which the Leviathan – death of the devil – is caught" (Jung 1981: 112).

island: "[Laguna's] early traditions and beliefs point to [an] island, for such it must have been, as the cradle of the Queres nation. The island is Spipap. Now, in the water which surrounded this island lived a monstrous animal or fish, the 'Wa-wa-keh,' that vomited water. Thus fish came up and threw such quantities of water over the land that it was submerged and all the people who had remained on the island perished. These traditions … are peculiar in one way, showing that these Indians were at one time a sea-faring people." https://nmsta tehood.unm.edu/node/75050 (Accessed 22nd May 2018).

Acres of pits: The Jackpile-Paguate mine, owned by Anaconda Minerals Corp. See Laguna Cracked.

May: On the fifth day of the fifth month the Boys' Festival, celebrating boys of ages six or seven having survived early childhood, is held in Japan. Pennants depicting carps are flown, the carp symbolizing good luck. (*Yu* = "fish" and "abundance." Both characters share the same sound but are written differently.)

bulging eyes: "satchel and sword, too, / displayed for Fifth Month: / carp streamers." (M. Basho. From, "The Narrow Road to the Deep North." D. L. Barnhill, trans.) Basho is referring to the sword of Minamoto Yoshitsune (1159–89), who was the greatest romantic hero of premodern Japan. Yoshitsune is said to have had bulging eyes. The pannier belonged to the warrior-monk Saito Musashibo Benkei. After being defeated by the young Yoshitsune on a bridge in Kyoto, Benkei became his loyal retainer.

drink the ruins: "To cure childhood illnesses, a reliable medicine consists of potsherds gathered from old ruins, ground fine, and drunk in water. The sherds are impregnated with power because they were made in one of the four epochs of the distant past, in each of which people were created by 'Our Mother' (Iyatik) but later destroyed (not having proved entirely satisfactory), and replaced by a presumably better group" (Tyler 1984: 253).

Mother's cloaked lap: "'Naiya iyatik said that she would never come out of the earth. If I go out into the world and people see me they will not prosper. If they do not see me, they can pray to me and I can help them.' And my old woman informant added, 'For this reason there is no face on the iyatik [the corn ear fetish], so they will not see her'" (Parsons 1920: 90).

discrete blooming: "In the late nineteenth century the church, which had finally admitted trees into cemeteries, turned its attacks on funeral wreaths, a pagan rite if ever there was one" (Regon 1983: 116).

Laguna with Fish

Before the Christian Fish hooked itself, marshes flourished, wild game gamboled in the bracken; cornfields, melons, apple, apricot orchards were lovingly tended.

> A garden is an island.
> A fish-baiting man is a man-eating fish.
> A deep hole is a quarry filled to the brim.

Acres of pits and underground mines, the earth turned inside out, hauled up, refined.

Caught in the combers of May winds, in Japan arching fishtails celebrate boys who survived the contaminants of growing up while hooked on the past, anguished fins beating against invisible currents and bulging eyes---

> What's become of History's carping voices?
> Bone dry.

We drink the ruins as if elixir, whispering to children sitting in Mother's cloaked lap, adding stories to stories, ancestral remains flowering from the depths, a discrete blooming drowned in devotions deeper than our shallow selves.

> This world keeps bobbing up,
> groundless;
> each corpse replaces another.

contamination: "Soil vapor studies conducted in 2007 by Sandia Lab, for example, show that cancer-causing volatile organic solvents are moving deeper beneath the Mixed Waste Landfill. Sandia has also reported that tritium concentrations are ten times higher, and found at deeper levels, than a decade ago; tritium is a radioactive form of hydrogen that binds well with oxygen to form radioactive fluids" (Hiller 2013: 3).

weave at night: The first mammal to be active in the daytime probably lived around 66 million years ago, about 200,000 years after the mass extinction that wiped out the dominant saurian species.

toying: "It remained for the theory of 'total war' to banish war's cultural function and extinguish the last vestige of the play-element" (Huizinga 2016: 90).

Hell's Canyon: Bisects the two mesas on which the Sandia National Laboratory's facility is located.

Stegosaurus: "Roof lizard." Plated dinosaurs who walked on all four legs, rearing to browse trees.

Triceratops: "Three-horned face." Both sexes had horns, which identifies the horns as weapons, not implements for intraspecific combat.

Allosaurus: "Other lizard." A flesh eater whose tail was over half its length. It is believed that Allosaurus ate only carrion, being too clumsy to hunt.

Tyrannosaurus rex: "Tyrant lizard." This king of the dinosaurs was the most savage hunter that ever lived on land.

extinction: "Extinction may be the first scientific idea that kids today have to grapple with. One-year-olds are given toy dinosaurs to play with, and two-year-olds understand, in a vague sort of way at least, that these small plastic creatures represent very large animals" (Kolbert 2014: 23).

X-rays: The Particle Beam Fusion Accelerator (PBFA II) began operation in 1985 at Sandia National Laboratories, located in Albuquerque. In 1996, it was converted into the Z facility. Another overhaul was completed in 2007, making the Z Machine the largest X-ray generator in the world designed to test materials in conditions of extreme temperatures and pressures, and gather data for the computer modeling of nuclear weapons.

the daughters: The daughter isotopes of hydrogen, used as fuel for fusion reactions, are deuterium and tritium.

Sandia Dinosaurs

Stone Age relics lumber to the edge of a desktop zoo, or wander across
the floor, emerging from trash cans, from the rank contamination of
mephitic swamps, peat moss bogs, liana-laden swales---rodent-size
mammals weave at night
between massive saurian feet.

We dream of toying with the naturalized forces of a nervous system
rumbling up from Hell's Canyon like an armor-plated Stegosaurus,
spiked Triceratops, Allosaurus, Tyrannosaurus rex threatening to
flatten our disjunctive lives.

Species are measured for extinction
like X-rays created
in the same mind as
the daughters of hydrogen light.

LAMPF: "The Los Alamos Meson Physics Facility (LAMPF) [is] a national center for medium energy physics investigations of nuclear structure, providing beams of nucleons and mesons, some ten thousand times more intense than now available. These beams [are] generated by impinging an intense beam of protons on a target. The proton beam is generated by a linear accelerator (linac) about 2600 feet long which forms the heart of the facility and incorporates many substantial advances in the state-of-the-art of microwave power technology" (Hagerman and Amerson 1968: 75–9).

turtle's: According to the Kalabari tribe of Nigeria, a supernatural tortoise, "old man of the forest," demolished the world in a dance of destruction.

Columns: "There is reason to believe that the [atom] bomb actually exploded approximately 50 meters southwest of the Aioi Bridge where Shima Hospital stood, because concrete columns flanking the entrance of this hospital were driven straight into the ground" (Hachiya 1955: 64).

A hat drifts: One day, while still a child, the poet Georg Trakl walked into a lake, and before he was noticed had submerged himself. It was only by his floating hat that rescuers were able to find and save him from drowning.

nuclear sprites: The second stage of the LAMPF accelerator is the drift-tube Alvarez unit, four tanks connected in tandem, in which the protons are accelerated to almost half the speed of light.

Tartarus' ova: When foreseeing a flood, tortoises bury their eggs in safer, higher places.

darker: The lowest region of hell, "three times as dark as the darkest night," where Zeus confined the rebellious Titans.

Hunting: "the age of the hunter, the Paleolithic, comprises by far the largest part of human history ... From this perspective, then, we can understand man's terrifying violence as deriving from the behavior of the predatory animal, whose characteristics he came to acquire in the course of becoming man" (Berkert 1985: 17).

LAMPF

Tubular guts of a labyrinthine machine shatter a world of assumptions,
reinforcing the illusion of protons dancing on a turtle's back.

Columns were driven through horizons of anatomy, ionizing malignancies
that thrive in the greatness of complex events.

A hat drifts...
       then seeks its fate in the blue depths of materialized heights,
dips into a children's story of nuclear sprites bubbling to the top,
churning in a gargantuan belly, in support of a malleable dream.

Myths fish the ambiguous rivers of tradition;
Tartarus' ova, "darker than the darkest night,"
buried in higher places.

Hunting predatory odors, unfledged thoughts evolve---
summarily trapped,
methodically clubbed
to death.

Tibbets: "[A]t the instant of the blast [Lieutenant Colonel Paul Tibbets] had 'a tingling sensation in my mouth and the very definite taste of lead upon my tongue.' According to Tibbets, scientists later told him that this was caused by an interaction between the fillings in his teeth and the radiation released by the bomb" (Preston 2005: 301).

Lucky Dragon: The Fukuryu Maru was a 93-ft. Japanese trawler with a crew of twenty-three. On March 1, 1954, fishing eighty-five miles east of Bikini Atoll, it was caught in the fallout from a U.S. nuclear test. All of its crew suffered radiation sickness; one sailor died 9 months later. Although in medieval Europe a dragon was symbolic of the Devil, in the Far East one aspect of the dragon represents good luck. (In China, a red dragon is the guardian of "higher science.")

eyes cried: When biophysicist Yasushi Nichiwaki held his Geiger counter to the fish from the Fukuryu Maru, "his instrument rattled away to the tune of 2,000 counts per minute! Personifying the situation, the bystanders murmured in awe, 'The fish are crying.' Thereafter, radioactive fish became known as 'crying fish'" (Lapp 1958: 90).

Snark: Coined by Lewis Carroll (Charles Lutwidge Dodgson), English mathematician and author of children's books, with reference to his poem, "The Hunting of the Snark." Here the Snark is a cruise missile with a self-contained celestial navigation system. The Snark was an interim weapon, used until ICBM's became operational, and was phased out in the 1960s.

smoke rings: A characteristic of the Minuteman ICBM is a smoke ring from its first-stage exhaust.

its shape: "It is possible to speak of the true form of a kimono only after it has been put on the human body. In other words, it is the wearer who, according to his proficiency, creates the form" (Yamanaka 1982: 9).

St. George: "The town of St. George, Utah, which lies about 242 km east of Yucca Flats [Nevada nuclear test site], has become known as Fallout City. On May 19, 1953, an unspecified accident with the detonation of a bomb called 'Harry' exposed St. George to more fallout than was ever to be measured in any other populated area" (Zimmerman and Dennis 1984: 314).

fried rice: "I saw Professor Takenaka standing at the foot of the bridge [in Hiroshima] ... he had a rice ball in his right hand ... His naked figure standing there before the flames with that rice ball looked to me as a symbol of the modest hope of human beings" (Inoue 1977: 10).

skeletal fish: "In [Professor Shogo] Nagaoka's home piles of fragments and remnants [from Hiroshima] grew taller, memorials to a technological civilization entering the suicidal phase" (Jungk 1961: 25).

Nuclear Sushi Museum

The taste that surfaced on Tibbets' tongue nine years later was deadly
to a Lucky Dragon swallowing fish whose eyes cried poisoned tears.

> We can't live without breathing the air of Hiroshima,
> no drink without swallowing waters of Bikini Lagoon.

"Unclassified nuclear weapon shapes" are displayed like trophies
curated out of context, emasculating history with their laser taxonomy,
in which a Snark is "handy for striking a light" to a Minuteman missile
blowing smoke rings that blacken the sun; each generation cloaking the
next in metaphors no longer fitting.

> In a dark closet,
> a kimono tries on
> the trajectory of its shape---
>
> Kimono and obi,
> the pride of straight lines,
> like missile designs.

Heaven cooks with thermonuclear heat, sautéing St. George's dragon
and fried rice served with the soul of sailor and the eyes of skeletal fish.

monstrous: "When I came in this game [of fractal shapes], there was a total absence of intuition. One had to create an intuition from scratch. Intuition as it was trained by the usual tools – the hand, the pencil, and the ruler – found these shapes quite monstrous and pathological" (Mandelbrot 2008: 102).

plowed into: On December 8, 1953, a few months after the Soviet Union exploded its first hydrogen bomb, President Dwight Eisenhower delivered his "Atoms for Peace" proposal to the United Nations. Included was the short-lived Plowshare Program, of which, on December 10, 1961, 25 miles southwest of Carlsbad, NM, Project Gnome became the first test.

twice-born: Conventional explosives above ground were set to fire 5 minutes after the A-blast; instead, they went off a moment after the shock.

seep through: "Although it had been planned as a contained explosion, GNOME vented to the atmosphere. A cloud of steam started to appear at the top of the shaft 2 to 3 minutes after the detonation. Gray smoke and steam, with associated radioactivity, emanated from the shaft opening for about 7 minutes after the detonation." "Projects Gnome and Sedan." www.dtra.mil/Portals/61/Documents/NTPR/1-Fact_Sheets/25_PLOWSHARE.pdf (Accessed 29th May 2018)

sensitive instruments: The shock wave traveled at 20,000 foot per second along extremely hard strata as much as 10 miles deep. A second wave traveled deep in loose layers of the earth's crust at approximately 10,000 foot per second.

administrators: One derivation of "gnome" is from the ancient German Kuba-Walda, "home administrator." There are various other claims, including the Greek *gnosis*, "knowledge."

flattened cap: "a gnome without a cap is not a gnome, and he knows it" (Huygen 1977: unpaginated).

Bacon's philosophy: Francis Bacon (1561–1626).

lionizing: "Our way through the desert of life or any moment in life is the awakening to it as a desert, the awakening of the beast, that vigil of desire, its greedy paw, hot and sleepless as the sun, fulminating as sulphur, setting the soul on fire" (Hillman 2014: 66).

stars: "In earlier times the gnome was an accepted member of society … But that was when waters were clear and forests virginal, when roads led peacefully from one settlement to another, when the heavens were filled only with birds and stars" (Huygen: ibid.).

Project Gnome

Where the desert shrinks bloated dreams into feats of engineering,
an intuitively monstrous breccia of fractal patterns rolls chaotically
inward, refiguring political objectives as a five kiloton-device
sighted at the end of a crook-shaped tunnel.

Forged into a "physics package"
and plowed into the earth, twice-born puffs of vapor
seep through the arms of sensitive instruments.

A dwarfish race of administrators,
who salted the earth's mineral wealth into their own veins,
exploded into a saline puddle,
their insidious breath bunged by a flattened cap.

Before electricity and Bacon's philosophy
fingers served as souls on cellular retreats,
lionizing the scars from Industry's greedy paw,
guarded by angels who dance once more
on this trackless sand,
igniting the feathers of surrounding stars.

Desire's fantasy: "Desire 'travels,' moves from one representation to another. This movement is destructive in two ways. First of all, images are constantly being abandoned for other images; secondly, the entire movement is generated by the need to get rid of the irritating lack of desire, to replace the emptiness in even more ecstatic fantasy by the imaginary plentitude of satisfaction" (Bersani 1977: 85).

unleashing: "I finally unleash your metallic bridle … You launch yourself, / intoxicatingly, into the liberating Infinite!" (E. Marinetti. From, "To the Automobile.")

Pegasus: This winged horse, born of Medusa's blood, is also the child of Poseidon, "Master of Horses."

love gasoline: Refers to Marcel Duchamp's, The Bride Stripped Bare by Her Bachelors, Even (The Large Glass). "(T)he Bride is a tank of love gasoline or timid power … The other name for this timid power is automobile: love gasoline" (Paz 1990: 51).

prime ribs: The gods always demand the choice part of the kill.

burnt offerings: Rocket Lounge is located in Alamogordo, NM. With reference to the first test of an Atomic Bomb 65 miles to the northwest, "Alamogordo could be the altar on which the whole earth was set up as a burnt offering" (Charlton 1986: 260).

talked about: "In March 1944, the director of engineering of Peenemuende, Professor von Braun, and two of his leading men were put in jail by the German Gestapo because they had thought and talked too much about space travel and not about the rocket as a weapon" (Dornberger 1964: 45).

These same men: "A peculiarity of the language of American rocketeers is its use of technical expressions taken bodily from the German" (Jungk 1954: 26).

The Friendliest Place on Earth: Alamogordo, NM, was a center for the development of the United States' space program.

the moon: Addressing the Mystery rites at Eleusis: "Two priestesses presided over the rites, representing Demeter as the Mother of Life and Persephone as Queen of Death and Mistress of the Underworld – the light and dark sides of the moon" (Hall 1991: 83).

let her down: In the myth of Persephone, Hades drives "his horses out of the gaping earth in heroic style. He lifts the girl into his chariot and takes his ravished bride on a long journey over the earth before turning back to his subterranean realm" (Kerenyi 1967: 35).

Rocket Lounge

Americans fall for Desire's fantasy of mobility, unleashing horses
beneath metallic hoods, stretching Pegasus to hundreds of cylindrical
feet, burning
billions of barrels of love gasoline.

In Rocket Lounge prime ribs sizzle,
burnt offerings frying beneath
a reddening sky.

Darkness lengthens behind the brightest scientists who talked about
flying into the cosmos, while the missiles they designed rained death
down on another country's population.

These same men were invited to "The Friendliest Place on Earth,"
designing rockets to reach the moon in the shadow of a terrified girl
raped and kidnapped by a god
who drove her to a life that let
her down.

little man: Harry Gold was "A pudgy, sad-faced little man," and a spy for the Soviet Union. "About him, the federal prosecutor had said: 'Harry Gold, who furnished the absolute corroboration of the testimony of [David and Ruth Greenglass], forged the necessary link in the chain that points indisputably to the guilt of [Julius and Ethel Rosenberg]'" (Schneir and Schneir 1983: 70, 155).

Jell-O: "At the [Rosenbergs'] trial, despite the addition of a number of other espionage allegations, the events of June 3, 1945, formed the core of the government's case. The matching pieces of a jello box as a means of identification is today one of the best-known cloak-and-dagger episodes of history" (Ibid: 372).

blossoms: "When her husband joined her in Sing Sing prison, where they would both await their execution for treason, Ethel Rosenberg wrote: 'My dearest husband, what heaven and what hell to welcome you to monotonous days and joyless nights, to endless desire and endless denial. And yet here shall we plight our troth anew, here held fast by brick and concrete and steel shall our love put forth gripping root and tender blossom'" (Hyde 1981: 232). The couple was electrocuted on June 19, 1953, one day after their fourteenth wedding anniversary.

kitchen: Harry Gold and David Greenglass met at 209 High Street, Albuquerque, NM, Apt. 4.

a sketch: "Of the Greenglass sketch showing a cross section of this bomb, Morrison said, it is 'barren of any meaningful or correct *quantitative* information'" (Radosh and Milton 1997: 433). Philip Morrison was the Los Alamos physicist who designed a magnesium-carrying case for the Fat Man bomb that destroyed Nagasaki, Japan.

cockroaches: The female cockroach secretes a chemical (pheromone) that attracts male roaches. The CIA had an inspiration to use pheromone for tracking suspected spies. The suspect would be unknowingly stained with the attractant, in order to be positively identified later – caught in the act of espionage by the roaches stampeding toward him?

the White House: "It all starts with that devilishly creative act of imagining something which is infinitely destructive. Then they go to Franklin Roosevelt or Harry Truman or Ronald Reagan and say, 'Here's this thing. Do you want it?' The answer is invariably, you bet we do!" (Taylor 1987: 166)

enemy's heart: "When you defeat an enemy you are required to eat his heart. In this way is your victory recorded with the Gods ... You consume the heart of your enemy so that it can no longer be said of him that he exists – except as he exists in you" (Doctorow 2007: 235).

Spies like Flies

One day in June, a little man in a trench coat, collar turned up, hat brim down, rapped on the door, an empty box of Jell-O torn in half and held in a hand. Its red gelatin blossoms had been molded and chilled into the shape of his cause. Invited into a greasy kitchen, he was handed a sketch of a cartoonist's vision of a nuclear bomb.

A fly with a tiny transmitter clung to a slippery wall, while cockroaches scurried behind cold gas stove, secreting evidence of the undercover act, while a clandestine army of ants ferried the transcripts to a classified formicary hidden beneath the White House in Washington D.C.

In an ornate room in the Kremlin's dark belly, red flecks clinging to his moustache's stiff broom, Uncle Joe Stalin is laughing uncontrollably, dining on a dish of gelatin dessert in the shape of his enemy's heart.

Classroom: "Consider a [classroom] informed by the spirit of Venus or Aphrodite … There would be no dry lectures or dry books coming from this moist [green] goddess. Growth in new ideas, new forms, new styles would be prominent. Relationship, sensuality, concern for beauty and comfort, gracefulness, care for the body and for emotions – these would be both the benefits and the problems of this kind of dominance" (Moore 1990: 61).

bony helmets: "In 7th grade the teacher blasted / her whistle and we dove / under our desks. Our hands / made frail bony helmets / to cut the risk of brain damage." (D. Hilton. From, "1952.")

soiled conditions: "[S]ince radon travels the path of least resistance through soil, it enters a house in localized spots; concentrations can vary from one side of a room to another, and from day to day, depending on soil conditions" (Cole 1990: 18).

fumes: "When you get down to lower dose levels, for example from natural background radiation or inhaling radon, then you do not get these cell-killing effects … What you get are more subtle effects in the cell. These are modifications to the cell, conventionally of mutations in DNA. They do not kill the cell, but can lead to changes, such that in several years' time this can develop into a cancer" (Dacey 2019: 1/7).

animal bladders: The history of protective respiratory equipment can be traced back to the first century, when Pliny the Elder (circa A.D. 23–79) used animal bladder skins to protect workers in Roman mines from red lead oxide dust.

sulphurous: Refers to an alchemical theory of two "exhalations," or principles, which form the difference between metals and minerals. Some alchemists believed these to be an "ideal" form of sulphur and mercury, "'secret sulphur,' sometimes green in color, a 'male and universal seed,' the Holy Ghost, the life-spirit itself. Celestial sulphur is the first and most potent cause of generation" (Grinnell 1973: 27).

apple: "The unexpected relationship between the Demon of Death to the most ecstatic moments of life is … illuminated by the fact that the apple [was] particularly holy to Aphrodite – the apple appears as a symbol embodying both death and renewal" (Herzog 2000: 85).

progenies sealed: "If [anyone wants to] know how a gas mask feels, let him seize his nose with a pair of fire tongs, bury his face in a hot feather pillow, then seize a gas pipe with his teeth and breathe through it for a few hours while he performs routine duties. It is safe, but like the deadly poison which forced its invention, it is not sane" (Anonymous 1968: 35).

Radon Classroom

Children curl beneath hardwood desks,
hands clasped behind their "frail bony helmets,"
spines like trees bending toward the classroom's dusty green carpet,
bearing poisonous fruit from soiled conditions.

As fumes infiltrate young minds, obscure roots spread and take refuge
in animal bladders, a savage progeny of radioactive gases lodged in
bronchial branches,
attacking cell nuclei,
diluting sulphurous life into
                     quicksilver death.

An apple for the teacher, her progenies sealed in rubbery gas masks.

Vaughn: U.S.60 and U.S.54 meet at Vaughn, NM, where they continue south as U.S.285, heading for the 10,240-acre Waste Isolation Pilot Plant (WIPP) site east of Carlsbad.

roadrunners: *Geococcyx californianus* is the State Bird of New Mexico. "Few brains, topped / by a crown– / And a flair for swift in-fighting–" (P. Whalen. From, "The Road-Runner.")

feathered garb: "Tim and Kim and Don and I were talking about / what an awful authoritarian garb Doctors / and Nurses wear, really, how spooky it is. / 'What should they wear?' – 'Masks and Feathers!'" (G. Snyder. From, "The Blue Sky.")

*lung-gom-pa***:** Tibetan "trance walkers" who are able to travel vast distances without tiring. "The deeper meaning of *lung-gom* is that matter can be mastered by the spiritual, i.e., consisting in strict seclusion and mental concentration upon certain elemental forces and their visualized symbols, accompanied by the recitation of *mantras*" (Govinda 1970: 81).

pentagon: "According to the old view, five is the number of the natural ('hylical') man, whose outstretched arms and legs form, with the head, a pentagram" (Jung 2005: 219). The Pentagon is also the headquarters of the United States Department of Defense, in Arlington, VA.

evil spirits: "Because two toes [of a roadrunner] point forward and two backward, it can be difficult to determine the direction the bird is going. One belief of the Pueblo [Indians of New Mexico] is that a safe afterlife for the deceased can be ensured by placing roadrunner tracks around the house of the dead. This will confuse evil spirits as to the direction taken by the spirit of the dead" (Meinzer 2003: 8).

Naturally good: The Cowboy, in pulp novels, was drawn to be "naturally good, sound to the core, though he may appear unruly and devilish on the surface." He also had "a natural understanding of world affairs" (Dressain 1970: 480, 481).

mercurial god: "[Jung's] choice of Hermes-Mercurius as the darkener, as the *psychopomp* to the underworld, echoes the Homeric hymn to Hermes, where this God is 'the only recognized messenger to Hades,' as he is Bringer of Dreams" (Hillman 1979: 89).

coffins: Slang for containers that transport nuclear waste.

trains don't stop: In 2018, Vaughn's population was down to 412, and its police department consisted of Nikka, the drug-sniffing dog. The Santa Fe and the Southern Pacific railroads intersected here, but the last depot was shut down in the 1980s.

Vaughn

Where roadrunners rot in the sun, technicians of the sacred shed
feathered garb for regular pay, lopping like tireless *lung-gom-pa,*
a pentagon with wide eyes trained on a long-dead star.
No confusion in directions; evil spirits are too engaged

At the close of the Civil War, teenaged boys, "Naturally good, sound
to the core"---in floppy hats and leather chaps, high-heeled boots with
jingle-jangle spurs, bellies full of red beans and chicory, maneuvered
frisky ponies along spooky routes...

where a mercurial god is now the dream of bright red trucks
hauling coffins through towns like Vaughn,
                        where the trains don't stop
                                        anymore.

Rio Puerco: Located about 50 miles south of Albuquerque, the Rio Puerco is a tributary of the Rio Grande. Its Spanish name is usually translated as Muddy River, as it normally only runs part of the year.

sheep: For centuries, sheep have been central to Navajo economic life and spirituality.

uremic: "Flood myths frequently represent the flood as urine, thereby revealing their dream origin" (Roheim 1988: 169).

thorium: Thorium 230, with a half-life of 80,000 years, tends to deposit in the liver, bone marrow and lymphatic tissue, where it can cause cancer and leukemia.

dam: The dam, owned by United Nuclear Corporation, was built of earth with a clay core, 25 foot high, 30 foot wide. At the time it broke it was retaining a load more than 2 foot higher than allowed for in its design.

downstream: "In the early morning of July 16, 1979 – fourteen weeks after the accident at Three Mile Island ... the dam at Church Rock burst, sending eleven hundred tons of radioactive mill wastes and ninety million gallons of contaminated liquid pouring [down the Rio Puerco] toward Arizona" (Wasserman and Solomon 1982: 177).

glyphs: This glyph is allegedly the sign for water on Neolithic vases.

Kweo Kachina: Hopi. A blue wolf kachina, Kweo is a "side dancer" who appears with Deer and Antelope, calling forth the Hopi gift for elaboration.

liquored: "Liquor" is a term used for liquid waste from the milling of uranium ore.

distance: "For whatever we do today in physics – whether we release energy processes that ordinarily go on only in the sun ... or disperse radioactive particles, created by us through the use of cosmic radiation, on the earth – we always handle nature from a point in the universe outside of earth" (Arendt 1958: 262).

Clouds: "The cloud-mask and the conception of the dead to which it relates, the cloud-people, are highly *aitherialised forms* ... To the Greeks aither, which means blazing, was an acceptable home for the departed spirits. To the Pueblos, water rather than fire represents the purest essence of the heavens and the likely transfiguration of the dead" (Tyler 1964: 57).

feral tongues: "The market of Argos stood under the protection of Apollo, worshipped here as 'Lykeios,' a name which was taken to mean 'wolf-like,' in this context Sophocles calls him 'wolf-killer'" (Berkert 1983: 108).

Rio Puerco

Hoof prints of sheep point across a land suffering with an incubus
of hot uremic isotopes, acid-leached uranium, polonium and
silvery thorium, breaching a dam,
raising manhole covers far downstream,
scored with watery glyphs.

Kweo Kachina,

liquored up
leans back,
feet dangling over an edge,
falling from a distance that rebounds in a seamless horizon
evolving with mesas wallowing in marl, cacti, mesquite,
quenching their thirst with addled mud.

Clouds haunt this river filled
with gods and sentient beings
sluicing over feral tongues.

aardvark: The name *aardvark*, Afrikaans for "earth pig," is unrelated to any present-day animal. It is the last survivor of a family of mammals 60 million years old.

Anteater of the air: The F-111 Aardvark, designed under the doctrine of Massive (nuclear) Retaliation, was the attempt the Kennedy Administration's Secretary of Defense, Robert Strange McNamara, made to develop a high-performance aircraft that could carry both conventional and nuclear weapons for both the Air Force and Navy. The overall concept proved to be a failure.

wings swept back: In the original design of the TFX's (F-111) Stable Variable Sweep Wing, the pivot point was inside the fuselage, which shifted the longitudinal stability with each angle of sweep. NASA engineers made the breakthrough by moving the point of pivot outside the body.

Southeast Asia: Originally designed to deliver nuclear bombs, the Aardvark was used in the Vietnam War with, at first, mainly negative results because of its underpowered engines, a condition later corrected.

Libyan Desert: On April 14, 1986, under code name Operation Eldorado Canyon, 24 F-111Ds of the U.S. 48th Tactical Fighter Wing, based at Lackenheath, England, in the longest fighter combat mission in history, raided Libya. Several civilians, including at least one child, were killed.

a pig: In 1386 the tribunal of Falaise, France, condemned a pig to be tortured and then hanged for having mangled a child who later died. The pig was dressed in a man's clothes, then executed in public. The hangman was paid 10 sous and 10 deniers, plus a pair of pigskin gloves.

intelligent eyes: "The men threw themselves on [the pig]. For a moment he was invisible beneath the heap of men, and he lay still. I could see one of his eyes. The pig has intelligent eyes, and his fear was now intelligent" (Berger 1980: 42).

Here: Cannon AFB, Clovis, NM.

a unit: The 27th Tactical Fighter Wing was the only wing in the Air Force equipped with the "D" model F-111.

calmly observing: "Such calm can be read as a sign of the way that the Bomb has been neutralized in the minds of our children and transformed into just another weapon. This neutralization may well have begun with the first *Star Wars* film in which a child could see an entire world destroyed without any noticeable disruption in the lives of the story's heroes" (Solomon 1988: 92).

Cannon AFB

An aardvark's long snout, snake-like tongue, ears of a donkey, camel's
hump, kangaroo's tail, tubular teeth of a shark; with the claws of a bear
probing roots,
        a little something for everyone---

Anteater of the air: 20 mm M61 cannon, two 340 kg. conventional bombs,
two AIM-54 Phoenix long-range air-to-air missiles, one nuclear bomb.

With wings swept back, there were sorties from Southeast Asia to the
Libyan Desert, where new species hunt in the skin of the old.

What's the meaning of the image of a pig whose appetite turned an
inquisitive child into a pail of slops? Penned and tortured, the swine
was hung dressed as a man in formal attire: clean white shirt, sunglasses hiding its intelligent eyes, watching his old school tie become
the fatal knot,

Here flies flags of
                a nation,
                a state,
                a unit...

calmly observing
                what it can destroy.

Ram Mesa: One of the mesas overlooking the Rio Puerco and the site of the United Nuclear Corporation's (UNC's) uranium mine. Located in McKinley Co., NM, it covers about 125 acres, 17 miles northeast of Grants and 1 mile from the Navajo Reservation. The mill operated from mid-1977 until mid-1982.

The ram is associated with Mars, the god of war, who "leaves us exposed to the return of the repressed, as rude eruptive violence … and as paranoid defenses against delusional enemies" (Hillman 2007: 133). Hillman makes a distinction between "the ram of territory and head-on collision [and] the eagle of piercing surprise and the uplifting rapture of nuclearism" (Ibid: 135).

there are only victims: On July 16, 1979 a dam at the UNC mill broke, releasing 90 million gallons of radioactivity into the Rio Puerco, contaminating water at least 70 miles downstream. More than 350 Navajo families depended upon this water for their livestock.

drained and buried: The UNC mill "used an acid leach, solvent extraction method [lixiviation] to extract uranium from the ore. The acid leach process produced a wet, acidic waste, commonly known as tailings, which were pumped to a disposal area. An estimated 3.5 million tons of tailings were disposed of in ponds until discharge ceased in May 1982." ("Superfund Project Update, July 15 2019." U.S. Environmental Protection Agency, Dallas, TX.) https://cumulis.epa.gov/supercpad/SiteProfiles/index.cfm?fuseaction=second.Cleanup&id=0600819#bkground

monstrous myth: Cliff Monster, "conceived by the self-abuse of a chief's daughter with a feather quill [is known as] He-throws-against-the-rocks, named from his habit of catching people in his long sharp claws and throwing them to his children lower among the rocks" (Reichard 1974: 422).

gives birth: According to a tale of the Siberian Buryats the first shaman was conceived from the union between an eagle (the first totemic shaman) and a woman sleeping beneath a tree.

human figure: "When the old Eagles came home at night, they took off their downy garments, which opened down the front, revealing human forms in white suits which were never removed" (Reichard: ibid: 432)

Black Eagle: The black eagle, along with "the dragon, the roaring fiery lion, and the night raven," are alchemical "synonyms for the devil" (Jung 1967: 198).

Tree of Life: "Probably this bird's association with healing is very ancient for according to the *Avesta (Yasht, xii.17)* it dwells on a tree called 'All-healing'" (Armstrong 1970: 125).

United Nuclear

Ram Mesa butts against heroic piles of lixiviated grammars
and apocalyptic spoils.

Here there are only victims, hunter and prey drained and buried
by the same legislation whose quills penned a monstrous myth
in which bodies are thrown to the foot of a tree where a woman,
pregnant from flight in an eagle's arms, gives birth in a dream
to a human figure in the skin of a radiation protective suit.

The Black Eagle builds his nest in the Tree of Life,
where even designers, makers and planners
of nuclear weapons and wars
                    may be healed.

Nike/Hercules: Nike was a child of the river Styx (*stygeo*: to hate). "Her children [Nike's sisters are Bia: 'violence,' Zelos: 'jealousy,' and Kratos: 'force'] provide the prototypes for that crusading morality which accompanies the ego on its righteous tasks of destroying in order to maintain itself" (Hillman 1979: 86).

"The cults of the Gods are cults of epithets that image the divine figures in concrete terms: Aider Hercules, Protector-from-Evil Hercules, Warlike Hercules, Victor Hercules – the name gives an image and suggests a mytheme" (Ibid.: 62).

The Nike/Hercules system was a surface-to-air missile. It was normally armed with the W31 nuclear warhead.

boar: The Erymanthian boar was run to ground by Hercules, and presented alive to King Eurystheus.

man-eating mares: Hercules tamed the Thracian horses of King Diomedes by slaying their master.

ravaging birds: Building their nests near Lake Stymphalus, the birds ravaged the surrounding fields until Hercules, and his faithful companion Iolaus, shot them down.

Hydra: The "grisly-minded" Hydra lived in the swamps of Lerna. With arrows, sickle and torch Hercules and his nephew, Iolaus, attacked the ogre, who assumed a new head for each one decapitated. The warriors' solution was to cauterize the wounds, thus promoting healing and death at the same time! Here, the Lernian Hydra presages MIRVs (Multiple Independently targetable Reentry Vehicles).

weakening: The last Hercules missile was launched in Italy on November 24, 2006. It was replaced by the more advanced Hawk and Patriot missiles.

standing guard: The Nike/Hercules monument overlooks White Sands Missile Range, NM State Highway 70, St. Augustine Pass.

santos: Fashioned primarily from home-crafted local materials, these images of saints were "for the people of New Mexico in the last century an instrument within a network or system of such related activities as prayer, penance, pilgrimages, processions, and the like" (Steele 1974: 26).

hi-tech god: "it is claimed that the NIKE can out maneuver bombers, fighters or transport planes, and it can operate regardless of weather conditions and visibility" (Burgess 1957: 151).

mechanical bird: One of the earliest known experiments with flying was the "pigeon of Archytas," an aeolipile in the form of a bird suspended from strings, with counterweights, and propelled by steam emitting from its body. The bird of course didn't actually fly, but circled on its axis.

Nike/Hercules

Each inch of earth is a threshold,
                    another step,
                            another dream.

Behind a scrim bleached with their blood, animals stalk: lion and boar,
man-eating mares, ravaging birds, and a Hydra with multiple heads.

Looked at from the future:

Gathered before a hero whose strength gives peaceful pretensions
the stigma of a bloody nose,
to whom Victory is cognate with Death's cold stare
shooting from one side of Hell
                        to the Other.

Sirocco winds sharpen themselves on flanges of the Hero's weakening
flanks standing guard with his nose in the air.

While pilgrims bathe in a vision of sunset,
their children hold *santos* of a hi-tech god
in a land that double-crosses itself.

In what have we come to believe?

        A rocket flying like the Holy Ghost,
                        a mechanical bird of prey,

Mortandad: Sp. "Loss of life," "slaughter," etc.

spongy ground: "The U.S. Energy Department is still uncertain about the extent of contamination from a massive plume of chromium that resulted from decades of poor waste management at Los Alamos National Laboratory. Doug Hintze with the Energy Department's environmental management field office in Los Alamos told state lawmakers during a recent hearing that cancer-causing chromium and other chemicals have continued to seep from the soil in Mortandad Canyon into the groundwater." "Extent of Los Alamos chromium contamination still uncertain." Associated Press, September 25th 2017. www.abqjournal.com/1068856/extent-of-los-alamos-chromium-contamination-still-uncertain.html (Accessed 26th May 2018)

screech: In Hebrew, one meaning of Lilith is "screech owl." "There is only one reference to Lilith as a night or screech owl in the Old Testament. It occurs in the midst of a prophecy in Isaiah. On the day of Yahweh's vengeance, when the land will be turned into a wildness, 'the satyr shall cry to his fellow; the screech owl also shall rest there, and find for herself a place of rest' (Isa. 34:14)" (Baring and Cashford 1991: 510).

pre-hostility: Military euphemism for peace.

collateral damage: Military euphemism for the killing of civilians.

environmental adjustment: Massive destruction of the environment.

Bombs and bowls: "What is the bomb? It is the wild in its modern guise … the very wilderness of old in a different shape – no longer out there, i.e., in nature, but in here, e.g., in technology" (Giegerich 1987: 107).

plutonium: "Plutonium is now a force that permeates cross-cultural relations along the northern Rio Grande, one that offers middle-class livelihoods, the possibility of taking back land and revitalizing Nuevomexicano culture through economic empowerment, or of losing it altogether through radioactive contamination, outsider gentrification, and cultural assimilation" (Masco 2006: 214).

migrating: "Because almost all plutonium released into the environment is ultimately attached to soil and sediment particles, the behavior of constantly changing natural transport systems such as water and sediment flows provides the key to understanding the ultimate geographic disposition of the element" (Graf 1994: 3).

little shrine: "In January Buffalo-Deer Dance … we observed in the center of the North Plaza (San Ildefonso Pueblo) a small shrine of four or five rocks and turkey down. When we inquired casually of a friend when this little shrine had been put there, she replied that it had been there all along. We did not press the point" (Whitman 1947: 119).

Mortandad Canyon

The people who baked clay pots prospered on these sunny mesas
in the niches of canyon walls by the steaming Jemez Mountains.

On this spongy ground, the sentinel's tall shadow curls into putrid balls,
sorcerer eyes dining on grains of fretted light.

This is the unseen kingdom where Lilith's ionized wings screech against
bitterly cold air, a disloyal breech with Top Secret clearance, her wild
heart beating in paralleled computers programmed with tropes of "pre-
hostility," "collateral damage," "environmental adjustment."

> Bombs and bowls---
> both handmade and
> wondrous to behold.

This earth is laced with a heavy effluence of plutonium mixed with clay,
a felony migrating
> downhill
>> to a little shrine
>> that was always there.

Organ Mountains: Mountains on the southwest border of the White Sands Missile Range.

white uranic glow: Uranium was discovered in 1789 by Martin Klaproth. "Taking his clue from the alchemists who had named elements after planets, Klaproth named this metal for Uranus [as the existence of this planet had been recently discovered]" (Asimov 1962: 72). Uranium ore, white before it oxidizes, is crushed, ground and chemically processed into "yellowcake," the color of this sky.

lies on its side: Uranus spins on its side with reference to the sun.

propped up: White Sands Missile Park was established in 1955 to exhibit examples of missiles and rockets that have been tested on the range.

a pilgrim: Juan Maria Agostini was born in Italy. For unknown reasons, he began a pilgrimage, first in Europe, then Latin America, walking with a cane and a bell. In 1863 he appeared in Las Vegas, NM, taking up residence on a mountain top now named Hermit Peak. After a stay of about 5 years, then journeys through Latin America, he settled in a cave in the Organ Mountains where, on April 17, 1869, he was found stabbed to death.

surprising harmonies: "The music of the spheres is not as sweet and seductive as the Greeks believed, yet it is full of surprising harmonies, strange rhythms and disturbing dissonances. Is this how the angels sing – or how the damned cry?" (Written at the top of St. Augustine Pass in the Organ Mountains) (Jungk 1954: 28).

Paiakyamu clowns: From *payetemu*, Keresan for "youth." These are Koshare, or Kossa, of the Tewa. "The clown's mystical liberation from ultimate cosmic fears brings with it a liberation from conventional notions of what is dangerous or sacred in the religious ceremonies of men" (Tedlock 1975: 108). There are six modern Tewa-speaking Pueblos in Northern New Mexico, including San Ildefonso, which borders on Los Alamos National Laboratory. In fact, "it [is] difficult to identify realistically where Los Alamos ends and San Ildefonso begins" (Masco 2006: 147).

bodies of contradictions: Cheyenne "visionary clowns" are called "Contraries," for doing everything backwards.

unmasked: "Originally, no doubt, all Kachina [sacred dancers representing Pueblos gods] were masked … but wherever the Catholic Church has attained power, they are performed secretly, or without masks" (Fergusson 1988: 32).

soft horns: "clowns used their horns in order to tunnel upwards to the earth's surface so that the people could come out" into the light of knowledge (Tedlock Ibid.: 113).

Missile Park

As seen from an aerie in the Organ Mountains, a white uranic glow
in the sky
    lies on its side.

Circles of missiles were tested then discarded,
propped up like mutant trees gloating over targets
they never hit in recurring tailpipe dreams.

With a lance planted deep in his side, a pilgrim heard again
the "surprising harmonies, strange rhythms and disturbing
dissonances" of his martyrdom,
his fading world murmuring like Pan's pipes, not super-heated,
but passing cold from the old man's itinerant lungs.

Dancing Paiakyamu clowns are bodies of contradictions. Raccoon eyes
unmasked by the Church with thin lines of red lips, dry husks and dull
wooden knives, thrums and vesicles of rabbitskin pelts, soft horns
mocking these endless horizons; neckties choking blackened throats...

dancing in the glaring light
                       of a rocket's last stand.

Trinity: Trinity Site, located on the White Sands Missile Range in southwestern New Mexico, was dedicated as a National Historical Landmark by the National Park Service on October 4, 1975.

lava: "The last phase of the Paleogene Period, about 25 to 40 m.y. ago, was an earth-shaking time in New Mexico – and the first explosion of an atomic bomb in 1945 on the Jornada del Muerto … was a relatively low-energy-yield compared with the late Paleogene earth movements" (Kottlowski 1972: 37).

salty tongue: "By the middle of Permian [Paleozoic] time … from Santa Fe south to White Sands and southeastward almost to Carlsbad, very shallow marine waters were alternately stifled by pale-red sandy mud or evaporated by the sun. The results were … thick deposits of rock salt which now is the site of WIPP [Waste Isolation Pilot Project]" (Ibid.: 46).

Dactylic fingers: The Dactyls were priests of Cybele, long-haired, wearing bells and playing flutes and tambourines – engaged in self-castration.

obelisk: "The close connection between the obelisk and the sun, implied by the Egyptian word *tehen*, is reflected in the common practice of erecting obelisks to honor the sun god, Ra. The obelisk can, in fact, be understood as the sign of solar religion" (Taylor 1987: 116).

commanded the sun: "John and I rang the doorbell and an old man came out. He looked quizzically at us (John and I were wearing white coveralls with gas masks hanging from our necks). Then he laughed and said, 'You boys must have been up to something this morning. The sun came up in the west and went on down again'" (Hirschfelder 1986: 102).

Alone: The Hiroshima Bomb was dropped from the Enola Gay, a Boeing B-29 Superfortress named after the mother of its pilot, Paul W. Tibbets, Jr. "Enola," spelled backwards, is "alonE."

stones wept: "In the uniquely high temperature produced by the atom bomb [stones] had begun to 'weep' or to 'bleed'" (Jungk 1961: 25).

a temple: The "aiming point" at Hiroshima was a bridge over the Ota River, close to a Buddhist temple.

paper crane: Sadako Sasaki was two years old when the Bomb was dropped on Hiroshima. There's an old Japanese belief that a crane lives for a thousand years; thus, folding a thousand paper cranes will cure one's illness. When Sadako was confined to hospital she took to folding cranes. Legend has it that she was thirty-six short when she died from radiation-related leukemia.

Wings over Trinity

Old signs of modernity posted on a monument still warm from lava
and the sea's salty tongue. Dactylic fingers, bleached ribs, with
O'Keeffean flowers sprout twice a year from the sweat of tourists'
brows ... then cool into breccia shaped like magi's hat coming to a
point, what can this be?

The spire of a half-buried buried church?
An erect black nipple of Cybele's breast pointing
to a future that makes her lactation bittersweet?
An obelisk in whose shadow the Cabiri of technology
recode the runes of their stoic dreams?

      Ground Zero chants in the voice that commanded
      the sun to rise in the West as a new form of death;
      then rise in the East as an old way of life.

Alone in their moment of infamy, until stones wept,
and a temple bowed---

      For a plane
          like a paper crane
          had flown from a child's hand.

Endarkened fathers: "In *Star Wars* we are given the image of 'Darth Vader,' a pun on dark father ... As political and mythological kings die the father loses the radiance he once absorbed from the sun, or from the hierarchy of solar beings, he strikes society as being endarkened" (Bly 1990: 99).

next generation: "The Air Force's issuing last week of the contract for the advanced nuclear-tipped missile ... starts a 12-year effort to replace an older model. The updated weapon is to eventually fly on a yet-undeveloped nuclear bomber. The plan is to produce 1,000 of the new missiles, which are stealthier and more precise than the ones they will replace, and to place revitalized nuclear warheads on half of them." (Sanger and Broad 2017: A1).

plumage: "The feathers, for example, might be those of an owl to help [the shield bearer] see at night ... [The Plains Indians] all placed [red cloth] on the top margins of their shields, possibly as a symbol of the blood they intended to shed" (Wright 1976: 13).

cathedral: "The [Nagasaki] bomb exploded directly above the Catholic cathedral of Urakami, immediately killing the priests and those who had gathered to worship. The dead were scattered in endless concentric circles, with the cathedral at the center" (Dower and Junkerman 1985: 87).

brilliant pebbles: Smaller than "smart rocks," "brilliant pebbles" are kinetic energy projectiles with no external guidance systems.

BONZO: "Bulwark Order Negating Zealous Offensive."

WIMP: "Western Intercontinental Missile Protection."

HOPE: "Hostile Projectile Elimination."

WACKO: "Wistful Attempts to Circumvent Killing Ourselves."

SAFE: "Mutual Assured Safety."

inertia: "Ronald Reagan, starring as heroic Secret Service agent Brass Bancroft in the 1940 movie *Murder in the Air*, blasted a spy's plane out of the air with 'a new super-weapon': the 'inertia projector' ... a ray machine designed to 'make America invincible in war' and thus to become 'the greatest force for world peace ever discovered'" (Franklin 2008: 202).

shield: In 1984 President Reagan called his Strategic Defense Initiative, popularly known as Star Wars, a "peace shield."

political aims: "One of the most important things to understand about these Shields is that they were never intended to give physical protection in battle" (Storm 1985: 9).

Star Wars

Endarkened fathers look into the next generation's same eschatological storm. What are we facing?

The Gods of Prey wave sacred plumage boosted from silos beneath a moonless sky, while omens are smeared with the scent of enemy blood.

A cathedral radiates from its center endless circles of corpses, brilliant pebbles flying through a paradise of acronyms:

BONZO dreams of the ultimate banana hanging like a
WIMP within
HOPE of beaming arms; a real
WACKO of an image consummated
in a seemingly
SAFE place.

But he awakes an impulse that keeps its inertia, a protective device that can shield a venture high on lucrative contracts, with scientists dazzled by inept political aims.

radiant ash: Holloman AFB is located 10 miles west of Alamogordo, in south-central New Mexico. It was in a corner of the then Alamogordo Army Airfield that Trinity Site was constructed, and, on July 16, 1945, the first atomic device was exploded.

chimponauts: At Holloman's 6571st Aeromedical Research Laboratory, two chimpanzees used in six separate tests were exposed to hyperbaric conditions equivalent to 50, 200 and 300 feet of seawater. "Chimponauts" Enos and Ham were launched 36 miles into space.

banana-flavored: "Nuclear War is Bad for Bananas" (Keyes Jr 1982: 115).

stealthy: F-117 Nighthawk stealth fighters were stationed at Holloman AFB 1993–2008. It was the first operational aircraft to be designed around stealth technology, and went into operation in 1983 and retired in 2008 and was replaced by the F-22 Rapier until 2014.

leaping from towers: "João Torto ascended the cathedral tower and stood upon a platform that the priests had allowed him to construct there for his flight. Using a rope and pulley, João Torto then pulled his wings and eagle helmet up to the platform. He suited up as the crowds watched in anticipation. With a final blessing from the priests, he stretched his winged arms outward and stood like an angel atop the cathedral. He began to flap as he jumped off the platform … Incredibly, he flew" (Van Hare 2012).

Right arm: "It is man's right arm that is dedicated to the god of war; it is the *mana* of the right shoulder that guides the spear to its target; it is therefore only the right hand that will carry and wield the weapon" (Hertz 1960: 108).

fading star: "This is the dead land / This is the cactus land / Here the stone images / Are raised, here they receive / The supplication of a dead man's hand / Under the twinkle of a fading star." (T.S. Eliot. From, "The Hollow Men.")

Holloman AFB

After radiant ash had settled into anonymous sand, two "chimponauts,"
were launched into space, cowering in a cockpit with a hollow reed for
air, with banana-flavored treats for the antics of humanized terror.

Naked metallic taste on tongues, in mouths of unbrushed teeth,
hairy panoply masked with the ardent intent of intelligent mutations
following an unlovely scent to a sorcerer's preparations
spread skin suited to stealthy lustrations.

The bones of body counts fly again, engineered to specifications
suspended between poles of secularized power; or leaping from
towers of blinding ambition.

What knowledge, gripped in the beak, condenses from beaker to
violent decisions?

Right arm raised, a uniformed effigy suns himself,
exposing the physics of an Old World mind
spinning on its axis like a fading star.

guano: Because of its rich content of nitrogen and phosphates, guano was highly valued as a fertilizer before the development of cheaper chemical substitutes. Also a source of saltpeter, guano was used in the production of gunpowder.

smoke: It is said that the bats rise like smoke from the Bat Cave at Carlsbad, NM. A smoke hole is also the entrance and exit of a kiva, a Pueblo Indian buried, or half-buried, ceremonial room symbolic of Earth Mother's womb. The kiva serves both sacred and secular uses. It also is from where the Kachina Gods emerge.

fluorescein: A green dye used in Navy survival kits.

fingers: "Let us remember that our fingers let us fly. Even phylogenetically our hands compare with bird's wings" (Hillman 2013: 213).

radar: Bats "see" by means of "echolocation," a term coined by Donald R. Griffin during the 1930s. They are able to produce both FM (broadband) and CF (narrow-band) signals to suit the topography and mission. The sounds are emitted from the throat and bounce off an object back to the bat's directional ears; its brain then instantly interprets and locates the object's origin.

crucified: "In ancient Rome, bats were nailed to the door of the house as a protection from witches and diseases. In fact it was believed at that time, that their silent presence announced the arrival of an accident or a great tempest." www.eniscuola.net/en/2012/06/11/bats-facts-and-fiction. (Accessed 5th May 2018)

Mexican bats: Mexican free-tailed bats, *Tadarida brasiliensis*, of the family Molossidae. Also known as "guano bats," they reside at Carlsbad, NM, and winter in Mexico.

lunatic scheme: Project X-Ray was proposed during World War II. During the tests, carried out in the Southwest desert, several military buildings were destroyed by armed stray bats. The project was abandoned shortly before the Atomic Bomb was tested nearby.

Dionysian god: In Mayan mythology a dying man had to pass through the "bat house" on his way to the depths of the earth. There he would meet the Death Bat, Camazotz, a "dismembering animal," with the body of a human and the head and wings of a bat.

Geiger counter: Hans Geiger, and others, upgraded the electrical counter he and Ernest Rutherford had first invented in 1908.

Bat Cave

A shadowy nation hangs upside down, mothers folding infants clinging with hooked thumbs, incubating guano in a chilly dripstone cave.

At the crack of night blind arms stretch the length of leathery wings rising like smoke into a fluorescein sky.

Comic masks conform to facts that can't be faced: an aviator's fingers poised with brutally ancient intent; while, wired with radar, bats yearn for echoes of delectable things.

Prey is devoured---
even as memories dawn
of ancestors crucified
on civilized doors.

During World War II, undocumented Mexican bats were drafted into a lunatic scheme. Dropped with incendiary bombs belted to their bellies, kamikaze bats were trained to roost in enemy barns, where, in a flash of glorious light, they would join their batty Dionysian god.

When a Geiger counter clicks...
        bones become stones,
        and bats
        like rats
        become bats.

Trestle: Twelve stories tall, billed as the world's largest wooden structure, the Trestle was located on Kirtland AFB, in Albuquerque. Inspired by a railroad bridge, the ATLAS-I (short for Air Force Weapons Lab Transmission-Line Aircraft Simulator) was a test platform for the world's largest electromagnetic pulse simulator, which tested how electromagnetic pulses, or EMP, like the kind made by an exploding nuclear bomb, affected the instrumentation of military aircraft.

Leonardo's: "The wooden bridge and wooden trestle are purely American products, although they were invented by Leonardo da Vinci in the sixteenth century" (Clarke 1889: 27).

Howe's: The Howe truss "was first used on all railways, old and new, from 1840 to about 1870. Had it been free from liability to decay and burn up, we should probably not be building iron and steel bridges now" (Ibid.).

hemorrhaging: In 1990, the Boeing Co., of Seattle, WA, agreed to pay more than $500,000 to a former employee who claimed his leukemia was caused by his exposure to radiation during company tests of electromagnetic pulses.

X: "X particles are able to mediate transmutations between particles that feel only the electromagnetic and weak forces. They ensure that during this fleeting era there is a complete symmetry between all these interactions" (Barrow and Tipler 1996: 370).

wings were pinned: In 1980, when the Trestle began operations, several owls set up housekeeping under its huge platform. "Palladius refers to [the owl's] magical efficacy in warding off hailstorms when nailed up with outstretched wings" (Armstrong 1970: 119).

Beasts: "The [Ark of the Covenant] was made of acacia wood sheathed in gold inside and out – the same principle as electric condensers, two conductors separated by an insulator. It was encircled by a garland, also of gold, and set in a dry region where the magnetic field reached five hundred to six hundred volts per vertical meter. It's said that Porsena used electricity to free his realm from the presence of a frightful animal called Volt" (Eco 2007: 266).

railroading: After the atomic bombing, Professor Shogo Nagaoka, of Hiroshima University, "found this first clear sign of renascent life: a thick covering of that 'railroad grass' which had been imported from the U.S.A. in the previous century to cover and bind railway embankments" (Jungk 1961: 24).

Trestle

From a forest of standing orders
Western Larch and Douglas fir were drawn
from Leonardo's brilliant mind and Howe's adjustable truss,
entering a fantasy of tall structures raised by the math of skeletal
design figured within a radius of hemorrhaging signs.

X
marks the spot where wisdom's wings
were pinned to history's cruel doors.

Now bobcats, crows, owls and red-tailed hawks fly in and out of
this ancient wizardry, on which the Beasts of Voltage stepped up,
railroading myths of ionized events.

Shiprock: The Town of Shiprock, NM, is spelled as one word; the monument with two. Shiprock is the location of a former uranium ore-processing facility within the Navajo Nation in the northwest corner of New Mexico, about 28 miles west of Farmington.

radioactive ordure: "Between 1950 and 1979, the region yielded more yellowcake than any other place in the United States. Hundreds of uranium mines and seven mills – many of them on or near Indian land – stocked the government's cold war atomic arsenal and, eventually, the nation's nuclear power plants" (Smithson 2009).

In 1983, the US Department of Energy and the Navajo Nation entered into an agreement for site cleanup. By September 1986, all tailings and associated materials were encapsulated in a disposal cell built on top of the piles of radio-active materials.

white bird: In Arabian folklore, the Roc is "a fabulous white bird of gigantic proportions that could lift elephants and carry them to its nest, where they would be eaten for dinner" (Mercatante 1974: 175). As Sinbad's bird, the Roc "was like a cloud that spread darkness over the earth" (Armstrong 1970: 128).

Tsé Bit'a'í: Navajo. "He hobbled in, leaving her to enjoy the view of Ship Rock. Even in the harsh afternoon light, Tsé Bit'a'í held majesty. Bernie knew the story of the winged monsters who once lived on Ship Rock and how the Hero Twins killed them but spared their children, transforming them into eagle and owl" (Hillerman 2015: 209).

inverted: "As a result of the dynamic tendencies of all contradictions, the world of phenomena becomes a system of perpetual inversions, illustrated, for example, in the hour-glass which turns upon its own axis in order to maintain its inner movement: that of sand passing through the central aperture–the 'focal point' of its inversion" (Cirlot 1983: 117).

Shiprock

Scrub landscape, stubble of houses, junked automobiles parked nearby. Trees felled and stripped for telephone posts, clumps of emaciated bushes pressed and scoured. This parody is gripped by fingers anxious as clocks having lost their hands to a digital display.

Monstrous tailings of radioactive ordure, the fabulous white bird ripped open the earth's stubborn womb and carried children to his nest, cleaving their tongues, bating their breath, in the marrow of scintillated bone.

Tsé Bit'a'í
an igneous spire
rises as a vision inverted between
maintenance
and despair,
no longer bloody
but still ticking:
we are almost there

Hekate: Queen of the dead, Hekate would appear at crossroads with a pack of hungry hounds.

drums: Each TRUPACT-II (TRansUranic PACaging Transporter), used to ship radioactive wastes from around the country to WIPP (Waste Isolation Pilot Plant), near Carlsbad, NM, can accommodate up to fourteen 55-gallon drums.

feeding holes: "Most of the jars are distinctive in that a hole from one to about four inches in diameter appears in one side of the jar, and the designs have been worked so this hole becomes an integral part of the pattern. This is the 'feeding' hole" (Kirk 1988: 22).

bitter love: "Bitter love is a salt cure, curing the tender soul, with tears, recriminations, and finally, some sort of stabilized pattern" (Hillman 2010: 69).

in a cave: "The Waste Isolation Pilot Plant, or WIPP, near Carlsbad has been utilized since 1999 for permanent disposal of radioactive waste from the nuclear weapons program. The waste is buried 2,150 feet below the land surface in ordinary steel drums in direct contact with damp salt, the most corrosive rock known to humanity. Proponents expected the salt beds to flow like plastic under the weight of the overlying rocks, thus encapsulating the steel drums and isolating the waste from the environment for 10,000 years. It took only 15 years for the WIPP site to fail. On February 14, 2014, plutonium and americium, the principal isotopes in the waste buried at WIPP, were detected by air monitors above ground" (Phillips 2014: N.pag.).

domes: "A young and careless man dreams of visiting C. G. Jung in his house, which turns out to be a laboratory in a huge salt-dome where the wizened Jung explains how he works on making salt" (Hillman 2010: 68).

unearthed: "It's the year 3988 ... Some things haven't changed. For example, humankind still uses oil for many purposes. To get oil you still must drill underground ... One of the sites you explore is a desert area about 26 miles southeast of the ancient city of Carlsbad ... Your crew begins to drill. About 3,000 feet down, the drill encounters brine" (Staats 1988: 21).

Waste Isolation

Hekate is wired with swarms of photons inwardly
glowing in slow radiogenic decay...

> on a journey of rags, gowns, white abalone shells, green
> plutonium powder secreting drops of turquois puncturing
> protective gloves...jars become 55-gallon drums,
> feeding holes sealed with locking rings,
> fourteen containers swaddled in foam
> and stainless steel skin.

Caustic fumes of bitter love inhaled in a cave, salting away memories
of domestic tranquility beneath domes of collective dreams.

As seen from a distance, history is high-backed and wide-drifted,
its corridors braced with six million cubic feet of noxious debris.

Here someday will be unearthed
the deadly remains of a civilization
that sacrificed future generations to
the radiant God of Unlimited Power.

Kwahu Kachina: An Eagle Kachina. Kachinas occupy the transcendent realm between humans and gods, comparable to what Jung termed the psychoid.

failures: The first known failure of a nuclear bomb was the "P.P. shot" (Puny Plutonium bomb). Of it Enrico Fermi said, "Now you're making progress!"

sounding: The Aerobee is a series of upper-atmosphere research "sounding" rockets, retired in 1985. www.astronautix.com/a/aerobee.html (Accessed 21st May 2018)

the Furies: "aroused, the Furies will turn all the ripe earth into a wasteland. In offering them a home, bringing them inside the archetypal cosmos, Athena is skillfully taming the untamable forces of destruction" (Rowland 2015: 128). Athena was also a solid-fuel multi-stage research vehicle used to study atmospheric reentry phenomena.

hissing: "Athena's aegis bears a snaky fringe around its border and the Medusa's head in its center. In psychoanalytic writings and in Greek literature the aegis is usually called a dreadful weapon. But just what harm does it do? Athena shakes it at her enemies" (Eisner 1987: 61).

apehood's fire: Along with other animals, monkeys were used in high-altitude experiments, to be recovered by parachute. Thus, to the possibility of a manned flight to Mars, "And gone and flown and landed there in White Whale craft, / Remember Moby here, this dream, this time which does suspire, / This kindling of your tiny apehood's fire." (R. Bradbury. From, "Old Ahab's Friend and Friend to Noah Speaks His Peace.")

mystic flowers: Talos, whose mother was a mystic flower, invented the compass, among many other things. Here Talos is long-range surface-to-air missile, the result of the U.S. Navy's *Bumblebee* program.

ropes: These strips of leather represent sacred butterflies, "symbols of temptation and foolishness, so despicable that their behavior, 'acting like a moth,' has come to stand for insanity, the punishment for breaking taboos" (Reichard 1983: 407). "Rope" is also long strips of electromagnetic reflectors, sometimes attached to parachutes, used to confuse enemy radar.

biodegrades: "Is not the word 'biodegradable' a recent artefact … a modern and unstable graft of Greek and Latin in order to designate primarily that which is opposed to the signature of certain products of modern industry, products that are themselves artificial and synthetic, from plastic bags to nuclear waste?" (Derrida 1989: 816)

Kwahu Kachina

In how many guises do we fly?

A man in a bird's integument blesses a would-be deadly manufactured aviary,
failures of body and mind.

When we finally stood up, we were Man yet Bird
dreaming of vertiginous flight.

A world of loops sounding the Furies of untamed stars,
harmlessly hissing as their "apehood's fire" parachutes
down to Athena's newest app.

Wars begin in testicular mazes: even the gods suffer pains
as metaphors of their illusionary games.

Red-beaked, red-eared mystic flowers bloom, petals flying
in all directions; with a belt of ropes, shells, bells, and earth-
bound agravic shoes.

After a feast of recidivist blood, and life biodegrades into
molecular mud, only he will ascend: Kwahu Kachina—

AFTER THE END

Afterword

Seventy-five years ago, near the end of World War II, some of the brightest men of that generation watched their Frankensteinian device set fire to the dark stormy morning of a New Mexican desert. Applause for their amazing scientific accomplishment soon died into a question: what kind of monster had they borne into the world?

This morning myriad wildfires are burning not far from my home, the result of an accelerating global warming; while the "rough (nuclear) beast"[1] continues to evolve into ever more powerful iterations, spreading its potential for a fiery chaos of mass destruction. "The disaster is everything," Maurice Blanchot wrote.[2]

During the two years it took me to research and write *The Nuclear Enchantment of New Mexico*, I often thought about Pablo Picasso's powerful 1937 painting, "Guernica," that symbolizes the destruction of a small Basque town and its helpless population by Nazi dive bombers announcing Germany's military capabilities to the world. Eight years later, the total destruction by atomic bombs of two Japanese cities by the United States was meant, in part, to send the same ominous message.

How may these poems help mitigate the disaster? As the Bomb sprang from a "collective unconscious," as C. G. Jung called it, and from "the dismembering science of the subject / object split," as Susan Rowland has written, the poems, as a form of arts-based research, offer one path toward the re-membering; e.g., the healing within ourselves necessary before a viable relationship with respect to each other, and to the planet, can begin.

Lastly, I want to thank Susan Rowland for her thoughtful and insightful essays that demonstrate the mysteries and responsibilities of being human; and, on a personal note, have helped me see *The Nuclear Enchantment of New Mexico* in shades of many different lights.

Joel Weishaus
Ojai, CA

Notes

1 W. B. Yeats, From, "The Second Coming."
2 M. Blanchot (1986) *The Writing of the Disaster*. Lincoln: University of Nebraska Press.

References

Accidental H-Bomb

Hillman, J. (1979) *The Dream and the Underworld*. New York: Harper & Row.
Hillman, J. (2007) 'Apollo, Dream, Reality', in *Mythic Figures: Uniform Edition of the Writings of James Hillman*. Putnam, CT: Spring Publications, Inc.
Tsipis, K. (1983) *Arsenal: Understanding Weapons in the Nuclear Age*. New York: Simon & Schuster.

Alamogordo Chamber of Commerce

Burgess, E. (1957) *Guided Weapons*. New York: Macmillian.
Marvin, E. (1988) *Bullfight*. Oxford: B. Blackwell.
Rhodes, R. (1988) *The Making of the Atomic Bomb*. New York: Touchstone Press.
Tondriau, J. and R. Villeneuve. (1968) *Devils & Demons: A Dictionary of Demonology*. New York: Pyramid Communications, Inc.

Atomic Muse

Campbell, J. (2008) *The Hero with a Thousand Faces*. Novato, CA: New World Library.
Gray, George W. (1943) *Science At War*. New York: Harper and Brothers.
Jung, C. G. (2003) *Collected Works Volume 14, Mysterium Coniunctionis*. London: Routledge.
Onians, R. B. (1988) *The Origins of European Thought about the Body, the Mind, the Soul, the World, Time, and Fate*. Cambridge: Cambridge University Press.
Reik, T. (1973) *The Creation of Woman*. New York: McGrawHill.

Atomic Wrecking

Ansky, S. (1971) *The Dybbuk: A Play*. ed. C. Zhitlowsky. New York: Liveright.
Jung, C. G. (1965) *Memories, Dreams, Reflections*. New York: Vintage.
Masco, J. (2006) *The Nuclear Borderlands*. Princeton, NJ: Princeton University Press.
McPhee, J. (2000) *The Curve of Binding Energy*. New York: Farrar, Straus and Giroux.
Moss, R. (2017) 'Three Los Alamos Lab Workers Contaminated in Accident', *Santa Fe New Mexican*. 26 October.
Romanyshyn, R. D. (1989) *Technology as Symptom & Dream*. London: Routledge.

Bat Cave

Hillman, J. (2013) 'Puer Wounds and Ulysses' Scar', in G. Slater, ed. *Senex & Puer*. Putnam, CT: Spring Publications, Inc.

Bradbury Museum

Atherton, K. D. (2013) 'FYI. What are Cruise Missiles, and How Do They Work?' *Popular Science*, 29 August. www.popsci.com/technology/article/2013-08/fyi-cruise-mis siles (Accessed 14th May 2018).

Giedion, S. (1960) 'Space Conception in Prehistoric Art', in E. Carpenter and M. McLuhan, eds. *Explorations in Communication*. Boston, MA: Beacon Press.

Hersh, J. (1982) 'Model-making and the Promethean Ego', Dallas: *Spring*.

Leitner, L. (1978) *Fragments of Isabella: A Memoir of Auschwitz*. New York: Open Road Media (ebook).

Perlman, M. (1988) *Imaginal Memory and the Place of Hiroshima*. Albany, NY: State University of New York Press.

Takakura, A. (1977) in Japanese Broadcasting Corporation, ed. *Unforgettable Fire: Drawings by Atomic Bomb Survivors*. New York: Pantheon Books.

Younger, S. M. (2000) 'Nuclear Weapons in the Twenty-First Century', https://fas.org/nuke/guide/usa/doctrine/doe/younger.htm (Accessed 14th May 2018).

Cannon AFB

Berger, J. (1980) *Pig Earth*. New York: Pantheon Books.

Solomon, J. (1988) *The Signs of Our Time*. Los Angeles, CA: J.P. Tarcher.

Chaco Ruins

Balter, M. (2017) 'Ancient DNA Yields Unprecedented Insights into Mysterious Chaco Civilization', *Scientific American*. www.scientificamerican.com/article/ancient-dna-yields-unprecedented-insights-into-mysterious-chaco-civilization/# (Accessed 17th May 2018).

Bensinger, C. (1988) *Chaco Journey*. Santa Fe, NM: Ancient City Press.

Metcalf, R. (2015) 'NM No1 in Dependency on Federal Funds', *Albuquerque Journal*. August 12, Accessed 17th May 2018.

Sandler, D. (1991) *Navaho Symbols of Healing: A Jungian Exploration of Ritual, Image, & Medicine*. Rochester, VT: Healing Arts Press.

Stack, L. (2017) 'Plague Is Found in New Mexico. Again', *The New York Times*. June 27.

Stuart, D. E. (2010) *Ancient Southwest*. Albuquerque, NM: University of New Mexico Press.

Fusion Reactor

Opler, M. E. (1936) 'A Summary of Jicarilla Apache Culture', *American Anthropologist*, *38* (2), April-June.

Simmons, M. (1980) *Witchcraft in the Southwest: Spanish and Indian Supernaturalism on the Rio Grande*. Lincoln: University of Nebraska Press.

Gasbuggy

Coffer, W. E. (1981) *Where Is the Eagle?* New York: Van Nostrand Reinhold Company.

Hillman, J. (2013) 'Puer Wounds and Ulysses' Scar', in G. Slater, ed. *Senex & Puer*. Putnam, CT: Spring Publications, Inc.

LeFleur, W. R. (1983) *The Karma of Words*. Berkeley, CA: University of California Press.
Opler, M. E. (1936) 'A Summary of Jicarilla Apache Culture', *American Anthropologist*, *38* (2), April-June.
Reid, R. (1974) *Marie Curie*. New York: HarperCollins.
Schneidau, H. N. (1977) *Sacred Discontent*. Berkeley, CA: University of California Press.

Goddard High

Derrida, J. (1977) *On Grammatology*. Baltimore, MD: Johns Hopkins University Press.
Goddard, R. H. (1968) in A. Rosenthal, ed. *Venture Into Space: Early Years of Goddard Space Flight Center*. Washington, D.C.: National Aeronautics and Space Administration.
Lehman, M. and M. K. Lehman. (2016) 'Robert Goddard', *Encyclopedia Britannica*. www.britannica.com/biography/Robert-Goddard (Accessed 10th July 2019).
Romanyshyn, R. D. (1989) *Technology as Symptom & Dream*. London: Routledge.
Shaffer, P. (2005) *Equus*. New York: Scribner.

Holloman AFB

Hertz, R. (1960) *Death & the Right Hand*. Glencoe, IL: Free Press.
Keyes Jr., K. (1982) *The Hundredth Monkey*. Camarillo, CA: DeVorss & Company.
Van Hare, T. (2012) 'João De Almeida Torto Flies', *Historic Wings*. http://fly.historicw ings.com/2012/06/joao-de-almeida-torto-flies (Accessed 19th May 2018).

Homestake Mining

Harding, M. E. (1971) *Woman's Mysteries: Ancient & Modern*. Boston, MA: Shambhala.
Jung, C.G. (2014) *Collected Works Volume 13, Alchemical Studies*. Hove: Routledge.
Kiefer, A. (1988) Quoted in 'Anselm Kiefer, Interview with Donald Kuspit', in J. Siegel, ed. *Art Talk: The Early 80s*. Ann Arbor, MI: UMI Research Press.
Lamperti, J. (1982) 'Uranium: The Yellowcake Road', in J. Dennis, ed. *The Nuclear Almanac*. Reading, MA: Addison-Wesley.
Reichard, G. A. (1974) *Navaho Religion*. Princeton, NJ: Princeton University Press.
Silberer, H. (1971) *Hidden Symbolism of Alchemy and the Occult Arts*. New York: Dover.

Kirtland AFB

Hollinger, F. B. and A. Martin. (2013) 'Hepatitis A. Virus', in D. M. Knipe, and P. Howley, eds. *Fields Virology* Sixth Edition, Vol. 1. Philadelphia, PA: Lippincott Williams & Wilkins.
Kight, B. (2005) 'Nesting Birds: Their Brains are Small but Their Will Is Strong', www.aopa. org/news-and-media/all-news/2005/april/pilot/nesting-birds (Accessed 21st May 2018).
Spence, L. (2005) *The Magic and Demonology of Babylonia and Assyria*. Whitefish, MT: Kessinger Publishing.

Kwahu Kachina

Derrida, J. (1989) 'Biodegradables: Seven Diary Fragments', *Critical Inquiry*, *15* (4), Summer.

Eisner, R. (1987) *The Road to Daulis*, Syracuse, NY: Syracuse University Press.
Reichard, G. A. (1983) *Navaho Religion*. Princeton, NJ: Princeton University Press.
Rowland, S. (2015) *The Sleuth and the Goddess*. New Orleans, LA: Spring Journal Books.

Laguna Cracked

Cheetham, T. (2012) *All the World an Icon: Henry Corbin and the Angelic Function of Beings*. Berkeley, CA: North Atlantic Books.
Deleuze, G. (1987) in G. Deleuze and C. Parnet, eds. *Dialogues*. New York: Columbia University Press.
Douglas, M. (1966) *Purity and Danger*. London: Routledge.
Ortiz, A. (1969) *The Tewa World-Space, Time, Being, and Becoming in Pueblo Society*. Chicago, IL: University of Chicago Press.
Parsons, E. C. (1918) 'War God Shrines of Laguna and Zuni', *American Anthropologist*, *20* (4).

Laguna with Fish

Gunn, J. M. (1917) *Schat-Chen–History, Traditions and Narratives of the Queres Indians of Laguna and Acoma*. Albuquerque, NM: Albright & Anderson.
Jung, C. G. (1981) *Aion: Researches into the Phenomenology of the Self*. London: Routledge.
Parsons, E. C. (1920) 'Notes on Ceremonialism at Laguna', in *Anthropological Papers of the American Museum of Natural History*. Vol 19, Pt.4. New York: American Museum of Natural History.
Regon, M. (1983) *The Space of Death*. Charlottesville, VA: University of Virginia Press.
Tyler, H. A. (1984) *Pueblo Gods and Myths*. Norman, OK: University of Oklahoma Press.

Lampf

Berkert, W. (1985) *Homo Necans*. Berkeley, CA: University of California Press.
Hachiya, M. (1955) *Hiroshima Diary*. Chapel Hill, NC: University of North Carolina Press.
Hagerman, D. C. and R. A. Amerson. (1968) 'The Los Alamos Meson Physics Facility Accelerator', *Journal of Microwave Power*, *3* (2).

Manzano

Bachelard, G. (1968) *The Psychoanalysis of Fire*. Boston, MA: Beacon Press.
Jung, C. G. (2017) 'The Spirit Mercurius', in *Collected Works. Volume 13: Alchemical Studies*. Hove: Routledge.
Kafka, F. (1999) 'Letter to Max Brod', in M. Brod, ed. *The Dairies of Franz Kafka*. London: Vintage.
Layard, J. (1975) *A Celtic Quest*. Zurich: Spring Publications, Inc.
Weller, G. (1982) in H. Wasserman and N. Soloman, eds. *Killing Our Own*. New York: Delacorte Press.

Missile Park

Asimov, I. (1962) *The Search for the Elements*. New York: Basic Books.
Fergusson, E. (1988) *Dancing Gods*. Albuquerque, NM: University of New Mexico Press.
Jungk, R. (1954) *Tomorrow Is Already Here*. New York: Simon & Schuster.
Masco, J. (2006) *The Nuclear Borderlands*. Princeton, NJ: Princeton University Press.
Tedlock, B. (1975) 'The Clown's Way', in D. Tedlock and B. Tedlock, eds. *Teachings from the American Earth*. New York: Liveright.

Mortandad Canyon

Baring, A. and J. Cashford. (1991) *The Myth of the Goddess*. New York: Viking.
Giegerich, W. (1987) 'Saving the Nuclear Bomb', in V. Andrews, R. Bosnak and K. W. Goodwin, eds., *Facing Apocalypse*. Dallas: Spring.
Graf, W. L. (1994) *Plutonium and the Rio Grande*. New York: Oxford University Press.
Masco, J. (2016) *The Nuclear Borderlands*. Princeton, NJ: University of Princeton Press.
Whitman, W. (1947) *The Pueblo Indians of San Ildefonso*. New York: Columbia University Press.

Nike/Hercules

Burgess, E. (1957) *Guided Missiles*. New York: Macmillan.
Hillman, J. (1979) *The Dream and the Underworld*. New York: Harper & Row.
Steele, T. J. (1974) *Santos and Saints: The Religious Folk Art of Hispanic New Mexico*. Santa FE, NM: Ancient City Press.

Nuclear Sushi Museum

Inoue, M. (1977) Quoted, in Japanese Broadcasting Corporation, ed. *Unforgettable Fire: Drawings by Atomic Bomb Survivors*. New York: Pantheon Books.
Jungk, R. (1961) *Children of the Ashes*. New York: Harcourt, Brace & World.
Lapp, R. E. (1958) *The Voyage of the Lucky Dragon*. New York: Harper & Brothers.
Preston, D. (2005) *Before the Fallout: From Marie Curie to Hiroshima*. New York: Berkley Publishing Group.
Yamanaka, N. (1982) *The Book of Kimono*. Tokyo: Kodansha International Ltd.
Zimmerman, C. and J. Dennis. (1984) 'Nuclear Accidents,' in J. Dennis, ed., *The Nuclear Almanac*. Reading, MA: Addison-Wesley.

Project Gnome

Hillman, J. (2014) *The Thought of the Heart*. Putnam, CT: Spring Publications, Inc.
Huygen, W. (1977) *Gnomes*. New York: H.N. Abrams.
Mandelbrot, B. (2008) Quoted, in J. Gleik, ed. *Chaos*. New York: Penquin.

Radiation Therapy

Almond, P. R. (1976) 'Radiation Physics of Electron Beams', in N. duV. Tapley, ed. *Clinical Applications of the Electron Beam*. New York: R.E. Krieger Publishing Company.

Carter, A. B. (1985) 'The Relationship of ASAT and BMD Systems', *Daedalus*, *114* (2), (Spring).
Lockhart, R. A. (1977) 'Cancer in Myth and Dream', Dallas: *Spring*.
Von Franz, M.-L. (1987) *On Dreams and Death: A Jungian Interpretation*. Boston, MA: Shambhala.

Radium Springs

Bleakley, A. (1988) *Fruits of the Moon Tree*. Bath: Gateway Books.
Corbin, H. (1971) *The Man of Light in Iranian Sufism*. New Lebanon, NY: Omega Publications.
Layard, J. (1975) *A Celtic Quest*. Zurich: Spring Publications, Inc.
Reid, R. (1974) *Marie Curie*. New York: HarperCollins.
Von Franz, M.-L. (1998) *On Dreams and Death*. Boston, MA: Open Court.

Radon Classroom

Anonymous. (1968) in F. J. Brown, ed. *Chemical Warfare*. Princeton, NJ: Princeton University Press.
Cole, L. A. (1990) 'Much Ado about Radon', *The Sciences*. January/February.
Dacey, J. (2019) 'Chernobyl's Legacy and Why Assessing Radiation Risk Is so High', https://physicsworld.comla/chernobyls-legacy-and-why-assessing-radiation-risk-is-so-difficult Online 9 July 2019, Accessed 13th July 2019.
Grinnell, R. (1973) *Alchemy in a Modern Woman*. Zurich: Spring Publications, Inc.
Herzog, E. (2000) *Psyche and Death*. Woodstock, CT: Spring Publications, Inc.
Moore, T. (1990) *The Planets Within*. Great Barrington, MA: Lindisfarne Books.

Rio Puerco

Arendt, H. (1958) *The Human Condition*. Chicago, IL: University of Chicago Press.
Berkert, W. (1983) *Homo Necans*. Berkeley, CA: University of California Press.
Roheim, G. (1988) 'The Flood Myth as Vesical Dream', Quoted, in A. Dundes, ed. *The Flood Myth*. Berkeley, CA: University of California Press.
Tyler, H. A. (1964) *Pueblo Gods and Myths*. Norman, OK: University of Oklahoma Press.
Wasserman, H. and N. Solomon. (1982) *Killing Our Own*. New York: Delacorte Press.

Rocket Lounge

Bersani, L. (1977) *Baudelaire and Freud*. Berkeley, CA: University of California Press.
Charlton, M. (1986) Quoted, in R. Raymond, ed. *Out of the Fiery Furance*. University Park, PA: Penn State Press.
Dornberger, W. R. (1964) 'The German V-2', in E. M. Emme, ed. *The History of Rocket Technology*. Detroit, MI: Wayne State University Press.
Hall, N. (1991) *The Moon and the Virgin*. London: The Women's Press.
Jungk, R. (1954) *Tomorrow Is Already Here*. New York: Simon & Schuster.
Kerenyi, C. (1967) *Eleusis: Archetypal Image of Mother and Daughter*. Princeton, NJ: Princeton University Press.

Paz, O. (1990) *Marcel Duchamp: Appearance Stripped Bare*. New York: Arcade Publishing.

Sandia Dinosaurs

Hiller, S. (2013) 'Cover-up and Collusion at the Sandia National Laboratory Corral', *Lajicarita*. April 11. https://lajicarita.wordpress.com/2013/04/11/cover-up-and-collusion-at-the-sandia-national-laboratory-corral/ (Accessed 2nd June 2018).
Huizinga, J. (2016) *Homo Ludens*. Kettering, OH: Angelico Press.
Kolbert, E. (2014) *The Sixth Extinction*. New York: Henry Holt and Company.

Shiprock

Armstrong, E. A. (1970) *The Folklore of Birds*. New York: Dover.
Cirlot, J. E. (1983) *A Dictionary of Symbols*. New York: Philosophical Library.
Hillerman, A. (2015) *Rock with Wings*. New York: Harper.
Smithson, S. (2009) 'Radioactive Revival in New Mexico', *The Nation*. June 10. www.thenation.com/article/radioactive-revival-new-mexico (Accessed 4th June 2018).

Spies like Flies

Doctorow, E. L. (2007) *The Book of Daniel*. New York: Random House.
Hyde, H. M. (1981) *The Atomic Bomb Spies*. New York: Ballantine Books.
Radosh, R. and J. Milton. (1997) *The Rosenberg File*. New Haven, CT: Yale University Press.
Schneir, W. and M. Schneir. (1983) *Invitation to an Inquest*. New York: Doubleday.
Taylor, T. (1987) in R. D. Tredici, ed. *At Work in the Fields of the Bomb*. New York: Harper & Row.

Star Wars

Bly, R. (1990) *Iron John*. Reading, MA: Addison-Wesley.
Dower, J. W. and J. Junkerman. (1985) *The Hiroshima Murals*. Tokyo: Kodansha International Ltd.
Franklin, H. B. (2008) *War Stars: The Superweapon and the American Imagination*. Amherst, MA: University of Massachusetts Press.
Sanger, D. E. and W. J. Broad. (2017) 'Trump Forges Ahead on Costly Nuclear Overhaul', *The New York Times*, August 27.
Storm, H. (1985) *Seven Arrows*. New York: Ballantine Books.
Wright, B. (1976) *Pueblo Shields*. Flagstaff, AZ: Northland Press.

Trestle

Armstrong, E. A. (1970) *The Folklore of Birds*. New York: Dover.
Barrow, J. D. and F. J. Tipler. (1996) *The Anthropic Cosmological Principle*. Oxford: Oxford University Press.
Clarke, T. C. (1889) 'The Building of a Railway', in T.M. Cooley, ed. *The American Railway*. New York: Charles Scribner's Sons.

Eco, U. (2007) *Foucault's Pendulum*. New York: Houghton Mifflin Harcourt.
Jungk, R. (1961) *Children of the Ashes*. New York: Harcourt, Brace & World.

Trinity Site

Christiansen, P. W. (1972) 'Of Indians, Spaniards, and Americans', in P. W. Christiansen
    and F. E. Kottlowski, eds. *Mosaic of New Mexico's Scenery, Rocks, and History*. Soc-
    coro: New Mexico Bureau of Mines and Mineral Resourses.
Eisner, R. (1987) *The Road to Daulis*. Syracuse, NY: Syracuse University Press.
Jung, C. G. (1997) *Visions*. ed. C. Douglas. Princeton, NJ: Princeton University Press.
Lamont, L. (1965) *Day of Trinity*. New York: Scribner.
Otake, E. (2010) *From Trinity to Trinity*. trans. K. Hayashi. Barrytown, NY: Station Hill.
Rhodes, R. (2012) *The Making of the Atomic Bomb*. New York: Simon & Schuster.

United Nuclear

Armstrong, E. A. (1970) *The Folklore of Birds*. New York: Dover.
Hillman, J. (2007) 'Wars, Arms, Rams, Mars', in *Mythic Figures: Uniform Edition of the
    Writings of James Hillman*. Putnam, CT: Spring Publications, Inc.
Jung, C. G. (1967) *Alchemical Studies*. London: Routledge.
Reichard, G. A. (1974) *Navaho Religion*. Princeton, NJ: University of Princeton Press.

University Reactor

Lifton, R. J. (1982) 'Beyond Nuclear Numbing', *ScholarSpace*, *2* (3). https://scholar
    space.manoa.hawaii.edu/bitstream/10125/47208/1/EDPVol21%233_10-18.pdf
    (Accessed 8th June 2018).
Mercatante, A. S. (1974) *Zoo of the Gods*. New York: Harper & Row.
Noel, D. C. (1988) 'Realizing Dreams–Star Wars, 'Star Tours,' and the *Anima Machinae*',
    Dallas: *Spring*.
Romer, A. (1984) 'Toward Fission and Fusion 1913-1942', in J. Dennis, ed. *The Nuclear
    Almanac*. Reading, MA: Addison-Wesley.

Vaughn

Dressain, K. (1970) 'Once in the Saddle, the Meaning and Romance of the Trail Driving
    Cowboy', *Journal of Popular Culture*, (Fall).
Govinda, L. A. (1970) *The Way of the White Clouds*. Berkeley, CA: Shambhala.
Hillman, J. (1979) *The Dream and the Underworld*. New York: Harper & Row.
Jung, C. G. (2005) *Collected Works Volume 11, Psychology and Religion: West and East*.
    Hove: Routledge.
Meinzer, W. (2003) *The Roadrunner*. Lubbock, TX: Texas Tech University Press.

Waste Isolation

Hillman, J. (2010) 'The Suffering of Salt', in *Alchemical Psychology, Uniform Edition of
    the Writings of James Hillman*. Putnam, CT: Spring Publications, Inc.
Kirk, R. F. (1988) *Zuni Fetishism*, Santa FE, NM: Avanyu Publishing.

Phillips, R. H. (2014) 'Reader View: WIPP Incident Cause for Concern', Santa FE, NM: New Mexican. (March 17). www.santafenewmexican.com/opinion/my_view/reader-view-wipp-incident-cause-for-concern/article_848fd5eb-c18a-5744-a5b6-fef5a33a98c3.html (Accessed 9th June 2018).

Staats, D. (1988) 'WIPP Scientists Look Forward 10,000 Years', Albuquerque, NM: *Albuquerque Journal*. (May 22).

Wings over Trinity

Hirschfelder, J. O. (1986) in B. C. Hacker, ed. *The Dragon's Tail*. Berkeley, CA: University of California Press.

Jungk, R. (1961) *Children of the Ashes*. New York: Harcourt, Brace & World.

Kottlowski, F. E. (1972) 'Rocks that Shape the Enchanting Landscape', in P. W. Christiansen and F. E. Kottlowshi, eds. *Mosaic of New Mexico's Scenery, Rocks, and History*. Soccoro: New Mexico Bureau of Geology and Mineral Resources.

Taylor, M. C. (1987) *Altarity*. Chicago, IL: University of Chicago Press.

Index

Made in the USA
Las Vegas, NV
20 September 2021